GREAT BRITISH MENU
COOKBOOK

Great British Menu is an Optomen Television Production

LONDON, NEW YORK, MUNICH, MELBOURNE, DELHI

Editor Laura Nickoll
Executive Managing Editor Adèle Hayward
DTP Designer Traci Salter
Art Editor Nicola Rodway
Production Controller Luca Frassinetti
Operations Publishing Manager Gillian Roberts
Art Director Peter Luff
Publisher Stephanie Jackson

Project Manager and Editor Norma MacMillan
Art Direction and Text Design Smith & Gilmour, London
Photographers Dan Jones (food), Noel Murphy (location), Adrian Reay,
Joff Wilson and Ross Blair (chefs)
Food Stylist Stephen Parkins-Knight
Recipe Consultants Angela Nilsen and Jeni Wright

First published in Great Britain in 2007 by Dorling Kindersley Limited
80 Strand, London WC2R ORL

A Penguin Company
2 4 6 8 10 9 7 5 3 1

By arrangement with Optomen Television
Optomen logo © Optomen Television 2006
Optomen Television Production Team: Executive Producer Nicola Moody,
Series Producer Gary Broadhurst, Production Manager Raewyn Dickson,
Assistant Producer Ross Blair, Researchers Christopher Monk and Sam Knowles,
Personal Assistant Vanessa Land, Home Economist Karen Taylor.

By arrangement with the BBC
BBC logo © BBC 1996
The BBC logo is a registered trademark of the British Broadcasting Corporation
and is used under licence.

A CIP catalogue record for this book is available from The British Library.
ISBN-13: 978 1 4053 2210 2

Printed by Mohn in Germany

See our complete catalogue at **www.dk.com**

CONTENTS

4

It's one o'clock on a warm June afternoon and I'm trying to look inconspicuous as the Queen and the Duke of Edinburgh walk past. They're about to sit down to a four-course banquet created by the nation's finest chefs to celebrate the Queen's 80th birthday. I'm pinching myself because I can't believe it's all happening. But it is.

The banquet was the climax of Great British Menu, the BBC Two television series that my company, Optomen Television, brought to viewers in 2006. It was a simple idea – 14 of Britain's top chefs battled it out to represent their region of the UK and for the chance to be chosen by the public to cook for the Queen – that, to our delight, became a national talking point.

Earlier on that summer's day I had watched nervously as the four victorious chefs worked on their dishes in the grand kitchens of London's Mansion House, so I was very relieved when the Queen and her guests started to eat. As the empty plates were collected at the end of each course it was clear that the menu had been a resounding success.

It wasn't just the Queen and her guests who enjoyed the Great British Menu – millions of viewers tuned in regularly over the eight weeks of the contest. The plan had been to celebrate the abundance of fine cuisine in Britain today, and the success of the banquet and the series proved that we'd achieved that. But once the diners had gone home, we all wondered if the story was truly over. We reminisced about the extraordinary creativity we'd witnessed in the kitchens and thought 'surely British food deserves even further recognition?'

But where to fly the flag for British cooking next? The answer was clear. It was time to face the ultimate test. If there has been one nation that has been consistently resistant to our culinary charms, it is the French. Only a couple of years ago the French President, Jacques Chirac, was overheard saying that he couldn't trust the British as our cuisine was 'so bad'. British foodies struck back and denounced the French, but underneath it all I suspect many people did ask, 'Can we really cook as well as they do?' Now the time has come to prove we can.

The climax of the second series of Great British Menu will take place in the magnificent ballroom of the British Ambassador's Residence in Paris, at the heart of a city that loves fine food so much it gave birth to 'haute cuisine'. The Ambassador, Sir Peter Westmacott, and his wife, Susie, will host a glorious dinner showcasing the finest modern British cuisine. The Embassy has a proud reputation for celebrating the best that Britain can offer so it's the perfect location for this banquet, and it means that for the chefs the stakes could not be higher – the reputation of British food and cooking is in their hands.

Once again, 14 of Britain's top chefs, including the winners from the first series, will compete to win the opportunity to represent Britain. First of all they have to impress the panel of judges: doyenne of the cookery world, Prue Leith, esteemed food critic Matthew Fort and renowned restaurateur Oliver Peyton. In the end, though, only four chefs can triumph and it will ultimately be up to the British public to pick the food to be served in Paris. The guest list will read like a gastronomic Who's Who, so the food served up by our four kings of the kitchen will have to be superb if they're going to receive French applause.

The *Great British Menu Cookbook* serves up all of the mouthwatering dishes the 14 chefs have put together to showcase the very best of British cuisine. The stunning range of recipes they've created explodes the myth that British cooking lacks class and originality. The chefs have re-interpreted some classics as well as created some wonderful new recipes, and employed modern and traditional techniques to show off their talents. Whether it's a witty take on ham, egg and peas, a glorious recipe for the tried and tested trifle, or a succulent plate of slow-cooked lamb, the chefs have paid homage to the dedication of local producers by creating dishes that make Britain proud. Do try them at home and enjoy some of the best modern British food around.

NICOLA MOODY
EXECUTIVE PRODUCER GREAT BRITISH MENU

Renowned for his vibrant, exquisitely spiced food, Atul Kochhar became the first Indian chef to be awarded a coveted Michelin star as Head Chef of Tamarind in 2001. He opened his own restaurant, Benares, in London's exclusive Mayfair two years later and in 2007 it, too, was awarded a Michelin star. With such consistently excellent and innovative food it's no surprise Atul has been hailed as the best Indian chef in London.

Atul was born in eastern India in 1969 as one of six children. He started his cooking career at The Oberoi group of hotels, quickly progressing to Sous Chef at the much-fêted five-star Oberoi Deluxe in New Delhi. While cooking for these hotels, Atul learned the full spectrum of international cuisine, including French and Italian. It's this melding of Eastern and Western approaches that lies at the heart of all his cooking.

Always keen to reinvent and reinvigorate his food, Atul regularly returns to his homeland to research new recipes and ingredients. Cooking for Atul is all about being faithful to the origins of each recipe: the presentation and execution may be modern, but the true foundation of each dish he prepares can be traced to households across India.

Atul's cutting edge approach to Indian cookery was evident in the first series of Great British Menu, where he defeated the highly respected Gary Rhodes with dishes such as Sea Bass in Coconut Milk and Ginger Sauce. Merging potent Indian spices with the very best British produce, Atul continues to break conventional boundaries, opening our eyes and mouths to multicultural cuisine. As he puts it, "Multicultural cuisine hasn't happened overnight; it's been happening over centuries, and now its time has really come!"

ATUL KOCHHAR'S COMPETITION MENU
Starter Seared scallops with grape and mint dressing
Fish course Crisp-fried spicy john dory with grilled tomato chutney, cucumber salad and crushed peas
Main course Lamb rack and pan-fried lamb patties flavoured with rose petals
Dessert Apple tasting of the South East

STUART GILLIES

Stuart Gillies is famed for bringing New York-style café dining to London. His combination of exceptional food and a relaxed informal atmosphere has proved a massive success amongst the capital's food lovers. He currently holds the prestigious title of Executive Chef of the Boxwood Café at the Berkeley Hotel, a joint venture with Gordon Ramsay.

Stuart grew up in Crawley, Sussex, a town that he describes as a "culinary desert". After graduating from catering college, he worked at a local hotel for a year as part of a YTS scheme. It was an inauspicious start to what has been a meteoric rise through the culinary ranks. Stuart made a huge step up with his arrival at the Michelin-starred Connaught, where he worked as Head Chef alongside Angela Hartnett. He then progressed to London's famous celebrity haunt, Le Caprice.

Stuart's cooking has a vibrant international flavour, influenced by his experiences in New York working with legendary chef Daniel Boulud. "Cooking in this country has evolved so quickly in the last 15 years," he says. "I think that's because a lot of chefs went abroad to learn to cook and brought the knowledge back with them." The Big Apple's influence is clear to see on the Boxwood's contemporary menu: the foie gras and veal burger is a favourite amongst the regulars.

Seasonality is key to Stuart's cooking, and his menu evolves throughout the year to reflect the availability of ingredients. Making the most of terrific local produce, he believes that British cooking is back on the map. "It would be arrogant to say that British food is the best in the world, but it's certainly as good as anywhere else."

STUART GILLIES' COMPETITION MENU
Starter Pea and leek tarts with glazed asparagus and herb salad
Fish course Pan-fried john dory with lobster mash, broad beans, samphire and courgette flowers
Main course Roasted loin of suckling pig with mustard sauce
Dessert Vanilla and gingerbread cheesecakes with fresh raspberries and raspberry sorbet

MICHAEL CAINES MBE

Adopted into a large family in Exeter, Michael Caines grew up surrounded by good food. "Mum was a good English cook who used fresh, seasonal ingredients and baked great cakes, whilst Dad cultivated vegetables and apples. Meals were always a big family affair."

With a passion for all things culinary instilled at a young age, Michael quickly developed a real flair for cooking, winning the 'Student of the Year' award at Exeter Catering College in 1987. Raymond Blanc was impressed, and offered him a three-year mentorship at Le Manoir aux Quat'Saisons.

Michael went on to spend a number of years in France, sharpening his skills under the guidance of chefs Bernard Loiseau and Joël Robuchon. He returned to Britain in 1994 to take up the position of Head Chef at Gidleigh Park, the country house hotel on the edge of Dartmoor. It was here that he made his reputation, gaining two Michelin stars for his food, despite an appalling car accident in which he lost his right arm.

Michael pairs his French training with the best ingredients that the South West can offer, creating unique results. His enthusiasm for the quality and diversity of British produce is infectious. "In modern Britain it's impossible to define a typical British person; similarly, it is equally impossible to define exactly what is typical British cuisine."

But Michael is also keen to spread the gospel of good food beyond the trappings of haute cuisine: he formed Michael Caines Restaurants Ltd in 1999 and opened restaurants in Exeter and Bristol. He has also recently launched a boutique hotel chain called 'ABode', each hotel containing a Michael Caines restaurant. Locations so far include Exeter, Glasgow and Canterbury. "The UK has a great larder. We need more really good local restaurants, for a more relaxed experience that's real value for money."

Michael's position in the league of top chefs was cemented when he was awarded an MBE for services to the hospitality industry in the Queen's Birthday Honours List of 2006.

MICHAEL CAINES' COMPETITION MENU

Starter Galantine of quail spiked with raisins, served with a salad of walnuts

Fish course Devon crab and ginger dumplings with a lemon thyme and ginger sauce

Main course Honey roast Cornish duckling with cabbage and smoked bacon

Dessert Cox's apple tart

MARK HIX

As a youngster growing up in Dorset, Mark Hix quickly realised that it was home economics rather than metal work that held his full attention. So after leaving school he studied catering and got a job at the staff canteen at the Hilton Hotel in London. He craved more experience, and when the opportunity arose to go to the Grosvenor House Hotel and work with legendary chef Anton Edelmann, he seized it with both hands.

The job offers continued to roll in and after a while Mark found himself working at the Dorchester as a Commis Chef under Anton Mosimann, where he quickly got promoted to Chef De Partie. His big break came when, aged just 22, he was offered the job of Head Chef at the Candlewick Room. After his stint there he progressed to the position of Head Chef at Le Caprice and has stayed with the Caprice group ever since. Today Mark is Chef Director for Caprice Holdings Limited, overseeing all their restaurants, including J Sheekey, The Ivy and Le Caprice as well as the newly relaunched Scott's.

Mark is also a cookery writer and in 2003 was awarded the 'Glenfiddich Newspaper Cookery Writer of the Year' prize for his column in the Independent on Saturday. On top of his day job, Mark has spent the last two years researching his book about British regional food.

He is a champion of good British cuisine and lists one of his passions as discovering artisan food producers throughout the UK. "We're now out of the roast beef scenario and are finally getting respect from our overseas friends. There's great produce on our doorsteps and it's getting better, so there's no need to fly produce in from other parts of the globe anymore."

MARK HIX'S COMPETITION MENU
Starter Mixed beets and asparagus with Woolsery goat's cheese
Fish course Scallops, lobster and spider crab with wild seashore vegetables and oyster butter
Main course Rabbit and crayfish stargazy pie
Dessert Perry jelly and summer fruits with elderflower ice cream

10 GALTON BLACKISTON

Galton Blackiston's career began as a cash-strapped 17-year-old selling his own culinary creations on a market stall in Rye. After failing his A-levels he focused his attention on selling a home-made range of biscuits, cakes and preserves known as 'Galton's Goodies'. It proved such a success he turned his attentions to a career as a chef. Though not the most orthodox route into the industry, it proved a wise choice.

Honing his talents at work rather than in the classroom, he got his break under the guidance of TV chef John Tovey whilst working at the Miller Howe hotel in the Lake District. Steadily he progressed up to being Head Chef there before work experience overseas helped him develop even further.

In 1992 Galton and wife Tracey took a gamble and turned an 18th-century manor house in Norfolk into 'Morston Hall'. As well as a Michelin star it also showcases the best local produce around. In Galton's eyes, its style represents the best of modern British cuisine. "I love the tradition in British cooking, be it fish, chips and gravy or roast beef and Yorkshire pudding. These are unique parts of British cooking that can be modernised but never lost."

Galton has twice been named 'East Anglian Chef of the Year', and also honoured as 'Craft Guild of Chefs' Chef of the Year'. Not content with these accolades he has also written two books – *Cooking at Morston Hall* and *A Return to Real Cooking*.

He is a great ambassador of seasonal produce and grows plenty of it in his own garden. "Just about all the produce I use comes from my 'backyard', when it is in season – from mussels when there's an 'r' in the month to asparagus for just six weeks in the year."

GALTON BLACKISTON'S COMPETITION MENU

Starter Terrine of ham hock with piccalilli and toasted spelt bread with English mustard butter

Fish course Mousse and grilled fillet of wild sea bass served on samphire with a brown shrimp and tarragon sauce

Main course Roast saddle and slowly braised shoulder of spring lamb with fried new potatoes, Norfolk asparagus and young carrots

Dessert English trifle with a sorbet of Norfolk raspberries and sugared nuts

SAT BAINS

Sat Bains' food philosophy is all about giving diners a completely unique experience. As he says, "Why bother coming to a restaurant and spending good money if you can do better at home?" This bold, forward-thinking attitude has already reaped considerable rewards: he is the only chef in Nottingham to be awarded a Michelin star and his restaurant won the coveted AA 'Restaurant of the Year' award for 2007.

Born into a Punjabi family in Derby, Sat admits his main reason for joining catering college was "to meet girls". But whilst there he discovered a love of cooking too, and quickly developed into a hugely talented and passionate chef.

Sat got his big break when he became part of the team that opened the first of Raymond Blanc's brasseries, Le Petit Blanc, in Oxford in 1996. He then moved to a Head Chef's job at the Martin's Arms in Nottingham. Building on his growing successes, in 1999 Sat won the prestigious Roux Scholarship, and was awarded the chance to flex his culinary muscles at the world-renowned, three Michelin-starred Le Jardin de Sens in the south of France. This moulded him into the chef he is today: contemporary and cutting edge.

But despite the lofty heights of his culinary achievements, Sat has never lost sight of his roots in the Midlands, and the rich variety of produce it offers. "We need to back the artisan producers and keep the food bloodline of the Midlands going," he says. And through his much-lauded Restaurant Sat Bains, that's exactly what he's doing. "I'm very excited about modern British cooking. It's on par with any country in the world right now and we need to all celebrate that." We're sure all his Great British Menu competitors would agree.

SAT BAINS' COMPETITION MENU
Starter Ham, egg and peas
Fish course Lemon sole and oysters with muscovado jelly and sweet and sour chicory
Main course Dry-aged beef with textures of the onion family
Dessert Raspberry sponge with raspberries, goat's milk ice cream and black olive and honey

12 BRYN WILLIAMS

In 2006 Bryn Williams became a high profile champion of Welsh food when he secured the Head Chef's position at Odette's in North London. By using the best seasonal produce from the area that first inspired him, he has succeeded in turning the fashionable Primrose Hill set on to his classic Welsh dishes. Born and raised in Denbigh, North Wales, Bryn has always felt that "Wales has a fantastic larder from land and sea" and "the pure land gives pure ingredients I love to work with".

Bryn first became interested in food at primary school when he went on a trip with his classmates to a local bakery and got to spend a day making bread. Whilst training at the Llandrillo College in North Wales he got invaluable work placements at several world-class restaurants, including the Michelin-starred Restaurant Chateau Neercame in Maastricht and the Hotel Negresco in Nice. On his return to Britain in 1997, Bryn headed to London, where he started out at Le Gavroche, training under two of the capital's greatest chefs – Marco Pierre White and Michel Roux Jr.

After three years at Le Gavroche, Bryn was ready to take up the position of Senior Sous Chef at The Orrery, Conran's flagship Michelin-starred restaurant. It was whilst working at The Orrery that Bryn triumphed over one of the UK's top female chefs, Angela Hartnett, in the first Great British Menu with his Salt-Marsh Lamb. This and other dishes he served up in the competition are now regular fixtures on his menu at Odette's.

Even though he's been based in London for ten years Bryn hasn't lost touch with his Welsh roots. He is a judge at the 'Taste of Wales' awards, and regularly appears at The Royal Welsh Show and Conwy Feast. Bryn believes British cooking is in many ways "more advanced than the French, with a lighter touch. We're more with the times."

BRYN WILLIAMS' COMPETITION MENU

Starter Warm salad of lobster with summer vegetables and herbs and a Welsh water vinaigrette

Fish course Pan-fried wild salmon with Conwy mussels, crushed new potatoes and a horseradish sauce

Main course Roast rib of Welsh Black beef with onion purée

Dessert Strawberry soufflé with strawberry sorbet and Welsh shortbread

MATT TEBBUTT

When Matt Tebbutt was six months old his family moved to Newport, South Wales, and he has always classified himself as an "honorary Welshman".

His path to culinary success began in 1995 when he moved to London to study a diploma course at Prue Leith's School of Food and Wine. He followed this with a baptism of fire: working under Marco-Pierre White at The Oak Room and The Criterion. It was at the latter that Matt met his great friend and fellow Welshman Bryn Williams, and though they remain close, they are hugely competitive.

In 1998 Matt moved into the kitchens of Chez Bruce under the watchful eye of Bruce Poole. But it was whilst working under Alastair Little that Matt's cooking style really began to take shape. His fresh and flavoursome food bears the marks of his time with Little, a period in his life that shaped his view on British cuisine. "British cooking can be a mish-mash of ill-conceived rubbish or it can highlight the very best elements from the diversity of cultures in Britain today."

In 2001 Matt returned to Wales, transforming the Foxhunter pub in Monmouthshire into the AA 'Welsh Restaurant of the Year' in just three years. He strives to use only the best, most seasonal produce, which means the Foxhunter menu changes at least once a day to accommodate Matt's quest for freshness.

Though he spent a lot of time in England, Matt has never lost his passion for Welsh produce. "Welsh cooking has always been seasonal, fresh and simple, which are three of the most important aspects of cooking."

MATT TEBBUTT'S COMPETITION MENU

Starter Smoked eel and crisp pork belly with baby beetroot and horseradish cream

Fish course Sewin and soused vegetables with cockles and wood sorrel

Main course Poached fillet of Welsh Black beef with sautéed snails and asparagus on cauliflower purée

Dessert Rhubarb and ginger polenta crumble with soured vanilla ice cream

14

MARCUS WAREING

Despite still being in his thirties, Marcus Wareing is the chef behind three of London's best restaurants – Banquette, The Savoy Grill and Pétrus, the latter of which won its long-awaited second Michelin star in 2007. But Wareing's super chef status has never quelled his passion for honest Northern food. "The North has a fantastic tradition of cooking and farming, and I love the warm, earthy food that represents it as a region."

The son of a Merseyside fruit and veg merchant, Marcus trained at Southport College before starting at The Savoy in London at 18. A stint at Le Gavroche with Albert Roux followed, where he learned the art of classic French cuisine. Between 1991 and 1993 Marcus honed his skills at a number of famous restaurants, including The Point in New York and The Grand Hotel in Amsterdam, again with Albert Roux. In 1993 Marcus started working alongside Gordon Ramsay as Sous Chef at the newly opened Aubergine. In March 1999, with the backing of Gordon, Marcus opened Pétrus and within seven months it had won a Michelin star.

Even though his grounding is firmly in French cuisine, he has never lost his passion for British recipes and British ingredients. This was evident in last year's Great British Menu, where he presented his own interpretation of the classic Northern dish, Lancashire Hot Pot. His legendary Custard Tart was also chosen as overall winner in the dessert category and went on to be presented to the Queen at her 80th birthday banquet.

Marcus considers his amazing success to be part of a wider cooking renaissance in this country. "British cuisine is in the best state ever. We have some of the world's best chefs and it's great that we are becoming more aware of our fantastic British producers."

MARCUS WAREING'S COMPETITION MENU

Starter Crab and tea-smoked mackerel tarts with duck egg mayonnaise
Fish course Fillet of turbot in red wine with artichoke purée and pickled baby beets
Main course Slowly braised belly and roasted loin chop of pork with crackling
Dessert Earl Grey tea cream and Eccles cakes

MARK BROADBENT

Rochdale-born Mark Broadbent has been Executive Head Chef at Conran Bluebird restaurant since 2003. His career began at age 17, when he became a Commis Chef at The Rembrandt in Knightsbridge. A natural in the kitchen, Mark quickly moved on to work at the five-star Britannia Intercontinental. There he met his mentor, David Nicholls, and spent three years learning as much as he could with David's support.

Mark wanted to experience new cultures so he spent a year travelling around India, Australia and the US, working shifts in various restaurants to gain inside knowledge and experience of international cuisine. However, his travelling didn't shake his passionate commitment to British food and he wants people to rediscover British flavours. "What excites me is revisiting and redefining traditional dishes that have faded from our culinary consciousness, while caring deeply about the husbandry and provenance of the ingredients."

After returning to the UK in 1991, Mark put his new-found recipes and techniques to work, becoming a master of modern British cooking. His rise through the ranks – from Sous Chef at Restaurant 192 to Head Chef at Morton's Members Club & Restaurant – in just a decade is testament to his skill. Mark doesn't believe in combining international cuisines just for the sake of it, complaining that, "Our tastebuds have become jaded through an excess of lemongrass and a compulsion to embrace only what's new. Fusion? More like con-fusion." In 2003 his skilful use of flavours impressed Great British Menu judge, Oliver Peyton, enough to ask him to be the Head Chef at Isola in Knightsbridge. There Mark revolutionised their menu of traditional regional Italian cuisine by integrating British produce.

MARK BROADBENT'S
COMPETITION MENU

Starter Salad of duck livers, hearts, snails and bacon with dandelion and apple

Fish course Poached turbot and cockles with asparagus and brown shrimp butter

Main course Plate of aged mutton, potatoes and broad beans, with caper and herb relish

Dessert Strawberry knickerbocker glory

RICHARD CORRIGAN

Raised on a farm in County Meath in the Irish Midlands, Richard Corrigan was one of seven children. He was surrounded by food from the beginning. "We had no money, but no hunger," he recalls. "Father hunted, shot and poached everything we wanted. Regardless of the lack of money we ate like kings." Despite these humble beginnings Richard has become a world-renowned Michelin-starred chef.

Richard's career began earlier than most. Disillusioned with school, he began working at the local Kirwin Hotel with his father's friend, Ray Vaughan. At 21 he moved to London and worked under Michel Lorrain at the Meridian in Piccadilly and then at the Irish restaurant Mulligans. He went on to make a considerable impression at Searcy's in the Barbican Centre – an area of London that had hitherto been regarded as a culinary desert. In 1997 Richard bought his own restaurant, Lindsay House in Soho, and his first Michelin star soon followed. The restaurant remains a favourite for food lovers.

From opening a restaurant at the top of London's 'gherkin' building in 2004 to reviving the fortunes of the capital's iconic fish restaurant, Bentley's, a year later, it's little wonder Richard is known as 'the Irish chef in London'. As well as running his restaurants, Richard is also part of the select culinary council at British Airways, devising menus for long-haul and premier class flights.

Richard's food remains loyal to his Irish roots. In the first Great British Menu he skilfully demonstrated Irish food's earthy sophistication with dishes such as Venison Wellington with Pickled Cabbage and, of course, his overall winning starter of Wild Smoked Salmon, which wowed the judges. Passionate and committed, with an intense natural flair, Richard is now firmly established as one of the most remarkable chefs of his generation.

RICHARD CORRIGAN'S COMPETITION MENU

Starter Crubeens and beetroot with salad leaves and salad cream

Fish course Whole poached wild salmon and duck egg dressing with wheaten bread and country butter

Main course Slow-cooked shoulder of mountain lamb with leek-wrapped loin and champ

Dessert Carrageen moss pudding with apples, rosehip syrup and oatcakes

NOEL MCMEEL

Noel McMeel is Executive Head Chef of Castle Leslie in County Monaghan, Ireland. His unique cooking has helped Castle Leslie gain a spot among the top ten places to stay in the world.

Local produce is at the heart of Noel's cooking. Inspired by his farm upbringing, Noel strongly believes in using only the best local ingredients. However, his cooking is anything but parochial. It is his successful combination of traditional Irish ingredients and his extensive international professional experience that have cemented his reputation as one of the finest modern Irish chefs.

After training at the Northern Ireland Hotel and Catering College, Noel joined the kitchen at The Villager, in Crossgar, as an apprentice. He decided then to leave Ireland and worked in some of the most respected restaurants in the world, including a stint under Jean-Louis Palladin at the Watergate Hotel in Washington DC. In San Francisco he got the chance to work with his idol, Alice Waters, at Chez Panisse.

But Noel could not be away from his beloved Ireland forever, and so was delighted to take up the position of Head Chef at the Beech Hill Country House Hotel in Londonderry. In the late 1990s his dream of opening his own restaurant in his homeland finally came true. Trompets, his first venture, quickly received critical acclaim and soon he was in demand to cook at high profile events around the world. He joined Castle Leslie in 2000 and subsequently had the honour of cooking for the wedding of Paul McCartney and Heather Mills.

Quality, passion and flair are at the heart of everything Noel does. Firmly believing that "life is what you make it – you have to go after it, get it and deal with it", his life philosophy perfectly reflects his cuisine.

NOEL MCMEEL'S COMPETITION MENU
Starter Carpaccio of cured venison with horseradish, chive and roasted walnut cream
Fish course Tomato and fennel essence with oysters, Dublin Bay prawns and crab
Main course Canon of lamb with black pudding, minted pea purée and wild garlic potato cakes, garnished with lamb sweetbreads and rosemary gravy
Dessert Trio of rhubarb: rhubarb and ginger mousse, rhubarb ice cream, and rhubarb and whiskey compote

Not only is he Scotland's most famous chef, Nick Nairn was also the youngest chef north of the border to be awarded a coveted Michelin star – not bad for a self-taught cook who claimed that at the age of 25 he couldn't even boil an egg.

Nick developed his passion for food whilst travelling the world with the merchant navy, sampling delicious cuisine from all over the globe. Returning to his native Scotland he realised he wanted to open his own restaurant. The result was Braeval, which he opened close to his hometown of Stirling in 1986.

The year after its opening Nick was awarded the 'Scottish Field and Bollinger Newcomer' award. A key aspect of his success is using fresh Scottish produce, and he has campaigned vigorously to promote it. "Scottish food is all about the produce. We are in a bit of a melting pot at the moment and I think the true identity of modern Scottish food is in the process of being forged right now."

In 1997 Nick opened Nairn's Restaurant with Rooms in Glasgow. Never one to rest on his laurels, his next venture was Nairn's Anywhere in 2000, an event catering business providing food to any location. That same year he continued to diversify and launched The Nick Nairn Cook School. It was so successful that Nick sold his acclaimed Glasgow restaurant to concentrate his energies on the school and his other ventures.

As his profile has grown, Nick has added TV chef to his impressive CV. Since 1996 he has been a regular on Ready Steady Cook, though undoubtedly his finest achievement in front of the camera was having his roe deer main course presented to the Queen at her 80th birthday banquet after last year's Great British Menu.

NICK NAIRN'S COMPETITION MENU

Starter Cullen skink
Fish course Langoustines with summer vegetable stew
Main course A plate of Scottish pork
Dessert Cranachan with oatmeal praline

SCOTLAND

JEREMY LEE

Jeremy Lee grew up in the village of Auchterhouse near Dundee, and his deceptively simple cooking retains the freshness of his first encounters with food. "The foods of the sea, the coast, the lowlands and highlands of Scotland are equally glorious."

After working as a waiter at The Old Mansion House Hotel in Auchterhouse, Jeremy soon realised his future lay in the kitchen instead. He stayed there for four years before moving to London, where his career began at Boodles restaurant, before progressing to caterers Duff & Trotter. A meal at Bidendum convinced him just how much he missed the buzz of the restaurant kitchen. He managed to get work at Bidendum where he stayed for three years, creating the seemingly simple but unforgettable dishes for which he is now famous.

In 1991 he joined Alastair Little as Head Chef at the Frith Street Restaurant. In 1995 Jeremy launched Euphorium in Islington, then moved to The Blueprint Café as Head Chef where he has been ever since. A glance at the Blueprint's menu shows Jeremy's unswerving faith in Scottish produce, with dishes showcasing ingredients like Galloway beef and Arbroath smokies.

Though he has worked in London for many years he has never forgotten the culinary joys that Scotland offers. "The produce of Scotland is of such quality and flavour that the respect it commands is great." It's this respect for fine ingredients that leads Jeremy to believe British cuisine is going through something of a renaissance. "It is wonderful to work with producers who remain true to their splendid ingredients. Indeed, so good are these ingredients, British cooking is harking back to seemingly gentler times while striving to make its mark on very fast-paced modern times."

JEREMY LEE'S COMPETITION MENU
Starter Crab cakes and mayonnaise
Fish course A broth of Scottish shellfish
Main course Fillet steak, pickled walnuts and horseradish
Dessert Raspberry shortcake

CHAPTER ONE **STARTERS**

22

CRAB AND TEA-SMOKED MACKEREL TARTS
WITH DUCK EGG MAYONNAISE

SERVES 8
250g puff pastry
2 duck eggs
2 tbsp vinegar (any kind)
2 tsp finely chopped chives
juice of ¼ lemon
150ml mayonnaise
250g white crab meat, picked over
   to remove all shell and cartilage
salt and pepper

TEA-SMOKED MACKEREL
olive oil
1 large mackerel, filleted and with skin, pin
   bones removed
45g chamomile tea leaves
30g demerara sugar
30g risotto rice

1 Preheat the oven to 220°C/fan 200°C/gas 7.
2 To make the tea-smoked mackerel, you need a heavy roasting tin, a wire rack large enough to sit over the rim of the tin and an old wooden spoon. You will also need a sheet of foil folded double that is large enough to cover the rack and tuck in under the rim of the tin.
3 Dip a piece of kitchen paper in olive oil and lightly oil the rack and one side of the foil. Season the fish fillets and place skin-side down on the rack. Drape the foil oiled-side down over the fish, leaving the overhang loose.
4 Make the smoking mixture by mixing the tea, sugar and rice together in a bowl. Heat the roasting tin on the hob, moving it around to get an even heat. Scatter the smoking mixture over the bottom of the tin and stir it around with the wooden spoon. The sugar will melt and stick the tea to the rice, and then will start to burn. Immediately set the rack with the fish over the tin and remove from the heat. Protecting your hands with oven gloves or a tea towel, tuck the overhanging foil tightly all around the rim of the tin. When the foil is sealed really tight and no smoke is escaping from the sides, turn the heat back on and continue to move the tin around for 30 seconds. Then transfer to the oven to cook for 5 minutes.
5 Remove the tin from the oven and leave the fish to cool without unwrapping. Turn the oven down to 190°C/fan 170°C/gas 5. Line a large, heavy baking tray with baking parchment.
6 Roll out the pastry on a lightly floured surface to a large, neat rectangle about 3mm thick. Place the pastry on the parchment-lined tray. Cover with another sheet of baking parchment, then set a second heavy baking tray on top to act as a weight. Bake for 8–10 minutes or until the pastry starts to turn a very light brown. Remove

from the oven and take off the top tray and paper. Cut out eight discs from the pastry using a 7cm plain cutter. Return the discs to the oven on the parchment-lined tray and bake uncovered for 3–4 minutes or until golden and crisp. Leave to cool on a rack.

7 Take eight metal rings, about 8cm in diameter and 1cm deep, and tightly cover one end of each ring with cling film like a drum skin. Set the rings on their covered ends on a tray, and put into the fridge to chill.

8 Break the duck eggs into two separate cups. Bring 1 litre water and the vinegar to a gentle simmer in a large saucepan. Stir the water clockwise, then carefully drop the eggs into the vortex and poach for 6 minutes. Lift out the eggs with a slotted spoon and place in a bowl of iced water. Leave to cool. When the eggs are totally cold, remove from the water and drain on kitchen paper. Chop the eggs coarsely and place in a bowl, then cover and keep in the fridge.

9 When the mackerel is cool, remove it from the rack and peel away the skin. Check for any small bones with your fingers, then flake the fish into a bowl. Add the chives, lemon juice and one-third of the mayonnaise, then add the crab and lightly fold everything together, taking care not to break up the fish (you want to see nice chunks). Stir in half the chopped eggs, and check for seasoning.

10 Divide the mixture into eight equal portions and press into the chilled metal rings. Mix the rest of the chopped eggs with just enough of the remaining mayonnaise to bind, then taste and adjust the seasoning if necessary.

11 To serve, dab a little mayonnaise in the middle of each plate. Place a pastry disc in the top of each metal ring and carefully turn the ring over onto the plate, so the pastry is on the bottom and secured in place by the mayonnaise. Remove the cling film, push the fish mixture down in the ring with a small spoon so that it presses onto the pastry and lift off the ring. Using two teaspoons, make small quenelles of the egg mayonnaise to garnish the tops of the tarts.

24

WARM SALAD OF LOBSTER
WITH SUMMER VEGETABLES AND HERBS
AND A WELSH WATER VINAIGRETTE

SERVES 4

VINAIGRETTE
125ml spring water
2 tbsp Chardonnay wine vinegar
200ml olive oil
1 bay leaf
½ bunch of tarragon
1 small garlic clove, crushed
pinch of caster sugar
salt and pepper

LOBSTERS
1 onion, halved
1 carrot, halved
1 head of garlic, halved crossways
10 white peppercorns
4 live lobsters, each 400g
olive oil

SUMMER VEGETABLES
12 baby carrots
12 asparagus tips
100g freshly shelled broad beans
12 baby leeks
50g samphire
50g wood sorrel (or use watercress)
50g pennywort (or use mustard cress
 or rocket)

1 To make the vinaigrette, combine the spring water and vinegar in a bowl and season with salt and pepper. Whisk in the olive oil. When mixed and the seasoning is right, add the bay leaf, tarragon, garlic and sugar. Cover and leave to infuse at room temperature for 24 hours. After this, strain the vinaigrette and discard the herbs and garlic. Pour half the vinaigrette into a large bowl.

2 To cook the lobsters, three-quarters fill a heavy-bottomed pan with water and add the onion, carrot, garlic and white peppercorns. Bring to the boil and boil for 4–5 minutes. Season with a good handful of salt. Drop the lobsters into the boiling water and cook for 6 minutes.

3 Lift out the lobsters and place in iced water. Remove the claws, then put the lobsters back into the boiling water to cook for a further 2 minutes. Lift out into iced water again. When the lobsters are cold, crack the body/tail shells and remove the meat in one piece. Crack the claws and remove the meat. Set all the lobster meat aside.

4 To prepare the summer vegetables, blanch all the vegetables, including the samphire, in boiling salted water for 2–3 minutes. Drain. Slip the broad beans out of their skins, then add all the vegetables to the vinaigrette in the bowl. Leave to cool. As they are cooling the vegetables will absorb the flavours of the vinaigrette.

5 When ready to serve, cut the lobster meat into bite-sized pieces, season with salt and pepper, and pan-fry in a little olive oil to warm through. Drain the summer vegetables (discard the vinaigrette) and add to the frying pan to warm through. Remove from the heat and add the remaining vinaigrette just to warm it.

6 Spoon the warm lobster and vegetables onto four plates, scatter over the sorrel and pennywort, and drizzle with the warm vinaigrette. Serve immediately.

LIGHTLY CURED SEA TROUT
WITH PICKLED CUCUMBER

SERVES 4
50g sea salt
100g caster sugar
bunch of dill, roughly chopped
1 piece of sea trout fillet, about 1kg,
   skin on

CUCUMBER
2 cucumbers
sea salt
1 tbsp caster sugar
1 tbsp white wine vinegar
3 tbsp Dijon mustard
5 tbsp groundnut oil
1 tbsp chopped dill

1 Two days ahead of serving, rub the salt, sugar and roughly chopped dill together well. Rub this very well into the sea trout all over. Wrap the fish in a parcel of foil and place on a tray with a weight on top. Put the tray in the fridge and chill for 24 hours. Turn the parcel over and chill for a further 24 hours.

2 Early on the day of serving, peel the cucumbers. Cut them in half lengthways and remove all the seeds. Slice the cucumber diagonally across and not too thinly. Tip the slices into a colander, dredge liberally with sea salt and leave to drain for 2–3 hours. Rinse the cucumber very well, then drain thoroughly. Squeeze in a cloth until very dry.

3 Stir the sugar into the vinegar to dissolve. Add the mustard, then whisk in the oil a spoonful at a time. Use to dress the cucumber along with the chopped dill.

4 To serve, unwrap the fish and scrape away the dill, salt and sugar mixture on the surface. Cut slices, not too thin, from the trout and lay them on plates. Add a heaped spoonful of the cucumber salad on the side. (This makes more sea trout than you need for 4 servings, but it is good to cure more than you need as it keeps well for a week, and makes a delightful treat to have in the fridge.)

26

SALAD OF CRISP-FRIED SOUTH COAST SQUID
AND SPRING ONIONS IN SWEET CHILLI SAUCE

SERVES 4

SWEET CHILLI SAUCE
125g demerara sugar
2 tbsp red wine vinegar
1/2–1 tsp dried chilli flakes
2 tsp lime juice
2 tsp palm sugar
salt

SALAD
2 spring onions, diagonally sliced
1 medium red onion, thinly sliced
small bunch of rocket leaves
small bunch of bull's blood leaves
   or baby chard

SQUID
2 tbsp cornflour
1/2 tsp ground coriander
1/2 tsp chilli powder
1/2 tsp toasted cumin seeds
3 large squid, cleaned and tentacles kept,
   bodies cut into 1cm thick rings
vegetable oil for deep-frying

GARNISH
mixed micro salad leaves, or mustard cress
   mixed with coriander leaves

1 First make the sauce. Tip the demerara sugar into a heavy-based saucepan, mix in 2–3 tbsp cold water and let stand for 2 minutes (this helps dissolve the sugar). Heat slowly to dissolve the sugar, then bubble until lightly caramelised. Remove from the heat and slowly stir in 4 tbsp water. Return to the heat, add the vinegar and bring to a simmer. Stir in the chilli flakes, lime juice, palm sugar and salt. Simmer for 10–20 minutes, to a dipping consistency. Remove and cool to room temperature.

2 Mix all the salad ingredients together and keep wrapped in a wet cloth or damp kitchen paper in the refrigerator until required.

3 For the squid, stir the cornflour and spices together in a bowl, then mix in 5–6 tbsp water to make a batter. Add the pieces of squid and toss in the batter to coat. Set aside for 10 minutes.

4 Heat oil in a deep-fat fryer to about 180°C. Deep-fry the squid in batches for 3–4 minutes or until golden and crisp, reheating the oil in between each batch. Remove the squid with a slotted spoon and drain on kitchen paper.

5 Gently toss the fried squid with the salad. Drizzle 2 tbsp of the chilli sauce on top and lightly mix. (Any remaining chilli sauce will keep in the fridge for up to 3 weeks and is good as a dipping sauce or in salad dressings.) Place in a loose arrangement on each plate. Garnish with the mixed micro leaves, or mustard cress and coriander, and serve immediately.

28

CRAB CAKES
AND MAYONNAISE

SERVES 6

CRAB CAKES
1 large live crab
400g floury potatoes, such as King Edward
grated zest of 1 lemon
small handful of flat-leaf parsley,
  stalks discarded
1 garlic clove, finely chopped
1 egg yolk
3–4 drops of Tabasco sauce
plain flour for coating
vegetable or groundnut oil for frying
sea salt and freshly ground white pepper

MAYONNAISE
3 egg yolks, at room temperature
1 rounded tbsp Dijon mustard, plus 1 tsp
1 tbsp lemon juice
400ml groundnut oil

TO SERVE
6 little bunches of watercress
lemon quarters

1 The most humane way to kill the crab is to put it to sleep in the freezer first for about 1 hour. If you don't have time, simply plunge a large spike through its purse.
2 Put a large saucepan of water on to boil and add enough salt to give the taste of the sea. Plunge the crab into the boiling water, place a lid on the pan and boil for 12 minutes. Remove the crab from the water and leave to cool on a tray.
3 Peel the potatoes and rinse them very well in a colander until the water runs clear. Cut the potatoes into even-sized large pieces and place in a pan of water. Lightly salt the water and bring to the boil over a high heat. Lower the heat to a simmer and cook the potatoes quite gently for 10–15 minutes or until tender. Drain well and mash. Cover and set aside.
4 Remove the meat from the crab. Reserve the brown meat for another dish (this can be used to make a pâté by mixing with some Tabasco and Worcestershire sauces and a pinch of ground mace, then covered with clarified butter). Once you have removed all the white meat, pick through it to remove and discard any bits of shell and cartilage. Put the crab meat in a large bowl.
5 Combine the lemon zest, parsley leaves and garlic in a heap on a board and chop together finely. Add to the white crab meat along with the egg yolk, Tabasco, salt and pepper, and beat well until thoroughly mixed. Taste to check the seasoning. Let the mixture sit in the fridge for an hour or so to settle.
6 Shape the crab mixture into 18 little cakes about 2.5cm in diameter. Lay them on a tray and keep cool until ready to cook.

7 To make the mayonnaise, beat the egg yolks with the heaped tbsp of mustard and lemon juice in a bowl, then slowly whisk in the oil. Season with salt and pepper. Stir in the remaining mustard to spike up the taste. Turn the mayonnaise into a serving bowl.

8 Lightly flour both sides of the crab cakes. Heat a heavy-based frying pan, then add a little oil and heat through. Gently sit the cakes in the hot oil and fry until pale golden on the base. Turn over and continue cooking for 2–3 minutes or until thoroughly heated, lowering the heat if they start to get too brown.

9 Place three crab cakes on each plate and put a small bunch of watercress and a lemon quarter alongside. Serve immediately, with the mayonnaise.

MARK HIX

MIXED BEETS AND ASPARAGUS
WITH WOOLSERY GOAT'S CHEESE

SERVES 4
250g raw beetroots, preferably mixed
  varieties and colours, such as white,
  golden and red
250g asparagus
handful of silver sorrel leaves
150–200g Woolsery goat's cheese,
  broken into small nuggets
2–3 pickled walnuts, diced
salt and pepper

DRESSING
1 tbsp cider vinegar
3 tbsp cold-pressed rapeseed oil

1 Cook the beetroots in their skins in boiling salted water for about an hour or until tender. (If using different colours, cook them separately.) Drain and leave to cool, then rub off the skins.

2 Remove the woody ends from the asparagus, and cook the spears in boiling salted water for 5–6 minutes or until tender. Drain and leave to cool.

3 Cut the beetroots into bite-sized pieces (a mixture of slices and wedges). Cut the asparagus spears in half.

4 Make the dressing by whisking the vinegar and oil with seasoning to taste.

5 To serve, carefully arrange the beetroots and asparagus on plates with the sorrel leaves, then scatter the goat's cheese and pickled walnuts over the top. Drizzle over the dressing just before serving.

SEARED SCALLOPS
WITH GRAPE AND MINT DRESSING

SERVES 4
12 king-size scallops, coral removed
1 tbsp black sesame seeds
1½ tsp each chilli and garlic flakes,
    mixed
½ tsp each ground coriander and
    cumin, mixed
3 tbsp olive or vegetable oil
100g unsalted butter
12 large black seedless grapes
12 large green seedless grapes
salt and pepper

GRAPE SAUCE
200g black and green seedless grapes
50g mint leaves
20g fresh ginger, chopped
1 small green chilli
1 tsp salt
1 tsp dried mango powder
    or chaat masala

GRAPE SAUCE DRESSING
20g unsalted butter
½ tsp black sesame seeds
½ tsp white sesame seeds
1 tbsp julienned fresh ginger
1 shallot, finely chopped
200ml Wickham Vineyard's 'special release
    fumé' or other dry white English wine
¼ tsp paprika
¼ tsp mango powder or chaat masala

GARAM MASALA CARAMEL
100g caster sugar
pinch of garam masala powder

GARNISH
1 young carrot, cut into julienne
micro salad leaves or pea shoots

1 Put all the ingredients for the grape sauce in a blender and blend until smooth. Set aside.

2 To make the grape sauce dressing, heat the butter in a pan, then add the black and white sesame seeds. As they pop, add the ginger and shallot. Sauté until translucent, then pour in the wine and reduce to one-third. Stir in 200ml of the grape sauce, the paprika, mango powder and salt to season. Remove from the heat and set aside.

3 Next make the caramel. Line a baking sheet with baking parchment. Place the sugar and 2 tbsp water in a heavy-based pan over a low heat and stir until the sugar has dissolved. Increase the heat to medium and boil, without stirring, until the syrup caramelises to a golden colour. Carefully pour the hot caramel onto the lined baking sheet, sprinkle immediately with the garam masala and place another parchment sheet on top. Carefully roll out with a rolling pin to make a thin sheet of caramel. Leave to set. Remove the caramel from the paper and break into small pieces. Set aside for the garnish.

4 Divide the scallops into three batches. Dip one batch, on one side only, in the sesame seeds; dip the second batch, on one side only, in the chilli and garlic flakes; and dip the third batch, on one side only, in the ground coriander and cumin. Cook the scallops in their separate batches. Heat 1 tbsp of the oil in a frying pan and add the sesame scallops, sesame-side down. Cook over a medium heat for 30 seconds, then add one-third of the butter. Cook for a further 30–60 seconds to give a golden colour, then turn and cook for 1 more minute. Transfer to a warm plate. Repeat with the remaining scallops, using fresh oil and butter for each batch.

5 After the last batch of scallops has been sautéed, add the grapes to the oil and butter mixture left in the pan (if there is too much fat, pour off a little). Sauté the grapes for 2 minutes. Add a spoonful of the grape sauce dressing to lightly deglaze the pan. Remove the pan from the heat and keep warm. Season the scallops lightly with salt and pepper.

6 To serve, warm the grape dressing, then spoon some into the centre of each plate. Drag the back of a spoon through the dressing and across the plate to make a long streak. Place three scallops, one of each spice flavour, on the streak. Place glazed grapes near the edge, then spoon over the grape sauce dressing and place small pieces of caramel leaning on the grapes. To garnish, sprinkle with the carrot julienne and micro salad leaves.

CURED SLICES OF **SALMON TROUT**
WITH ONION CONFIT AND SMOKED BACON

SERVES 6

1 side of salmon trout (sea trout),
  with skin, about 1kg, pin bones removed
200g rock salt
50g caster sugar
grated zest and juice of 3 limes
12 thin rashers of smoked bacon,
  preferably Cumbrian
4 tbsp extra virgin olive oil, plus extra
  for drizzling

2 tsp white wine vinegar
salt and pepper

ONION CONFIT
50g unsalted butter
3 small white-skinned onions,
  preferably new season's, halved
  and cut into 3mm slices
1 bay leaf
sprig of thyme

1 Lay the fish flat, skin-side down, on a tray with raised sides. Mix together the rock salt, sugar, and lime zest and juice. Press this mixture all over the flesh side of the fish. Cover with cling film and refrigerate for 8 hours. Don't leave for longer than this or the fish will over-cure and become solid.

2 Scrape off the salt and rinse the fish thoroughly under cold running water. Now put the fish in a large bowl, cover with cold water and leave in the sink with the cold tap trickling gently for 20 minutes. Lift the fish out and dry thoroughly with a cloth.

3 Remove the skin from the fish with a sharp knife. Cut the fish into thirty-six 1cm-thick slices, working from the tail to the head end. Arrange the slices, slightly overlapping in six groups of six, on a baking tray lined with baking parchment. Cover and keep in the fridge.

4 To make the confit, heat the butter in a large pan until it melts and starts to bubble. Add the onions and herbs, and season with a good pinch of fine salt. Cook over a medium heat for about 10 minutes or until the onions are very tender and have caramelised to a deep golden brown. Stir frequently and add a teaspoon of water from time to time, to prevent the onions from catching on the bottom of the pan. Remove from the heat, discard the herbs and keep the confit warm.

5 Preheat the oven to 200°C/fan 180°C/gas 6.

6 Line a baking tray with baking parchment. Lay the bacon rashers in a single layer on the tray and cook in the oven for 6–8 minutes or until crisp. Remove the bacon and keep warm on kitchen paper.

7 Drizzle the slices of trout with a little olive oil and warm in the oven for 5–6 minutes.

8 Meanwhile, make a simple dressing by whisking the 4 tbsp olive oil with the vinegar and a little salt.

9 Season the fish with a light sprinkling of sea salt and a twist of pepper, then lay six slices neatly on each plate. Make a quenelle of the onion confit and place next to the fish. Place two rashers of bacon on the confit and finish with a drizzle of dressing.

FLEETWOOD COCK CRAB
WITH POTATO DROP SCONES AND LAND CRESS

SERVES 4

1 large live crab, preferably a cock crab
200ml organic rapeseed oil
1 fennel bulb, sliced or chopped
2 carrots, roughly chopped
1 large onion, roughly chopped
4 ripe and juicy large tomatoes, chopped
1 star anise
strip of pared lemon zest
squeeze of lemon juice
good sprig of tarragon
120g land cress
salt and pepper

POTATO DROP SCONES

500g Maris Piper or King Edward potatoes
2½ tbsp plain flour
50ml full-fat milk
3 medium eggs
4 medium egg whites
2½ tbsp double cream
2 tbsp vegetable oil for shallow frying

1 Put the crab in the freezer for about an hour, to desensitize it, then plunge it into a large saucepan of boiling salted water. Boil for 12–18 minutes, depending on size (ask your fishmonger for advice on this when you buy the crab – cock crabs are larger than hen crabs, so they take longer to cook). Drain and leave until cool enough to handle, then crack the claws and prise open the body. Pick out all the white meat, keeping the chunks as large as possible; cover and keep the fridge. (The brown meat can be used for a soup or sauce.) Discard the dead man's fingers and crack the shells from the claws and body.

2 Preheat the oven to 180°C/fan 160°C/gas 4.

3 Heat the oil in a large flameproof casserole until hot. Add the cracked crab shells and the fennel, carrots, onions and tomatoes. Fry over a medium heat until nicely coloured. Add the star anise. Transfer the casserole to the oven and roast for about 1½ hours, turning the ingredients occasionally. Remove from the oven and add the lemon zest and juice and the tarragon. Stir, then cover the pot and leave to infuse overnight. The next day, strain the infused oil through a fine sieve lined with muslin. Discard the contents of the sieve.

4 To make the drop scones, cook the potatoes in their skins in boiling water until soft. Drain and peel, then work through a potato ricer or food mill (mouli). When cool, transfer to a food processor and add all the other ingredients for the scones (except the oil). Blitz until smooth, but be careful not to overmix. Pour the batter into a bowl, cover and chill for 2–3 hours.

5 Heat a large non-stick frying pan until hot. Add the vegetable oil and heat it, then drop six dessertspoonfuls of the batter into the pan, keeping them far apart. Fry for about 2 minutes in total until the scones are puffed up and lightly browned on both sides, turning once. Drain on kitchen paper and keep warm in the oven while frying the remaining batter in the same way, to make 12 scones altogether.

6 To serve, dress the land cress with the crab oil and some salt and pepper. Arrange on plates with the white crab meat next to it, then place three scones alongside the crab. Drizzle a little crab oil on each plate to finish.

GALTON BLACKISTON

MOUSSE OF NORFOLK-GROWN PEAS
ON CREAMED CEPS WITH CRISP BACON

SERVES 6
25g salted butter, plus extra for greasing
   the ramekins
275g freshly shelled peas
1 medium egg, plus 1 medium egg yolk
200ml whipping cream
6 very thin slices smoked streaky bacon
salt and pepper

CREAMED CEPS
white truffle oil or olive oil
2 shallots, finely chopped
1 garlic clove, finely chopped
250g fresh ceps (porcini) or other wild
   mushrooms, sliced
120ml double cream

1 Generously butter six 7.5cm diameter ramekins, then set them aside in the fridge. Preheat the grill.

2 Melt the 25g butter in a saucepan. Add the peas and 2 tbsp water. Season lightly, then cover with a lid and cook gently for about 3 minutes or until the peas are just tender. Remove from the heat and whiz the peas in a food processor or blender to a smooth purée. With the machine running, add the egg, egg yolk and whipping cream. Season. Pass the mixture through a sieve into a jug, then pour it into the cold ramekins. The mixture will only half fill the dishes, but it puffs up during cooking.

3 Place the ramekins in the top of a double boiler or bain marie pan, cover and steam gently over simmering water for 8–10 minutes or until the mousses are just set but still wobble in the centre.

4 While the mousses are steaming, cook the bacon and ceps. Place the bacon slices on a baking tray and grill until crisp.

5 Heat a frying pan over a high heat. Add a splash of truffle or olive oil, then quickly fry the shallots and garlic until soft and translucent. Add the ceps and fry very briefly, seasoning as you go. Remove from the heat and keep warm.

6 To serve, stir the double cream into the ceps and place a spoonful in the centre of each plate. Run a small, sharp knife around the inside of each ramekin and turn the pea mousses out onto the creamed ceps. Top each mousse with a slice of crisp bacon.

36

SMOKED EEL AND CRISP PORK BELLY
WITH BABY BEETROOT AND HORSERADISH CREAM

SERVES 4

1 piece of good-quality pork belly on the
  bone, with skin intact, about 2kg
coarse sea salt
1 head of garlic, cut crossways in half
small bunch of thyme
6 bay leaves
about 500ml duck fat or rendered pork fat
14 raw baby beetroots
olive oil

4 fillets of smoked eel, each 50–75g,
  sliced at an angle into bite-sized pieces
salt and pepper
flat-leaf parsley leaves, young beetroot
  leaves or baby salad leaves to garnish

HORSERADISH CREAM

5 tbsp freshly grated horseradish
4 tbsp crème fraîche
squeeze of lemon juice

1 Rub the pork belly all over with coarse sea salt, then with the cut sides of the garlic.
Scrunch the thyme and 3 of the bay leaves in your hands, and rub these all over the
joint too. Now sit the joint skin-side up in a container with the garlic and herbs.
Cover and leave in the fridge for 24 hours.

2 Preheat the oven to 140°C/fan 120°C/gas 1.

3 Remove the garlic and herbs from the pork and reserve. Quickly rinse off the salt,
then pat the joint dry. Warm the duck or pork fat in a roasting tin on top of the stove
until it becomes liquid, then slip in the joint, skin-side up. It must be submerged in
fat, so you may need to add more. Add the reserved garlic and herbs, and bring the
fat to the boil. Cover with a heavy lid, put in the oven and cook for about 3 hours. To
check if the pork is done, pierce it in the middle with a carving fork and try to pick
it up – it should slip off the fork. Leave the joint to solidify in the liquid by letting
it cool, then putting it in the fridge overnight.

4 The next day, wash the beetroots and place them in a pan of cold water with the
remaining bay leaves. Bring to the boil and simmer for 40–50 minutes or until
tender. Allow the beetroots to cool in the liquid, then lift them out and peel off the
skins. Purée 2 of the beetroots in a blender, then work through a sieve into a bowl.
Stir in about 50ml olive oil to give the purée a pouring consistency.

5 Make the horseradish cream by stirring all the ingredients together. Cover and
refrigerate until needed.

6 Remove the solid pork belly from the tin and place skin-side down on a board.
Prise away the bones with the tip of a sharp knife. Turn the pork over and trim
into a block, discarding any fat and gristle. You should end up with a 7.5cm square
of prime meat cut from the middle (the trimmings are good fried with eggs for
breakfast, or cut into lardons and used in salads). Cut the block into 5mm-wide

strips and pan-fry with a little olive oil (or use some of the duck or pork fat) in a very hot pan for 1–2 minutes on each side until brown and crisp.

7 To serve, spoon some horseradish cream onto each plate, add three beetroots (sliced if you like), a couple of slices of pork belly and some pieces of eel fillet. Finish by garnishing with your choice of leaves, and spooning beetroot purée around each plate.

SAT BAINS

HAM, EGG AND PEAS

SERVES 4
4 very fresh duck eggs
8 wafer-thin slices French stick
olive oil
3–4 tbsp good chicken stock
10g salted butter
100g freshly shelled peas
4 wafer-thin slices British air-dried ham, or similar, such as Serrano or Parma

100g fresh pea shoots, chilled
salt
PEA SORBET
40g liquid glucose, warmed
400g frozen petit pois
2 sprigs of mint, roughly chopped
caster sugar if needed

1 To make the pea sorbet, bring the liquid glucose and 200ml water to the boil in a saucepan to make a stock syrup. Add the frozen petit pois and mint. Pour into a blender and process on high speed to make a purée. Chill, then pour into your ice cream machine and churn for 20–30 minutes or until the sorbet looks like a soft scoop ice cream. Taste for seasoning and adjust with a pinch each of sugar and salt, if necessary. Transfer to a freezer container and freeze.

2 Next, poach the eggs. A rice cooker is the best thing to use, but if you don't have one, heat a pan of water to around 62°C, ideally monitoring the temperature with a digital probe. Carefully add the eggs in their shells and leave at 62°C for about 1¹/₂ hours – the whites will be just firm and the yolks runny. Remove the eggs with a slotted spoon and set aside.

3 Preheat the oven to 180°C/fan 160°C/gas 4. Arrange the bread slices on a large baking sheet, brush with olive oil and bake for 12 minutes or until golden brown.

4 Pour the chicken stock into a medium saucepan and add the butter, shelled peas and a good pinch of salt. Simmer gently for 3–4 minutes or until the peas are tender.

5 To serve, carefully peel the shells from the duck eggs. Spoon the braised peas into the centre of warmed shallow soup bowls. Sit the eggs on top of the peas. Lay a slice of ham over each egg, and spoon a quenelle of pea sorbet to one side. Lay a couple of pieces of toast on top of the ham. Dress the pea shoots with a drizzle of olive oil and a sprinkling of salt, then scatter them all around.

38 ASPARAGUS AND WILD HERB SALAD
WITH DUCK EGGS

SERVES 4
250g asparagus
4 duck eggs
seasoned flour, beaten egg, crumbs
  and oil for deep-frying (optional)
50–60g wild herb leaves, such as
  nasturtium, wild chervil, bittercress,
  chickweed, etc
salt and pepper

CELERY SALT
1 head of celery with plenty of leaves
sea salt

VINAIGRETTE DRESSING
6 tbsp cold-pressed rapeseed oil
2 tbsp cider vinegar
1 tsp English grain mustard
1 garlic clove, halved
few sprigs of tarragon

1 First make the celery salt. Set your oven to its lowest temperature (with some modern ovens you can get away with using just the fan; the warming oven of an Aga is also ideal). Remove all the leaves from the head of celery and roughly chop them (use the celery sticks themselves for a soup, stock or salad). Scatter the celery leaves over one or two baking trays lined with greaseproof paper, and leave in the oven overnight or until the pieces are dry and crisp. Don't let them go brown. Put them into a food processor with a handful of sea salt and grind to a powder-like consistency, as coarse or as fine as you wish. For a smaller amount of celery salt, spread the inner leaves of the celery head on kitchen paper, then microwave on Low for 5 minutes or until bright green and brittle. Cool, then blitz in a spice mill with some sea salt. Store in an airtight container or Kilner jar. (You'll have more celery salt than you need for this recipe, but it's great for gulls' eggs or other egg dishes – and in a Bloody Mary of course.)

2 Remove the woody ends from the asparagus, and cook the spears in boiling salted water for 5–6 minutes or until tender. Drain and leave to cool.

3 Lower the eggs into a saucepan of boiling water. Return to the boil and boil for 3–5 minutes, depending on their size (if yours are the size of hen's eggs, boil them for 3 minutes; if they are larger, which they usually are, allow 4–5 minutes). Drain and refresh under cold running water for a few minutes until they are cool enough to handle, then peel. If you like, you can then deep-fry the duck's eggs. Coat in seasoned flour and beaten egg, followed by fresh white breadcrumbs. Deep-fry in hot oil for 3–4 minutes or until golden, then drain on kitchen paper.

4 Make the vinaigrette dressing by shaking all the ingredients together in a bottle or jar with the lid on.

5 Cut each asparagus spear in half and arrange on plates with the herb leaves. Drizzle over the vinaigrette. Break the eggs in half crossways (or cut them if they have been deep-fried) and place two halves in the middle of each salad with their yolks facing up. Sprinkle each egg half with a pinch of celery salt, then serve.

BELLY PORK, LANGOUSTINES AND LARDO
WITH GRANNY SMITH APPLES

SERVES 4

1 piece boned belly pork, about 500g,
   skin and rind removed
2–3kg duck fat, or you can use lard
   or 2 litres groundnut oil
pared zest of 2 oranges
pared zest of 2 lemons
2 vanilla pods, split lengthways
big bunch of lemon thyme
8 live langoustines
5g lardo (Italian cured back fat),
   plus 8 wafer-thin slices to serve

SALT MIX
10 white peppercorns, crushed
20 coriander seeds
5 green cardamom pods

5 whole cloves
2 cinnamon sticks, broken in pieces
100g wet sea salt, such as fleur de sel
2 sprigs of rosemary
10 sprigs of lemon thyme
2 garlic cloves, crushed

SHERRY SYRUP
100ml good quality sweet sherry

APPLE PUREE
3 Granny Smith apples, thinly sliced
200ml apple juice

APPLE SALAD
1 Granny Smith apple
squeeze of lemon juice
sea salt

1 You need to start 2 days ahead. To make the salt mix, put the peppercorns and all the dry spices in a frying pan and toast over a medium heat for about 2 minutes, shaking the pan often so they don't burn. Remove the cardamom seeds from the pods and put into a spice mill or a small electric blender with the remaining toasted spices. Blitz for about 30 seconds to make a coarse mix. Add the wet salt, rosemary, thyme and garlic, and blitz again for 30 seconds.

2 Rub the salt mix into the flesh side of the pork belly. (If you don't use all the salt mix, keep in a jar for using another time.) Sit the pork on a tray, cover and refrigerate for 24 hours.

3 The next day, rinse off the salt mix and pat the pork very dry with kitchen paper. Put the fat of your choice in a deep roasting tin or other deep pan and add the orange and lemon zests, vanilla pods and thyme. Heat the fat on top of the stove to 70°C (use a thermometer to check), then carefully add the pork. Cover and leave to cook very gently until the meat is very tender – this can take up to 10 hours. During this time, check regularly to be sure the temperature remains at 70°C. (A temperature of 70°C is ideal, but if you have trouble keeping it that low, cook at 100°C for 5 hours.) To test if the meat is done, push a large two-pronged fork into the centre; it should come out clean and do so as easily and smoothly as if it were coming out of a piece of butter. If not done, continue to cook.

4 While the meat cooks, make the sherry syrup and apple purée. Bubble the sherry in a small pan until reduced to a thick balsamic-vinegar consistency, then set aside. Put the apple slices in a pan with the apple juice. Bring to a simmer and cook for about 5 minutes. Strain off some of the liquid (leave the apples moist enough to purée, but not too wet). Purée the apples in a blender until smooth, then pass through a sieve. Chill.

5 Preheat the oven to 190°C/fan 170°C/gas 5.

6 When the pork is done, lift it from its cooking fat and lay it on a rack to drain. Then place it on a tray, set another tray on top and press down with a heavy weight. Leave in the fridge overnight to flatten.

7 The next day, remove the heads and the middle tail bits (waste pipe) from the langoustines. Blanch the langoustines in boiling salted water for 5 seconds, then plunge into a big bowl of iced water to cool for a few minutes. Remove the shells and dry the langoustines. Keep chilled until needed.

8 When ready to serve, trim the pork into a square, then cut into four 5cm cubes. Lay the cubes fat-side down in a dry non-stick ovenproof frying pan and cook for about 5 minutes or until caramelised. Turn the cubes of pork over and transfer the pan to the oven to cook for 5 minutes. Remove from the oven but leave in the pan.

9 While the pork is cooking, make the apple salad. Slice the apple very thinly, preferably using a mandolin. Sprinkle the slices with lemon juice and a little sea salt.

10 To cook the langoustines, melt the 5g of lardo in a non-stick frying pan, add the langoustines and fry for 30 seconds on each side.

11 To serve, cut each cube of pork into four slices. Lay four slices on each warmed plate, sit two langoustines on top and drape a slice of lardo over the langoustines so it starts to melt and look translucent. Drop little spoonfuls of apple purée around the pork and finish with a scattering of the apple salad over the langoustines and pork. Finish with a drizzle of sherry syrup.

CARPACCIO OF CURED VENISON
WITH HORSERADISH, CHIVE AND
ROASTED WALNUT CREAM

SERVES 4
1 boneless loin of venison, about 1kg
rapeseed oil
150g sea salt
10 juniper berries, very finely crushed
3 star anise, very finely crushed
1 tbsp cracked black pepper
leaves of 1 sprig of rosemary,
   very finely chopped
leaves of 2 sprigs of thyme,
   very finely chopped
1 tbsp coriander seeds, crushed
1 tsp grated orange zest
1 tsp grated lemon zest
salt and pepper

ROASTED WALNUT CREAM
8 walnuts, shelled
300ml whipping cream
1 tsp freshly grated horseradish
1 tsp wholegrain mustard, preferably
   Castle Leslie
5 chives, finely chopped

GARNISH
olive oil
a few chives

1 Heat a heavy pan until very hot, then sear the venison in a little oil over a high heat until nicely coloured on all sides. This should take about 3 minutes. Remove from the pan.
2 Mix together the sea salt, juniper berries, star anise, pepper, rosemary, thyme, coriander seeds, and orange and lemon zests on a baking tray, then spread out in a 3mm-thick layer.
3 Roll the warm venison in the spice mixture, making sure it is well coated all over. Wrap tightly in cling film and leave to infuse at room temperature for about 2 hours, then freeze for at least 4 hours until solid.
4 Preheat the oven to 180°C/fan 160°C/gas 4.
5 For the roasted walnut cream, spread the walnuts out on a baking tray and roast for 5 minutes. Rub off the excess skin while the nuts are warm, then chop the nuts roughly and leave to cool. Whip the cream until it holds a peak. Mix in the walnuts, horseradish, mustard and chives. Add seasoning to taste. Keep in a covered bowl in the fridge until serving time.
6 To serve, unwrap the venison and slice very finely on a meat slicer or with a very sharp knife. Arrange the slices in a semi-circle on each plate and glaze with a little olive oil. Spoon the roasted walnut cream in the middle, in a quenelle shape if you like, and garnish with chives.

GALANTINE OF QUAIL
SPIKED WITH RAISINS, SERVED
WITH A SALAD OF WALNUTS

SERVES 4
4 boned quails
mixed salad leaves to serve
salt and pepper

RAISINS
15g jasmine tea leaves
250ml boiling water
100g raisins
1 shallot, finely chopped

QUAIL MOUSSE
75g skinned quail breast meat
  (2–3 breasts)
75g skinned chicken breast meat
  (1 very small breast)
80ml double cream
50g chopped onion
½ garlic clove, crushed
50g unsalted butter

50g wild mushrooms, finely chopped
20g raisins
20g toasted walnuts, finely chopped
50g toasted pistachio nuts
1 tsp chopped tarragon

CARAMELISED WALNUTS
100g caster sugar
100g walnuts halves
vegetable oil for deep-frying

WALNUT VINAIGRETTE
150ml walnut oil
50ml Champagne vinegar or white
  wine vinegar
small sprig of thyme
½ garlic clove, lightly bashed

1 Stir the tea into the boiling hot water, then leave to steep until the water is warm. Put the raisins in a jar or plastic container and strain in the tea through a fine sieve. Leave to soak for 12 hours.

2 To make the quail mousse, blend the quail and chicken breast meat in a blender three times for about 3 minutes each time, leaving to cool in the fridge between each blending. (This stops the mousse over-heating.) Add the cream, then remove from the blender and transfer to a bowl. Set the bowl on a bowl of ice.

3 Sweat the onion and garlic in the butter until soft and translucent, but with no colour. Add the mushrooms and continue cooking until all the moisture has gone. Allow to cool, then fold into the quail and chicken purée along with the raisins, toasted walnuts and pistachios, and tarragon. Season with salt and pepper.

4 Open out one of the boned quails skin-side down on a large piece of cling film. Season lightly with salt and pepper, then pipe (using a piping bag fitted with a small round nozzle) or spoon one-quarter of the quail mousse down the middle. Roll the quail around the mousse, keeping the mousse in the centre, then roll up in the cling film so the quail encircles the mousse neatly in a sausage shape. Make sure the quail is well wrapped in the cling film, then twist the ends like a cracker and fold them back on themselves to seal. Repeat with the remaining quails and mousse.

5 Poach the quail parcels in a bain-marie with the water at 80°C (or in a large saucepan, making sure they are well submerged while cooking) for 30–35 minutes. Remove from the hot water and place in iced water. Leave until cold, then drain and chill overnight in the fridge, still wrapped in cling film.

6 To make the caramelised walnuts, pour 100ml water into a saucepan, stir in the sugar and bring to the boil. When the sugar has dissolved, add the walnuts and cook until the sugar syrup reaches 110°C. Meanwhile, heat oil in a deep-fat fryer to 180°C.

7 Using a slotted spoon, remove the walnuts from the sugar syrup, letting any excess syrup drain off, then place carefully in the hot oil and fry for about 2 minutes or until golden brown. Remove with a slotted spoon to a metal tray. Season with a pinch of salt.

8 To make the vinaigrette, mix all the ingredients together in a bowl and pour into a jar or plastic bottle. Shake well before using.

9 When ready to serve, drain the tea-soaked raisins and season with some of the vinaigrette and the chopped shallot. Remove the cling film from each quail and cut 4–6 slices, leaving the rest of the quail whole (or slice the whole quail).

10 Place the quail on the plates, fanning the slices. Dress the salad leaves with some vinaigrette and arrange a little in the centre of each plate. Break up a few caramelised nuts and scatter around the outside of the plate along with the dressed raisins. Serve.

46

SALAD OF DUCK LIVERS, HEARTS, SNAILS AND BACON
WITH DANDELION AND APPLE

SERVES 4

100g slab of streaky bacon, skin removed

75g duck fat

12 duck hearts, trimmed

16 duck livers, cleaned

24 fresh snails, poached in court bouillon
and drained, or ready prepared snails,
thawed if frozen or drained and rinsed
if canned

best-quality sherry vinegar, preferable Xerez,
for deglazing

4 tbsp duck jus (below), or 4 tbsp rich
chicken jus or gravy

hazelnut oil

salt and pepper

DUCK JUS

1 uncooked duck carcass, chopped

mirepoix of finely diced vegetables (2 onions,
2 carrots, ½ head celery and 1 leek)

organic rapeseed oil

red wine

sprig of thyme

1 bay leaf

SALAD

2 tbsp organic rapeseed oil

1 tsp cider vinegar

150g mixed fresh salad leaves, such
as dandelion, onion cress, land cress,
watercress, purslane, red amaranth
and flat-leaf parsley

3 crisp, tart eating apples, peeled and
cut into 1cm dice

1 If making the duck jus, brown the carcass and mirepoix in a little oil in a large saucepan over a high heat, then deglaze with a good splash of red wine. Add the thyme and bay leaf, and cover the carcass with cold water. Bring to the boil, then simmer gently for 1½ hours. Strain the stock into a clean pan and boil to reduce to a gravy-like consistency. Taste for seasoning, taking care not to over-salt as the jus will be reduced further when it is used for deglazing later. Set aside.

2 Put the slab of bacon in a saucepan of cold water and bring to the boil. Take off the heat and leave for about 5 minutes or until you see the bacon puff up a little, then drain. Cut into strips about 2cm long and 1cm wide and thick.

3 Heat a large, heavy or non-stick frying pan until hot. Add the duck fat and sauté the hearts and bacon over a high heat for 2–3 minutes. Add the livers and sauté for about 30 seconds on each side until well caramelised. Now add the snails, and deglaze the pan with a splash of vinegar and the duck jus (or chicken jus or gravy). Cook for a minute until reduced to a light sauce. Check the seasoning, and adjust if necessary.

4 Make a vinaigrette dressing for the salad with the rapeseed oil, cider vinegar and seasoning. Dress the salad leaves with the vinaigrette, and toss with the apple cubes.

5 To serve, pile the salad in a small heap in the centre of each plate, then arrange the livers, hearts, bacon and snails around. Spoon the sauce over and finish with a drizzle of hazelnut oil.

PEA AND LEEK TARTS
WITH GLAZED ASPARAGUS AND HERB SALAD

SERVES 6

18 spears of young, tender English
   asparagus, woody ends cut off and
   peeled if necessary
leaves of 24 sprigs of tarragon, finely chopped
leaves of 24 sprigs of chervil, finely chopped
24 chives, finely chopped
100g baby salad leaves
salt and pepper

TART CASES

250g plain flour
pinch of caster sugar
160g chilled unsalted butter, diced
1 medium egg, lightly beaten
few drops of cold milk, if needed
2 medium egg yolks, beaten, for sealing

FILLING

1 small leek, finely shredded
2 tbsp olive oil
1/2 tsp very finely chopped rosemary
250ml whipping cream
125g frozen English petits pois
10g Parmesan, finely grated
pinch of caster sugar

GLAZE

100g unsalted butter
2 medium egg yolks
10g Parmesan, finely grated
1 tsp double cream, lightly whipped

WHITE WINE VINAIGRETTE

1 tbsp white wine vinegar
4 tbsp olive oil

1 First make the tart cases. Sift the flour into a bowl with the sugar and a pinch of salt. Rub in the butter until the mixture looks like breadcrumbs, then mix in half the beaten egg. Add the remaining egg a little at a time until you can bring everything together to form a dough. If it starts to get sticky, don't add all of the egg; if it feels dry, add a drop or two of cold milk as well as the egg. Turn the dough onto a floured surface and knead very lightly into a rough ball. Wrap the ball in cling film and chill for about 30 minutes.

2 Butter and flour six metal rings, about 7.5cm in diameter and 1.6cm deep. Stand the rings on a baking sheet lined with a non-stick mat or baking parchment, and chill with the dough.

3 Preheat the oven to 170°C/fan 150°C/gas 3.

4 Roll out the dough on a floured surface until 3mm thick. Cut out six discs about 11cm in diameter. Line each metal ring with a pastry disc, pushing it firmly into the bottom inside edge and letting the surplus hang loosely over the top. Prick the bottoms all over with a fork, then line each tart case with greaseproof paper or a double layer of cling film and fill with baking beans. Bake the tart cases blind for 12–14 minutes or until the pastry is fully cooked. Remove from the oven, and turn the oven down to 140°C/fan 120°C/gas 1.

5 Remove the paper and beans while the pastry is warm. Cool slightly, then brush all over the inside of the tart cases with the beaten egg yolks, sealing any cracks. Return to the oven to bake for 4 minutes to set the egg, then cool slightly. Trim off the overhanging pastry by gently sawing with a small serrated knife at a 30° angle. Set the cases aside, still in their rings on the mat or paper.

6 To make the filling, gently sweat the leek in the olive oil with the rosemary and 2 tbsp water in a covered pan for 10–15 minutes or until very soft but not coloured. Cool. Bring the cream to the boil in a separate pan. Add the frozen peas and simmer for 1–2 minutes or until soft, then immediately purée in a blender until smooth and thick. Leave until cold, then mix with the leek, Parmesan, sugar and seasoning.

7 Fill the tart cases three-quarters full with the creamy pea mixture. Bake for about 16 minutes or until the filling is almost set but still has a slight wobble in the centre. Remove from the oven and cool slightly until just warm.

8 Meanwhile, plunge the asparagus spears into a pan of boiling salted water and simmer for 4–5 minutes or until just tender. Drain and refresh in iced water. Drain again, cool and dry on a cloth.

9 For the glaze, gently melt the butter in a heavy saucepan. Pour off the clear butter into a bowl, leaving the whey in the bottom of the pan. Keep both warm. Put the egg yolks in a bowl with 1/2 tbsp cold water. Set over a pan of gently simmering water and whisk until thick and aerated – the mixture should triple in volume and hold a ribbon trail when the whisk is lifted. Transfer the bowl to an empty saucepan and slowly whisk in the clear butter until all is incorporated, adding some of the whey to help prevent the sauce from splitting, if necessary. Fold in the Parmesan and cream, and season to taste.

10 Preheat the grill so that it is warm, not hot. Remove the metal rings from the tarts. Arrange three asparagus spears on the top of each tart, with their tips resting on the edge of the pastry case. Spoon the glaze over the top in a smooth, even layer, then slide the tarts under the grill to warm them through for 2–3 minutes and lightly colour the glaze.

11 Meanwhile, make the dressing by whisking the vinegar and oil with salt and pepper, then toss with the tarragon, chervil, chives, and baby leaves.

12 To serve, place the warm tarts on individual plates, and pile the salad on the side in a little mound.

SALAD OF SLOW-ROASTED WOOD PIGEON
WITH HAZELNUTS AND APPLES

SERVES 4
4 wood pigeons, oven ready
olive oil
1 garlic clove, sliced
sprig of thyme
1 bay leaf
25g butter
salt and pepper

HAZELNUT VINAIGRETTE
150ml hazelnut oil
3 tbsp Champagne vinegar or white
  wine vinegar
sprig of thyme
½ small garlic clove, lightly bashed

PIGEON SAUCE
3 tbsp groundnut or vegetable oil
20g unsalted butter
50g shallots, sliced

½ head of garlic, cut crossways
100g button mushrooms, sliced
1 tbsp sherry vinegar
150ml Madeira
500ml chicken stock
100ml veal glacé
3 tbsp double cream
5 black peppercorns
2 sprigs of thyme

TO SERVE
2 Cox's apples, peeled and diced
mixed baby salad leaves
handful of toasted and skinned hazelnuts,
  halved
3 shallots, finely chopped
mixed herbs, such as chervil, chives
  and marjoram

1 Remove the breasts from the pigeons (reserve the carcasses) and tie each into
a cylinder shape using a fine string. Place on a deep tray, cover with olive oil and
add the garlic, thyme and bay leaf. Cover and marinate overnight in the fridge.
2 Meanwhile, to make the vinaigrette, mix all the ingredients together in a bowl
and transfer to a bottle. Set aside.
3 For the pigeon sauce, chop the reserved pigeon carcasses into small pieces. Heat
the oil in a roasting tin on top of the stove. Add the pigeon carcasses and fry to colour
lightly, then add the butter and continue to colour. Stir in the shallots and garlic,
and lightly colour the shallots. Add the mushrooms and sweat for 5 minutes. Pour
in the sherry vinegar and stir to deglaze the pan, then cook until reduced to nothing.
Pour in the Madeira and bring to the boil, then boil to reduce by two-thirds. Stir in
the chicken stock, veal glacé, cream, peppercorns, thyme and salt. Bring to the boil
and skim the scum, then reduce to a gentle simmer and cook for 30 minutes.
Pass through a colander, then a fine sieve into a clean saucepan. Boil to reduce
to a sauce consistency. Finish by whisking in a little of the hazelnut vinaigrette,
enough to taste. Set aside.
4 When ready to serve, remove the pigeon breasts from the olive oil and season with
salt and pepper. Heat the 25g butter in a frying pan, add the pigeon breasts and fry

for 4–6 minutes to colour; they will be medium rare. Remove from the heat and leave to rest for about 5 minutes.

5 To serve, reheat the pigeon sauce. Toss the apples with some of the remaining vinaigrette. Do the same with the mixed salad, then the hazelnuts, shallots and herbs. Carve each pigeon breast into three slices and place on serving plates. Pile the mixed salad on top. Scatter the apple dice and hazelnut mixture around the plate and finish with a drizzle of the pigeon sauce.

GALTON BLACKISTON

TERRINE OF HAM HOCK
WITH PICCALILLI AND TOASTED
SPELT BREAD WITH ENGLISH MUSTARD BUTTER

SERVES 8

PICCALILLI
600ml white wine vinegar
250g caster sugar
50g freshly grated horseradish
   (or creamed horseradish sauce)
2–3 sprigs of thyme
1 bay leaf
2 large red chillies, deseeded and diced
300g red peppers, deseeded
200g yellow peppers, deseeded
200g cucumber, peeled and deseeded
200g courgettes
200g fennel bulb
200g celery sticks
200g button or pickling onions
50g salt
40g cornflour
15g turmeric (2 tbsp)
75g Dijon mustard (6 tbsp)

TERRINE
3 green (unsmoked) ham hocks on the
   bone, each about 1.2kg
2 pig's trotters, split lengthways
1 tsp coriander seeds
1 tsp black peppercorns

bouquet garni (2 bay leaves, few sprigs of
   thyme, 2 sprigs of parsley and few optional
   sprigs of tarragon, tied together)
2 shallots, chopped
1 bottle (75cl) white wine
4 tbsp white wine vinegar
2 tbsp small capers, rinsed and drained
50g gherkins, rinsed and chopped
generous handful of parsley, finely chopped
salt and pepper

NORFOLK SPELT BREAD
350g Letheringsett spelt flour, sifted
1 tsp salt
1 tsp English mustard powder
40g soft salted butter
50g chopped walnuts
25g sultanas (optional)
10g fresh yeast
1 tsp caster sugar
60–75ml lukewarm milk
60–75ml lukewarm water
1 egg, beaten

ENGLISH MUSTARD BUTTER
50g very soft unsalted butter
1 heaped tsp English mustard powder

1 Make the piccalilli well ahead as it improves with keeping. Combine the vinegar, sugar, horseradish, thyme, bay leaf and half of the chilli in a saucepan. Heat gently until the sugar has dissolved, then bring to the boil. Simmer gently for a couple of minutes. Set aside to cool, then strain and set aside.

2 Meanwhile, cut all the vegetables into small cubes (the onions can either be left whole or cut into halves or quarters). Pour 2 litres of water into a large bowl and stir in the salt. Immerse all the vegetables in the salted water and leave to soak overnight. The next morning, rinse the vegetables and drain well, then place in a large bowl.

3 Put the remaining chilli, the cornflour, turmeric and mustard in a bowl and mix to a runny paste with about 150ml of the cold strained vinegar. Bring the rest of the strained vinegar to the boil in a clean saucepan over a moderate heat, then stir in the paste mixture. Cook for 2–3 minutes, stirring, until thickened.

4 Pour the hot mixture over the vegetables and mix thoroughly. Fill five sterilised 450g jam jars with the piccalilli. When cool, cover and seal. (The piccalilli will keep for up to a month in a cool place. Keep in the fridge once opened. It's good to make plenty, as it goes well with a lot of snacky foods.)

5 To make the terrine, put the ham hocks and pig's trotters in a large saucepan and cover with cold water. Bring to the boil and boil steadily for 10 minutes, skimming off any scum from the surface. Remove the hocks and trotters, and discard the water.

6 Return the hocks and trotters to the cleaned pan. Add the coriander seeds, peppercorns, bouquet garni and shallots. Pour in the wine and vinegar, and add enough cold water to just cover the ingredients. Bring to the boil, then simmer very, very gently (no need to cover the pan) for a minimum of 2 hours or until the hocks are tender and the meat flakes easily.

7 Leave the hocks and trotters to cool in the liquid for about an hour. Remove the hocks, cover with cling film and set aside. Discard the trotters.

8 Strain the cooking liquid through a muslin-lined sieve into a clean pan. Place the pan on a high heat and bring the liquid to a rapid boil. Boil to reduce down to 650ml, then pass it once again through a sieve lined with a clean piece of muslin into a jug. Set aside.

9 Line a 1.5-litre terrine with a double layer of cling film, leaving some film draping over the sides.

10 Peel the skin off the hocks, then shred the meat into nuggets. Place in a large bowl with the capers, gherkins and parsley. Mix well. Taste and season with pepper (add salt only if really necessary). Pile the mixture into the lined terrine and press down firmly. Slowly pour in the reduced liquid, adding just enough to cover the meat. As you pour, tap down well to ensure the liquid is spread throughout the terrine. Cover with the overhanging cling film and chill overnight.

11 To make the spelt bread, put the flour, salt, mustard powder, butter, chopped walnuts and sultanas (if using) in the bowl of a food mixer. Using the dough hook, mix thoroughly together.

12 Combine the yeast and sugar in a bowl, mixing with your fingertips so that the yeast breaks down and becomes smooth and almost liquid. Mix in 60ml each of the warm milk and water and the egg. With the mixer running, slowly pour the yeast mixture into the flour to make quite a soft dough (it will become firmer on kneading), adding a little more warm liquid if needed. Allow the machine to knead the dough for 5–8 minutes or until it comes away from the sides of the bowl and does not stick to your fingers. Remove the bowl from the mixer and cover with a damp tea towel. Leave in a warm place for 1–1¹/₂ hours or until the dough has doubled in volume.

13 Line a large baking tray with greaseproof paper. Turn the dough out onto a lightly floured surface and knead well with the palm of your hand, then shape the dough into a plump rectangle. Place it on the baking tray and leave in a warm place for 45 minutes (no need to cover) to prove and double in size again.

14 Preheat the oven to 220°C/fan 200°C/gas 7. Bake the bread for 20–25 minutes or until golden and it sounds hollow when you tap your knuckles on the top. Cool on a wire rack.

15 For the mustard butter, beat together the butter and mustard powder in a bowl until thoroughly mixed. Taste and season with salt and pepper. Press into small pots and firm up in the fridge.

16 The terrine is best eaten at room temperature. Serve it sliced, with the piccalilli, slices of toasted spelt bread and English mustard butter.

54

POTTED SALT BEEF
WITH LAND CRESS AND RYE TOAST

SERVES 8

1 piece of salted beef brisket, 500–600g
1 carrot
½ onion
¼ leek
½ celery stick
½ head garlic, cut crossways
large sprig each of rosemary and thyme
200g mayonnaise, preferably home-made
25g fresh horseradish, very finely grated
  on a Microplane
1 crisp red-skinned English apple, peeled
  and finely diced
salt and pepper

TO SERVE

4 small handfuls of land cress (or other
  cress)
2 tbsp white wine vinaigrette (page 47)
dill pickles, cut into wedges
rye sourdough bread, thickly sliced
  and toasted

1 If necessary, soak the brisket in a bowl of cold water for 24 hours in the fridge (ask your butcher for advice on this when you buy the beef).

2 Place the brisket in a large saucepan, cover generously with fresh cold water and bring to the boil over a high heat. When almost boiling, skim off any scum from the surface, and add the vegetables, garlic and herbs. Cover and bring back to the boil, then remove the lid and simmer gently for 3–3½ hours. The brisket must be submerged all the time during cooking, so check regularly and pour in more water if necessary.

3 At the end of cooking, the brisket should feel very tender when pierced in the middle with the tip of a small sharp knife. Remove the pan from the heat and leave the meat to cool in the liquid for 30 minutes, then remove to a tray and leave until cold. Cover with cling film and chill overnight.

4 The next day, remove any fat and sinews from the meat, then pull the meat into long strands with your fingers. Cut the strands across into 2–3cm strips and place in a bowl. Add the mayonnaise, horseradish and diced apple. Gently fold together until evenly mixed, then add seasoning to taste.

5 For each serving, place a metal ring measuring 5cm in diameter and 4cm deep on an individual serving plate. Fill the ring with potted beef and level it off, then lift the ring up and off while gently pressing down on the mix. Toss the land cress in the dressing and arrange in a small mound next to the potted beef along with wedges of dill pickle. Serve with rye toast.

56

CRUBEENS AND BEETROOT
WITH SALAD LEAVES AND SALAD CREAM

SERVES 4

BRINE
900g sea salt
450g light soft brown sugar
1 tbsp saltpetre (optional – it isn't essential,
    but it improves the colour of the meat)
1 clove
10 black peppercorns
6 juniper berries
4 garlic cloves, split in half
1 bay leaf
3 sprigs of thyme

CRUBEENS
6 pig's trotters, well cleaned and
    hairs removed
bouquet garni
mirepoix of diced vegetables (1 carrot,
    2 celery sticks, 1 leek and 1 onion)
1 small ham hock
1 bottle (75cl) dry white wine
olive oil
2 shallots, finely chopped
1 cup chopped parsley
2 tbsp made English mustard
100g fine fresh white breadcrumbs
2 tsp English mustard powder

75g plain flour
2 large eggs, beaten
corn oil for shallow-frying
salt and pepper

SALAD CREAM
1 tsp made English mustard
1 tsp caster sugar
2–3 tbsp white wine vinegar
1/4 tsp white pepper
150ml evaporated milk
150ml organic rapeseed oil

BEETROOT RELISH
4 small raw beetroots
1 onion, finely sliced
olive oil
2 tbsp red wine vinegar
50ml red wine
1 tbsp freshly grated horseradish
sugar to taste

TO SERVE
4 small raw beetroots
2 sprigs of thyme
1 garlic clove, unpeeled, pounded flat
organic salad leaves and herbs in season,
    such as frisée, flat-leaf parsley, wood
    sorrel, pea shoots and dandelion

1 Put all the ingredients for the brine in a large saucepan with 3 litres cold water. Bring to the boil, stirring until the sugar has dissolved and skimming off the foam that rises to the surface. Simmer for 10 minutes, then remove from the heat and leave to cool.
2 Put the trotters in a large bowl and pour over the cold brine. Cover the trotters with a plate to keep them submerged, then cover the bowl and leave in the fridge for 24 hours.
3 Drain the trotters and put them in a large saucepan. Cover with cold water, add the bouquet garni and bring to the boil. Reduce the heat, cover and simmer for 3 hours.
4 Preheat the oven to 160°C/fan 140°C/gas 3.
5 Make a bed of the vegetable mirepoix on the bottom of a heavy casserole. Set the ham hock on top and pour over the white wine. Cover the pan with cling film, then

tie a sheet of foil tightly over the top with string and cover with a tight-fitting lid. Braise in the oven for $3^1/_2$ hours.

6 Leave both trotters and ham hock to cool in their pans, then remove. Using a very sharp knife, score through the skin and split the trotters in half lengthways. Carefully take out the meat, discarding the bones and gristle but keeping the fat with the meat. Reserve the skins. Shred the trotter meat, and the meat from the ham hock.

7 Heat a splash of olive oil in a heavy frying pan and sweat the shallots, stirring frequently, over a low to medium heat for 8–9 minutes or until softened but not coloured. Remove from the heat and stir in the parsley, then mix with the shredded meats and fat, and the made mustard. Season lightly with salt and pepper. Divide the mixture into four portions.

8 Lay two large (catering-size) sheets of cling film on top of each other on a board and smooth out any wrinkles. Place the trotter skins on the cling film, opening them out and laying them flat. Arrange them close to each other in pairs so you have three rows that make a 'blanket' of skins. Put the meat mixture in the middle of the skins and form into a long sausage, then roll up the sausage so that it is completely encased in the skins. Now roll the sausage in the cling film and twist the ends to seal. Chill overnight.

9 The next day, make the salad cream. Whisk the mustard, sugar and vinegar with the white pepper and $^1/_2$ tsp salt. Add the evaporated milk and continue to whisk. Gradually whisk in the oil to make a cream consistency. Check the seasoning. Keep cool.

10 To make the beetroot relish, peel and grate the raw beetroots, sprinkle with salt and leave to stand for 30 minutes. Rinse off the salt. Sweat the onion in a splash of hot olive oil with some salt and pepper until softened but not coloured. Add the wine vinegar, wine and grated beetroot, and stir. Cover and cook until reduced. Uncover and fold in the horseradish with sugar, salt and pepper to taste. Set aside.

11 Preheat the oven to 180°C/fan 160°C/gas 4.

12 Place the whole raw beetroots on a large sheet of oiled foil, add the thyme and garlic, and sprinkle with olive oil, salt and pepper. Close the foil to make a parcel and place on a baking tray. Roast for 30–35 minutes or until the beetroots are tender. Cool, then peel and halve.

13 Remove the cling film from the sausage and cut it in half lengthways. Place each half cut-side down on a board and cut in half lengthways again. Now cut each quarter crossways into five 3–4cm nuggets or crubeens. Mix the breadcrumbs and mustard powder together on a plate. Coat the crubeens in the flour, then in the beaten eggs and finally in the crumbs. Shallow-fry in hot corn oil for 2–3 minutes or until crisp and golden brown. Drain well.

14 To serve, put five crubeens and two beetroot halves on each plate with a spoonful of beetroot relish. Lightly dress the salad leaves with olive oil and seasoning, then put a pile of leaves on each plate. Serve the salad cream in a bowl.

58

WARM SEARED PIGEON
WITH A CARAMELISED RED ONION TART
AND WILD GARLIC DRESSING

SERVES 4

4 pigeon crowns, boned and halved to
    make 8 suprêmes (boneless breasts with
    wing bones attached)
olive oil
4 small handfuls of mixed salad leaves
salt and pepper

RED ONION TARTS

25g salted butter
25g light soft brown sugar
2 red onions, sliced into half rings
75ml red wine

75ml red wine vinegar
1 star anise
1/2 x 375g sheet of ready-rolled puff pastry
1 medium egg yolk mixed with 1 tsp water

WILD GARLIC DRESSING

large handful of young wild garlic leaves
4 tbsp olive oil
juice of 1/2 orange
juice of 1/2 lemon

1 Ask your poulterer or butcher to make the pigeon suprêmes, and to scrape the
wing bones clean for an attractive presentation..

2 For the tarts, melt the butter in a saucepan, add the sugar and cook over a medium
heat for 3–5 minutes until becoming golden brown and caramelised. Mix in the
onions. The sugar will go into lumps, but don't worry. Add the wine, vinegar and star
anise, put the lid on and cook over a medium heat for 15–20 minutes or until the
onions soften and reduce down. Remove from the heat.

3 Preheat the oven to 160°C/fan 140°C/gas 3.

4 Lay the sheet of puff pastry on a floured surface and brush with the egg yolk
wash. Working from top to bottom, mark wavy lines across the pastry using the
tines of a fork. Cut out four 10cm squares and place them on a non-stick baking
sheet. Press a 5cm plain, round pastry cutter into the middle of one of the squares.
Spoon in some of the onions, allowing about 1 tbsp per square, then carefully
remove the cutter. Repeat with the remaining pastry squares and onions.

5 Bake the onion tarts for 10–15 minutes or until golden brown. Remove from the
oven and leave to cool. Increase the oven temperature to 200°C/fan 180°C/gas 6.

6 To make the dressing, plunge the wild garlic leaves into a saucepan of boiling
salted water and blanch for 1–2 seconds. Drain and refresh in iced water, then
drain again and squeeze out as much water as possible. Work the blanched garlic
to a purée in a blender with the oil, orange and lemon juices, and salt and pepper.
Pass through a sieve and set aside.

7 Season the pigeon suprêmes. Heat a heavy ovenproof frying pan until hot, then
add a little olive oil and put in the suprêmes, skin-side down. Sear for 1 minute or

until the skin is golden and crisp, then transfer the pan to the oven to roast for 3 minutes. Remove the pan from the oven and place the pigeon suprêmes on a wire rack to rest for 5 minutes.

8 Meanwhile, reheat the onion tarts in the oven for a few minutes, and toss the salad leaves with the dressing.

9 To serve, set the warm onion tarts on the plates. Link two pigeon suprêmes together with their wing bones and place skin-side up on top of each tart. Arrange the dressed salad leaves alongside.

RICHARD CORRIGAN

COLCANNON SOUP

SERVES 4
2 tbsp unsalted butter
1 large onion, chopped
4 garlic cloves, chopped
250g potatoes, preferably Romano or
   Desirée, peeled and thinly sliced
ham stock or chicken stock
bouquet garni

1 Hispi cabbage, shredded
300ml double cream
salt and pepper

TO SERVE
8 rashers of bacon, preferably O'Doherty's
   Black Bacon, grilled
slices of toasted wheaten bread (page 74)

1 Heat the butter in a large saucepan and sweat the onion, garlic and potato slices for 5 minutes without colouring. Pour over enough stock to cover all the vegetables, and add the bouquet garni and seasoning. Bring to the boil, then cover and simmer for about 15 minutes.

2 Add the cabbage and bring back to the boil, then remove from the heat right away. Pour into a sieve set in a bowl and immediately chill the stock and vegetables separately in the fridge.

3 When both stock and vegetables are chilled, purée together in a blender until smooth, then pass through a sieve into a clean saucepan. (If you prefer a more rustic texture, don't blend or pass.)

4 To serve, reheat the soup, enrich with the cream and check the seasoning. Serve piping hot in earthenware bowls, with grilled bacon on slices of toasted wheaten bread.

MUSSEL BREE

SERVES 4

1.5kg fresh mussels in the shell
175ml dry white wine
50g butter
2 shallots, chopped
2 celery sticks, finely chopped
1 carrot, finely chopped
1 garlic clove, crushed and finely chopped

200ml double cream
1 tsp lemon juice
pinch of cayenne
50g cooked basmati rice (you need about 20g raw rice)
2 tbsp finely chopped chives
olive oil for drizzling (optional)

1 To prepare the mussels, place them in a bowl of cold water and scrub well to remove any dirt or barnacles. Tip the water out and repeat this process until the water is clear. Pull out the beards, which are the tough fibres protruding from between the shells. Discard any open mussels that don't close when tapped on the work surface.

2 Heat a large pan with a lid until hot. Have the wine close at hand. Lift the mussels into the pan, add the wine and slam on the lid. Cook over a high temperature, shaking the pan from time to time, until all the mussels have opened. This should take 3–4 minutes. Discard any mussels that don't open during cooking.

3 Pour the mussels into a colander lined with muslin and set over a bowl. Reserve the liquid that drains into the bowl (you should have about 300ml). When cool enough to handle, shell the mussels, leaving a few in their shells to garnish. Set the mussels and the strained cooking liquid aside.

4 In a large pan, melt the butter over a medium heat and add the vegetables and garlic. Cook until soft; don't allow them to brown. Add 300ml of the mussel cooking liquid and bring to the boil. Add the cream and stir in, then add the lemon juice, cayenne and rice. Simmer for a couple of minutes.

5 Purée in a blender, then pass through a fine sieve. Pour the soup into a clean pan.

6 To serve, reheat the soup gently, then add the mussels and allow them to warm through. Divide among four warmed bowls and garnish with a sprinkling of chopped chives and an optional drizzle of olive oil.

62 CULLEN SKINK

SERVES 4
20g unsalted butter
2 banana shallots, finely diced
100g leek, white only, finely diced
2 medium garlic cloves, crushed
  then finely diced
200g Ratte potatoes, boiled until soft
  then peeled
2 Arbroath smokies, skin and bones removed
100ml whole milk
100ml double cream
pepper

FISH STOCK
2 tbsp olive oil
100g chopped white vegetables, such as
  white of leeks, fennel and onion
100ml dry white wine
2 Arbroath smokies, roughly chopped

GARNISH
1 Arbroath smokie, skin and bones removed
chopped chives

1 To make the fish stock, put the oil into a heavy saucepan and heat, then add the vegetables and stir well to coat with the oil. Cover and sweat over a low heat for about 10 minutes; do not allow them to colour. Take the lid off the pan and pour in the white wine. Boil for 1 minute. Now add 1.2 litres of water and the smokies. Bring up almost to the boil, then skim well. Reduce the heat and simmer very gently for about 20 minutes. Allow to cool. Once cold, strain the stock through a very fine sieve, preferably lined with a double layer of muslin. (The stock can be made 2 days ahead, then kept chilled until needed.)

2 To make the soup, put a large saucepan over a medium heat. Add the butter and, when it has melted, throw in the shallots, leek and garlic. Cover and sweat for 5–10 minutes, but don't allow the vegetables to colour.

3 Add the cooked potatoes. Flake the smokies and add to the pan. Cover and sweat for a further 2 minutes, then add 1 litre of the stock and season with pepper. Bring to the boil and simmer for 8–10 minutes.

4 Take the pan off the heat and allow to cool slightly. Carefully pour the mixture into a blender and put on the lid. Take the stopper out of the hole in the lid and cover the hole with a tea towel to stop the hot mix splattering. Blitz for a few seconds, then slowly add the milk and cream through the hole. When it's all added and the mixture is smooth, pass through a chinois to give a fine, velvety texture.

5 To serve, pour the soup into a clean pan and heat gently to avoid burning. Flake the remaining smokie and divide among four warmed shallow bowls. Ladle in the soup and garnish with chopped chives.

CAWL CENNIN
WITH CAERPHILLY CHEESE

SERVES 4
5–6 leeks, finely sliced
200g Caerphilly cheese
fresh crusty bread to serve

STOCK
1 piece of uncooked bacon (hock or collar),
   about 1kg
2 onions, cut in half
2 carrots, cut into rough chunks
4–5 celery sticks, cut into rough chunks
1 head of garlic, halved crossways
small bunch of thyme
3–4 bay leaves
1 tsp black peppercorns

1 To make the stock, put all the ingredients in a large saucepan, cover with cold water and bring to the boil. Turn the heat down to a gentle simmer and cook uncovered for 2–3 hours, skimming frequently.

2 Remove the pan from the heat and allow to settle, then pass the liquid through a very fine sieve into a bowl. Chill the stock overnight. Reserve the cooked bacon.

3 The next day, remove the fat from the surface of the stock, then reheat and taste it. If you prefer a stronger flavour, you can reduce and concentrate the stock, but be careful not to make it too salty.

4 Strain the stock into a clean pan, throw in the sliced leeks and simmer for about 5 minutes or until tender. At this point, you can add some chunks of the cooked bacon (this is optional, as all the flavour is now in the stock). Taste for seasoning, and season only if necessary.

5 To serve, ladle the soup into individual bowls and crumble the cheese over the top. Serve hot, with fresh crusty bread.

64

UNCLE ARWYN'S BEETROOT SOUP

SERVES 4
1 medium onion, sliced
olive oil
4 large raw beetroots, about 500g total weight
600ml vegetable stock
12 raw baby beetroots
sprig of thyme
150ml crème fraîche
salt and pepper

1 Cook the onion with a little olive oil in a heavy-bottomed saucepan for about 5 minutes or until just softened. While the onions are cooking, peel the large beetroots and cut into small dice. Add to the onions and cook for another 5 minutes. Pour in the vegetable stock, season and bring to the boil. Lower the heat and leave to simmer for 20–30 minutes or until the beetroot is tender.
2 Preheat the oven to 160°C/fan 140°C/gas 3.
3 While the soup is cooking, season the baby beetroots with salt and pepper, and place in a small roasting tin with the sprig of thyme. Roast for 20–25 minutes or until soft. Remove from the oven and peel off the skin.
4 When the soup is done, tip the contents of the pan into a blender or food processor and process to a smooth purée.
5 To serve, reheat the soup if necessary. Place the whole roasted baby beetroots in soup bowls. Ladle the soup over and finish each serving with a spoonful of crème fraîche.

CHAPTER TWO **FISH COURSE**

WARM SALAD OF
HOT-SMOKED SEA TROUT, ASPARAGUS AND CUCUMBER
WITH CAPER AND EGG DRESSING

SERVES 4

10 spears of English asparagus, peeled
  and woody ends cut off
250g hot-smoked sea trout fillets
olive oil for drizzling
60g lamb's lettuce
1/4 cucumber, peeled and shaved into strips
1/4 bunch of chives, finely chopped

CAPER AND EGG DRESSING

100g cornichons (baby gherkins),
  finely chopped
100g baby capers
1 shallot, finely chopped
1 hard-boiled egg, grated
50ml olive oil
1 tbsp coarsely cut tarragon leaves
1 tbsp chopped chives
1 tsp sherry vinegar
1 tsp Dijon mustard

1 Preheat the oven to 180°C/fan 160°C/gas 4.

2 Plunge the asparagus into boiling salted water and simmer for 4–5 minutes or until just tender. Drain and refresh in iced water. Drain again, cool and dry, then cut each spear across in half at an angle. Cut the trout into four equal pieces.

3 Make the dressing by mixing all the ingredients together.

4 Line a baking tray with baking parchment. Place the trout and asparagus on the baking tray, drizzle with olive oil and warm through in the oven for 2–3 minutes. Meanwhile, mix the lamb's lettuce and cucumber in a bowl.

5 Break the warm fish into large flakes. Add to the salad with 2 tbsp of the dressing and fold gently together.

6 To serve, arrange five pieces of asparagus on each plate like the spokes of a wheel. Carefully spoon the salad into the middle. Sprinkle with chopped chives and serve immediately, while the trout is still warm. The remaining dressing can be handed separately in a jug.

CRISP-FRIED SPICY JOHN DORY
WITH GRILLED TOMATO CHUTNEY, CUCUMBER SALAD AND CRUSHED PEAS

SERVES 4

4 john dory fillets, each 100–120g, skin on
1 tbsp lime juice
groundnut oil for deep-frying
1 tsp chaat masala
salt and pepper

CUCUMBER SALAD

1 small cucumber, peeled, deseeded
  and cut into julienne
2 medium tomatoes, deseeded and
  cut into julienne
½ medium red onion, halved and
  thinly sliced
10 sprigs of coriander

DRESSING

2 tbsp chilli jam
about 2 tsp lime juice
about 2 tsp vegetable or olive oil

GRILLED TOMATO CHUTNEY

4 medium tomatoes
2 garlic cloves, unpeeled
about 1 tbsp olive oil
1 small green chilli
3 tbsp chopped coriander leaves
1 tsp finely chopped fresh ginger
½ tsp toasted cumin seeds, crushed
2 tbsp lime juice

BATTER

1½ tsp each ginger and garlic pastes,
  mixed together
½ tsp ground turmeric
½ tsp red chilli powder or crushed
  black pepper
¼ tsp garam masala powder
½ tsp mango powder
¼ tsp ajwain seeds (optional)
100g gram flour
1 tbsp cornflour
120ml sparkling water

CRUSHED PEAS

100g freshly shelled peas
15g unsalted butter
2 tsp vegetable oil
pinch of asafoetida
½ tsp cumin seeds
½ tsp red chilli flakes
1 tbsp vegetable stock or water
1 tbsp single cream

1 Mix together all the ingredients for the cucumber salad. In a separate bowl, mix the dressing, adding just enough lime juice and oil to slacken the jam, and to your taste. Chill the salad and dressing.

2 Preheat the grill. To make the tomato chutney, lay the whole tomatoes and garlic on a baking tray and drizzle with a little oil. Grill until well charred. Peel the garlic, then place on a large board with the grilled tomatoes and the rest of the chutney ingredients. Chop together finely to combine. (Or pulse in a food processor to a chutney consistency.) Keep chilled until required.

3 Marinate the fish in the lime juice with a pinch of salt for 20 minutes.

4 To make the batter, mix all the dry ingredients in a bowl, then slowly pour in the sparkling water, whisking as you do so. Wipe the fish with kitchen paper to remove excess moisture, then add to the batter. Leave for 10 minutes.

5 Meanwhile, make the crushed peas. Lightly blanch the peas in boiling salted water for 1 minute, then drain. Heat the butter and oil in a frying pan. Add the asafoetida and, as it foams, add the cumin seeds. When the cumin seeds crackle, add the chilli flakes and the blanched peas. Cook for 3–4 minutes, then stir in the stock and cream, and season. Remove from heat and, with a wooden spoon, crush the peas. Keep warm while you fry the fish.

6 Heat some groundnut oil in a large wok over a medium heat, then deep-fry the fillets for 3–5 minutes or until golden and crisp on both sides. Remove and drain on kitchen paper. Sprinkle with the chaat masala.

7 To serve, toss the cucumber salad with dressing to taste. Spoon the crushed peas onto large warm plates. Place the fish on top, then pile some of the cucumber salad on the fish. Spoon a little tomato chutney around the plate.

GALTON BLACKISTON

MOUSSE AND GRILLED FILLET OF WILD SEA BASS, SERVED ON SAMPHIRE WITH A BROWN SHRIMP AND TARRAGON SAUCE

SERVES 8
8 small wild sea bass fillets, each
   just over 100g, skin on, scaled and
   pin bones removed
250g samphire, well rinsed
1 tsp caster sugar
25g unsalted butter
salt and pepper

WILD SEA BASS MOUSSE
350g wild sea bass fillet, pin bones
   removed, skinned and cubed
1/2 egg white
330ml double cream

BROWN SHRIMP AND TARRAGON SAUCE
1 tbsp lemon juice
1 tbsp white wine
1 tbsp white wine vinegar
1 medium shallot, finely sliced
175g salted butter
3 medium egg yolks
pinch of caster sugar
175g peeled brown shrimps
2 tbsp chopped tarragon

1 To make the mousse, place the sea bass in a food processor and blitz at high speed to purée. Add the egg white and blitz again. Scrape the purée out of the food processor and, using the back of a ladle, push the mixture through a coarse sieve (or tamis) into a bowl.

2 Season the purée with salt and pepper. Add the cream little by little, stirring well between each addition. The finished mixture should be smooth and of a dolloping consistency.

3 Next make up eight little parcels of the mousse. For each parcel, place a square of cling film on your work surface and put a spoonful of mousse into the centre. Bring the four corners up and tie together firmly as if you were tying up a balloon. Set the parcels aside in the fridge. (They can be prepared up to a day ahead.)

4 To make the brown shrimp and tarragon sauce, combine the lemon juice, wine, vinegar and shallot in a small pan and reduce by half. In another pan, melt the butter and allow it to bubble.

5 Put the egg yolks, sugar and a pinch of salt in a food processor and give them a quick whiz to blend. With the processor running, strain in the hot reduced shallot mixture, followed slowly by the hot butter. When all the butter has been added, pour the sauce into a bowl. Stir in the brown shrimps. (The sauce can be made up to 1 hour ahead and left in a bowl set over warm, but not too hot, water.) Add the tarragon at the last minute.

6 When ready to serve, place the cling film parcels in the top of a double boiler and steam over a gentle heat for about 10 minutes. The mousses are ready when they feel firmish to the touch.

7 Meanwhile, preheat the grill to high and bring a large saucepan of water to the boil, ready for cooking the sea bass and samphire. Score the skin of the sea bass fillets, being careful not to cut too deeply into the flesh. Season the flesh side, then arrange, skin-side up, on an oiled baking tray. Brush the scored skin with olive oil. Grill for about 4 minutes or until the skin has blackened and the flesh is just cooked. There is no need to turn the fillets.

8 While the fish cooks, drop the samphire into the pan of boiling water and add the sugar. Boil for 2 minutes, then test a sprig to see if it is cooked (the fleshy end should slip off the stem easily). Drain the samphire thoroughly and smear with the butter.

9 When the mousses are cooked, remove from the steamer. Place some samphire in the centre of each ovenproof plate. Set the grilled fillets of sea bass, skin-side up, on the samphire, then carefully peel off the blackened skin. Snip open the little mousse parcels with scissors, slip off the cling film and place a fish mousse on top of each fillet. Stir the tarragon into the brown shrimp sauce and spoon a little over each mousse. Place the plates under the still hot grill briefly to glaze the sauce (watching carefully), then serve immediately.

LEMON SOLE AND OYSTERS
WITH MUSCOVADO JELLY AND
SWEET AND SOUR CHICORY

SERVES 4

8 fresh oysters in their shells

4 tsp agar-agar

50g dark muscovado sugar, plus
a little extra for sprinkling

125g salted butter

juice of ½ lemon

50ml good chicken stock

50ml good fish stock

2–3 drops of sherry or balsamic vinegar

2 whole lemon soles (ask your fishmonger
to remove the head, fins and black skin,
and cut lengthways down through the
central spine, to give you 4 long pieces
– the fish is still on the bone)

olive or groundnut oil for shallow frying

1 tsp chopped parsley

SWEET AND SOUR CHICORY

1 head chicory

lemon juice

pinch of caster sugar

sea salt

olive oil

1 tsp chopped chives

1 Remove the oysters from their shells. Strain the juices and reserve. Chop each oyster into three and keep chilled until needed.

2 To make the muscovado jelly, mix the agar-agar with 100ml cold water in a pan and leave (off the heat) for a few minutes until softened, then stir in the muscovado sugar and boil for 1 minute. Pour in one-third of the reserved oyster juices. Strain through a fine sieve into a small container and leave to set at room temperature (this should take about 20 minutes).

3 Put 100g of the butter into a small pan. Melt, then heat until almost nut brown and starting to sizzle and caramelise on the bottom of the pan. As the butter foams, quickly mix in the lemon juice and the two stocks to create an emulsion. Add the vinegar for a touch of acidity. Remove from the heat and whiz with a stick blender to make a creamy sauce. Add half of the remaining oyster juices and whiz again with the stick blender. Drop in the chopped oysters. Set aside at room temperature.

4 Pat the pieces of lemon sole dry with kitchen paper. Add a smear of oil to a large non-stick frying pan and heat until you can feel the heat rising when you place your hand above the surface. Lay the fish pieces in the pan, white skin-side down, and cook gently for 2 minutes. Drop in the remaining 25g butter, which will melt and foam straightaway. Turn the fish over and cook gently for 1 more minute. Remove from the heat and leave the fish to continue to cook in the residual heat of the pan for a couple of minutes.

74

5 Meanwhile, finely slice the head of chicory lengthways on a mandolin. Put into a bowl and squeeze over a little lemon juice. Add the sugar, some sea salt, a drizzle of olive oil and the chives, then toss everything together and taste for seasoning. Add the chopped parsley to the oyster butter sauce.

6 To serve, drain the lemon sole on kitchen paper and carefully remove the bone from each piece. Place a piece of fish on each plate and brush with the remaining oyster juices (or spray on using an atomiser).

7 Spoon the warm oysters over the fish with some of the butter sauce, then dot tiny scoops of the muscovado jelly, taken with the tip of a teaspoon, between the chopped oysters. Sprinkle the jelly with just a little muscovado sugar. Scatter the chicory alongside the fish.

RICHARD CORRIGAN

WHOLE POACHED WILD SALMON AND DUCK EGG DRESSING
WITH WHEATEN BREAD AND COUNTRY BUTTER

SERVES 6-8
1 whole wild salmon, 3–3.5kg, gutted
  and scaled
salt and pepper

WHEATEN BREAD
250g plain flour, plus extra for dusting
10g salt
10g bicarbonate of soda
250g wholemeal flour
150g jumbo oatmeal
2 tsp clear honey
1 tsp black treacle
375ml buttermilk
125ml full-fat milk

CUCUMBER SALAD
1 cucumber, peeled, deseeded and
  finely sliced
100ml white wine vinegar
25g caster sugar

½ tbsp mustard seeds
handful of dill, chopped

COURT BOUILLON
1 bottle (75cl) dry white wine
bunch of flat-leaf parsley
2 small leeks, sliced
2 celery sticks, sliced
2 onions, sliced
1 tbsp sea salt
6 black peppercorns
2 bay leaves

DRESSING
150g good-quality organic unsalted butter
4 duck eggs
4 tbsp capers
small handful of flat-leaf parsley, chopped
2 tbsp chopped chives
lemon juice

1 First make the bread. Preheat the oven to 200°C/fan 180°C/gas 6. Line a baking sheet with baking parchment.

2 Sift the plain flour, salt and soda into a large bowl and mix in the wholemeal flour and oatmeal. Mix the honey and treacle into the buttermilk, then quickly and lightly fold the buttermilk and milk into the dry ingredients. Use five folds of the hand and do not overwork – when the ingredients are heavy, the action should be light.

3 Divide the dough into quarters with floured hands, then mould each into a round and place on the baking sheet. Dust lightly with plain flour and mark a cross in the top of each loaf. Bake for 20–30 minutes or until the loaves sound hollow when tapped on the base. Transfer to a wire rack, drape a damp cloth over the loaves and leave to cool. (Wheaten bread should be eaten on the day of baking, or toasted the next. This will make four loaves, but the bread freezes well.) Turn the oven down to 100°C/fan 80°C/gas 1/4.

4 While the bread is baking, make the cucumber salad. Sprinkle the cucumber slices with salt and leave to stand. Put the wine vinegar in a heavy pan with 100ml water, the sugar and mustard seeds. Heat gently until the sugar has dissolved, then boil to reduce by half. Remove from the heat. Rinse and drain the cucumber, then mix into the pickling liquid with the dill. Set aside.

5 Put all the ingredients for the court bouillon in a large fish kettle with 6 litres cold water. Bring to the boil and simmer for 20 minutes.

6 Lower the salmon into the court bouillon. Bring back to the boil, then cover the kettle tightly so no steam can escape. Transfer to the oven and poach for 25 minutes with the oven door ajar.

7 Meanwhile, make the dressing. Melt the butter and keep warm. Lower the duck eggs into a pan of boiling water and simmer for 4 minutes. Lift the eggs out of the water and cool a little under the cold tap, then carefully peel off the shells. Mash the eggs in a bowl with a fork, then mix in the capers, herbs and warm melted butter. Season with lemon juice, salt and pepper to taste. Keep the dressing warm.

8 Remove the salmon from the court bouillon as soon as the poaching time is up. Serve with the cucumber salad and warm dressing, with slices of wheaten bread and country butter on the side.

76

PAN-FRIED JOHN DORY
WITH LOBSTER MASH, BROAD BEANS,
SAMPHIRE AND COURGETTE FLOWERS

SERVES 4

2 live lobsters, preferably native South
  Coast, each 500–600g
200g freshly shelled broad beans
4 baby courgettes, with flowers attached
200g samphire
4 large fillets of john dory, each
  about 150g, skinned
200ml olive oil
50g butter
salt and pepper

LOBSTER SAUCE

mirepoix of finely diced vegetables (½
  onion, 1 carrot, 2 celery sticks, ¼ fennel
  bulb)
4 garlic cloves, finely diced
2 tbsp olive oil
1 tbsp tomato purée

large sprig of thyme
large sprig of basil
½ star anise
6 fennel seeds
6 coriander seeds
6 black peppercorns
4 tbsp white wine
2 tbsp brandy
500ml home-made chicken stock

LOBSTER MASH

4 large Desirée potatoes, peeled
  and quartered
125ml double cream
about 100g unsalted butter, diced
freshly grated nutmeg
8 basil leaves, coarsely chopped
6 tarragon leaves, coarsely chopped

1 Put the lobsters in the freezer for an hour to desensitize them (no longer than this or the meat will become frozen), then cut them in half lengthways and separate the heads, claws and tails. Cut the heads into about six pieces, reserving all the liquid that comes out. (If there are any corals, freeze them to use in another dish.) Blanch the claws and tails in boiling salted water for 4 minutes. Drain and leave on a tray until cool enough to handle, then remove the shells while still warm. Cut the meat into 1cm dice and set aside. Reserve all the shells and heads.

2 To make the lobster sauce, cook the mirepoix and garlic in the oil over a high heat for 10–15 minutes or until lightly browned. Add the lobster shells and heads with all the liquid, and mix well. Cook for 2 minutes, then add the tomato purée and cook for 1 more minute before adding the herbs, spices, wine and brandy. Cover with the stock and 500ml water and bring to the boil, then simmer for 45 minutes. Strain through a muslin-lined sieve into a clean pan and boil until reduced to 100ml. Keep the sauce warm.

3 Plunge the broad beans into boiling salted water and simmer for 3–5 minutes or until tender. Drain and refresh in iced water, then drain again and peel off the skins.

4 Remove the flowers from the courgettes and set aside. Cut each courgette lengthways into quarters, then dice each length into 1cm pieces. Cook in boiling

salted water for 2 minutes only. Drain, refresh in iced water and drain again. Split the courgette flowers lengthways in half and pick out the stamens, then split the flowers in half again.

5 Pick the roots off the samphire and blanch the stems in boiling water for 1 minute. Drain, refresh in iced water and drain again.

6 To make the mash, put the potatoes in a pan of cold salted water and bring to the boil. Turn the heat down and simmer gently for about 25 minutes or until the potatoes are just cooked. Meanwhile, boil the cream in a separate pan until reduced by half. Drain the potatoes, then dry off slightly and mash. Work the mash through a food mill (mouli), ricer or sieve into a clean pan and beat in 50g butter, a few pieces at a time, followed by three-quarters of the reduced cream. Now beat in another 50g butter, and season to taste with nutmeg, salt and pepper. If you think the mash needs it, you can add more butter at this stage.

7 Reheat the mash until hot, then gently fold in half the diced lobster meat along with the chopped basil and tarragon. Taste for seasoning and fold in the remaining cream. Cover the surface of the mash with greaseproof paper or cling film and keep warm by the side of the stove.

8 Cut each john dory fillet lengthways into three pieces. Season. Heat 150ml of the olive oil in a large heavy frying pan until hot but not smoking. Lower in the pieces of fish, skinned side up, and pan-fry for $1-1^1/_2$ minutes or until golden underneath. Turn the pieces over and repeat on the other side. When the fish is almost done, add the butter in small pieces and let it start to turn golden brown and foam around the fish. Remove the fish and drain well on kitchen paper.

9 In a small saucepan, gently reheat the blanched broad beans, courgette dice and samphire with all but 2 tsp of the remaining olive oil and 1 tsp water. When hot, add the lobster sauce and the courgette flower pieces, then the remaining diced lobster meat and oil. Taste and add seasoning if necessary.

10 To serve, quickly reheat the mash for 20 seconds or so, then spoon onto the centre of each plate. Top each serving with three pieces of fish and drizzle the lobster and vegetable dressing over and around.

FILLET OF TURBOT IN RED WINE
WITH ARTICHOKE PURÉE AND PICKLED BABY BEETS

SERVES 6

6 thick turbot fillets, each 125–150g, skinned

salt and pepper

18 small sprigs of lovage or very fine flat-leaf
   parsley to garnish

POACHING LIQUOR

2 litres red wine

2 sprigs of thyme

1/2 bay leaf

1 garlic clove, peeled

PICKLED BABY BEETS

9 raw baby beetroots

1 tsp demerara sugar

4 tsp balsamic vinegar

ARTICHOKE PUREE

25g unsalted butter

500g Jerusalem artichokes, peeled
   and very finely sliced

2 sprigs of thyme

1/2 bay leaf

1 garlic clove, peeled

50ml double cream

1 For the poaching liquor, pour the wine into a large saucepan and add the thyme, bay leaf, garlic clove and 1/2 tsp salt. Boil over a medium-high heat until reduced to 750ml. Strain through a fine sieve, preferably lined with muslin, into a large wide pan and set aside.

2 To make the pickled baby beets, peel the beetroots with a small, sharp knife or a very fine potato peeler, then place in a pan with 150ml water, the sugar, balsamic vinegar and a pinch of salt. Bring just to the boil. Cover the pan and simmer for 8–10 minutes or until tender. Remove the beetroots. Pass the cooking liquid through a fine sieve, then return to the pan and reduce to a nice glaze over a medium heat. Cut the beetroots in half and add to the glaze. Set aside.

3 Next, make the artichoke purée. Melt the butter in a heavy pan. Add the artichokes, season with a pinch of salt and add the thyme, bay leaf and garlic clove. Stir well. Cover with a sheet of greaseproof paper and sweat the artichokes for 10–15 minutes or until they are very soft. Stir regularly during cooking, and add a little water if they start to colour. Add the cream and boil for 3 minutes, then remove the thyme, bay leaf and garlic. Purée the artichokes in a blender until silky smooth. Check for seasoning, and keep warm.

4 Bring the poaching liquor to the boil, then remove from the heat. Carefully lower in the fish fillets, making sure they are submerged in a single layer and not sitting on top of each other. Leave the turbot off the heat like this for 7–8 minutes or until the fish is just cooked through, only returning the pan to a low heat if the liquor cools down too much before the fish is cooked.

5 While the fish is cooking, gently reheat the beetroots and the artichoke purée. When the fish is cooked, remove it very gently from the poaching liquor using a fish slice and drain on kitchen paper. Season each fillet with a pinch of sea salt.

6 To serve, place a piece of fish on each plate and garnish with a neat spoonful of artichoke purée and beetroot halves. Drizzle a little of the beetroot glaze around the fish, and finish with the lovage or parsley.

MATT TEBBUTT

SEWIN AND SOUSED VEGETABLES
WITH COCKLES AND WOOD SORREL

SERVES 4
4 sewin (sea trout) fillets, each
   about 175g, skin on
400g live cockles in their shells
100g wood sorrel
50ml extra virgin olive oil

POACHING LIQUOR
4 celery sticks
4 carrots
2 large onions
2 bay leaves
1 tsp black peppercorns
1 tsp coriander seeds
400ml dry white wine
200ml white wine vinegar

1 To make the poaching liquor, slice the celery and carrots on the diagonal, to the same thickness. Halve the onions, place the halves cut-side down and slice into semi-circles. Throw these vegetables into a wide saucepan and add the remaining ingredients and 100ml cold water. Bring to the boil and simmer for 30 minutes. Remove from the heat.

2 Slip the sewin into the poaching liquor. Return the pan to a gentle heat and cook, uncovered, for 6–7 minutes. Do not allow the liquid to boil. Remove the fish and keep warm. Lift the vegetables out of the poaching liquor with a slotted spoon and keep warm.

3 Pour most of the poaching liquor out of the pan, leaving behind just enough to cover the bottom. Bring this to the boil and throw in the cockles. Cover with the lid and cook, shaking the pan from time to time, until the cockles open – this should take 2–3 minutes. Drain the cockles and remove them from their shells, keeping some in the shell for the garnish.

4 To serve, place some soused vegetables on warm plates with the sewin on top, and scatter the cockles around. Finish with the wood sorrel, a splash of olive oil and the cockles in their shells.

SKATE WING,
NUT BROWN BUTTER, PARSLEY JELLY, CAPERS AND LEMON CONFIT

SERVES 4

4 skate wings, each 500g, skinned and
  filleted (ask the fishmonger to do this)
3 tbsp olive oil
knob of butter
squeeze of lemon juice
salt and white pepper

PARSLEY JELLY

100g parsley, stalks and leaves
2 tsp agar-agar powder

LEMON CONFIT

2 unwaxed lemons
50g caster sugar

BUTTER SAUCE

100g salted butter
juice of 1 lemon
5 tbsp chicken stock
50g small capers, rinsed and dried

1 To make the parsley jelly, put the parsley through a juicer, then pour immediately into an airtight container and chill. Sprinkle the agar-agar and a pinch of salt over 4 tbsp cold water in a small saucepan. Leave to soak for 2–3 minutes. Bring to the boil and boil for 1 minute, then pour in the parsley juice. Pour into a clean container and chill for about 1 hour or until softly set. Purée the jelly in a blender and pass it through a sieve. Keep in a plastic squeezy bottle in the fridge until ready to use.

2 For the lemon confit, wash the lemons, then thinly slice on a mandolin. Put the sugar in a saucepan with 200ml water. When the sugar has dissolved, bring to the boil. Carefully lay the lemon slices in the syrup. Remove from the heat and cool. (These are best made a day ahead; any extras will keep in the fridge for 2–3 weeks.)

3 To make the butter sauce, melt the butter in a saucepan until it foams and then turns to a nut-brown colour. Add the lemon juice, a pinch of salt and the chicken stock. Remove from the heat and blend with a stick blender to create an emulsified sauce. Throw in the capers and keep warm.

4 Cut each skate fillet in half lengthways. Roll each up into a long roll, rolling from the long side so you get a cigar shape that is plump in the middle and tapers off at the ends. Secure each with a wooden cocktail stick.

5 Heat the olive oil and butter in a non-stick frying pan. When the butter is foaming, add the rolls of skate and spoon over the oil and foaming butter as they cook. Allow about 5 minutes, turning occasionally. Remove, drain on kitchen paper and let rest for a few minutes.

6 To serve, season the skate with the lemon juice and some salt and white pepper. Place in warm bowls, spoon the butter sauce over and arrange some lemon slices on top of the fish. Dot the parsley jelly around the fish and into the sauce to give you bursts of fresh green colour and flavour.

PAN-FRIED BLACK BREAM
WITH MADRAS CURRY SAUCE AND
SEMOLINA POLENTA

SERVES 4

4 medium-sized black bream fillets, skin on

2 tbsp vegetable oil

15g butter

salt and pepper

mustard cress to garnish

MADRAS SAUCE

2 tbsp vegetable oil

2 cloves

1 tsp finely chopped fresh ginger

1 green chilli, deseeded and finely chopped

6 curry leaves (fresh or freeze-dried)

2 medium onions, thinly sliced

1/2 tsp ground turmeric

1/2 tsp ground coriander

1/2 tsp black pepper

1 large tomato, chopped

1 medium-sized, just ripe mango,
   flesh puréed

300ml coconut milk

SEMOLINA POLENTA

200g coarse semolina

3 tbsp vegetable oil

1 tsp black mustard seeds

1 tbsp unroasted peanuts, roughly crushed

1 red chilli, split

6 curry leaves

1 tbsp finely chopped fresh ginger

1 medium onion, finely sliced

1 tsp lime juice

1 tbsp chopped coriander leaves

4 tbsp dry breadcrumbs

butter and a splash of vegetable oil
   for frying

1 First make the sauce. Heat the oil in a wok, add the cloves, ginger, chilli and curry leaves, and sauté for 1 minute. Add the sliced onions and sauté for 2–3 minutes or until translucent, then add the turmeric, coriander and black pepper and sauté for 1 more minute. Add the tomato and sauté for 2 minutes, then add the mango purée. Cook for a further 2–3 minutes. Pour in the coconut milk and simmer gently for 2–3 minutes. Set aside. If the sauce goes a bit thick, add 1 tbsp warm water.

2 For the polenta, tip the semolina into a frying pan and toast over a medium heat, shaking the pan often, until lightly browned. Set aside. Heat the oil in a wok and add the mustard seeds, peanuts, whole chilli and curry leaves. Fry for 1 minute, then add the ginger. Stir in the onion and sauté until translucent. Pour in 450ml hot water and bring to the boil. Slowly add the toasted semolina, beating briskly as you pour to prevent any lumps from forming. If the mix seems a bit stiff to beat, add a little more boiling water. Mix well together, then stir in the lime juice, chopped coriander and salt to taste. Cook for a further 3–4 minutes. Discard the chilli. Spread the mixture in a 17cm square tin that is about 2.5cm deep. Leave to cool and set.

3 Cut the set semolina cake into 3 x 4cm rectangles and dust them lightly with the breadcrumbs on both sides. Melt a big knob of butter in a frying pan with a splash of oil, add the polenta cakes and fry to make a golden crust, adding more butter as needed. Keep warm. (Extra polenta cakes can be reheated for another time.)

4 For the bream, season the fillets with salt and pepper. Heat the oil in a non-stick pan, add the fillets, skin-side down, and fry for 2–3 minutes or until golden. Turn the fillets over, add the butter and fry on a medium heat for a further 1–2 minutes. Meanwhile, reheat the sauce.

5 To serve, place the fish on large plates. Pour some of the sauce over and around the fish, place a polenta cake alongside and top with some mustard cress.

MARK BROADBENT

POACHED TURBOT AND COCKLES
WITH ASPARAGUS AND BROWN SHRIMP BUTTER

SERVES 4
20 asparagus spears, preferably Formby
4 skinless pieces of turbot fillet, each
  about 200g
very finely shredded flat-leaf parsley
  to garnish

SOUSED COCKLES
125ml Chardonnay vinegar, preferably
  Forum
1 banana shallot, sliced into rings
sprig of thyme
2 bay leaves
5 black peppercorns
1 tsp pickling spice
450g live cockles in their shells, preferably
  from Morecambe Bay

BROWN SHRIMP BUTTER
450g cooked brown shrimps in their shells,
  preferably from Morecambe Bay
525g good salted butter, preferably
  Longley Farm Yorkshire, clarified
1 tsp blade mace
pinch of celery salt
2 pinches of cayenne pepper
pinch of grated nutmeg
black pepper
lemon juice

COURT BOUILLON
dry white wine, preferably English
1 tsp white peppercorns
large bouquet garni (1 large sprig of thyme,
  3 celery sticks, a few parsley stalks, 1/2 leek,
  2 bay leaves and pared zest of 1/4 lemon,
  tied together)

1 To souse the cockles, pour the vinegar into a heavy saucepan, add the shallot, herbs and spices, and bring to the boil. Simmer for 10 minutes, then add the cockles and cover the pan. Cook for 3–5 minutes only, just until the cockles open. Do not overcook. Drain the cockles, reserving the sousing liquor, and remove them from their shells. Set both cockles and liquor aside.

2 Trim the ends off the asparagus at an angle, and peel away any woody bits. Plunge the spears into a pan of boiling salted water to cook for 2 minutes. Drain and refresh in iced water, and drain again. Set aside.

3 Preheat the oven to 180°C/fan 160°C/gas 4.

4 For the shrimp butter, peel the shrimps and put the shells in a roasting tin with 125g of the butter. Roast for about 1 hour or until golden brown. Leave to infuse until cool, then pass the butter through a fine sieve lined with muslin into a clean pan. Add the remaining clarified butter, the mace, celery salt, cayenne and nutmeg. Simmer for 15 minutes. Take off the heat. Taste and balance the flavours with black pepper and a squeeze of lemon juice. If you've used a good salted butter, it won't be necessary to add any salt. Reserve in the pan.

5 To make the court bouillon, bring 1.2 litres water to the boil in a large saucepan with a healthy splash of wine, the peppercorns and bouquet garni. Lower the heat and simmer for 20–25 minutes, then remove from the heat and cover the pan. Leave to infuse until cold.

6 Strain the cold court bouillon into a straight-sided pan and bring to a simmer. Gently lower in the turbot fillets, arranging them in a single layer. Poach gently for 4–5 minutes.

7 While the fish is poaching, gently warm the asparagus in the reserved sousing liquor, then add the cockles and warm for no more than 30 seconds. Taste for seasoning. Warm the shrimp butter, add the peeled shrimps and gently warm through (do not cook). Taste for seasoning.

8 To serve, place a turbot fillet to the right side of each plate, and place the asparagus on the left. Spoon the cockles and a little of the sousing liquor over the asparagus and sprinkle with shredded parsley. Top the turbot with the shrimps and spoon the shrimp butter over and around.

PAN-FRIED WILD SALMON
WITH CONWY MUSSELS, CRUSHED NEW
POTATOES AND A HORSERADISH SAUCE

SERVES 4

500g fresh mussels in their shells
2 shallots, finely sliced
olive oil
250ml white wine
250ml single cream
lemon juice
5cm piece of fresh horseradish

200g Charlotte potatoes
bunch of chives, chopped
4 pieces of wild salmon fillet, each 120g,
   skin on
100g freshly shelled peas
50g pea shoots
salt and pepper

1 Prepare the mussels by washing them under cold water and removing the beards. Drain. In a heavy-bottomed pan, cook the shallots in a little olive oil until translucent. Add the mussels and pour on the wine. Place a lid on the pan and cook for 3–4 minutes or until the mussels have opened. (Discard any that do not open.) Drain the mussels in a colander set over a bowl. Pour the liquid from the bowl into a small pan and set aside. Pick the mussels out of their shells and keep, covered, in the fridge.

2 To make the sauce, bring the reserved mussel liquid to the boil. Add the cream and simmer for 5–6 minutes until reduced slightly. It should not be too thick, but more soupy. Season with salt, pepper and a squeeze of lemon juice. Remove from the heat, then grate in the fresh horseradish and leave to cool. When cool, taste the sauce. If the horseradish flavour is strong enough, strain through a fine sieve and leave to one side. If not, leave a little longer for the flavour to develop before straining.

3 Cook the whole potatoes in boiling salted water for 10–12 minutes or until tender. Drain and leave to cool. When cool, peel off the skins and put the potatoes back into the pan. Crush the potatoes with a fork. Season and add the chives. Keep warm.

4 Preheat the oven to 180°C/fan 160°C/gas 4.

5 Season the salmon with salt and pepper. Heat a non-stick, ovenproof frying pan, then add a splash of olive oil and cook the salmon skin-side down for 2 minutes, without turning. Place the pan in the oven to cook for 3–4 minutes.

6 Meanwhile, heat a little of the horseradish sauce in a pan. Add the peas and cook for 1 minute, then add the mussels just to warm through. Heat the remaining sauce in another pan. Season the pea shoots with salt, pepper, lemon juice and olive oil.

7 For each serving, place a ring, about 4cm diameter, in the middle of a shallow bowl. Spoon the crushed potatoes into the ring, lightly packing them. Remove the ring. Scatter the mussels and peas around the potato and place a salmon fillet, skin-side up, on top. Scatter the pea shoots on top of the mussels and peas, then finish with a light drizzle of the warm horseradish cream sauce all around.

BRAISED FILLET
OF WILD HALIBUT
WITH TRUFFLE AND WHITE BEAN SAUCE

SERVES 6

50ml good olive oil, plus extra for drizzling

3 skinless halibut fillets, preferably wild,
  each about 150g

2 tsp chopped chervil

20g unsalted butter

salt

fresh black truffles to serve (optional)

VEGETABLE NAGE

½ leek, outside leaves discarded, cut
  into 3cm lengths

2 carrots, cut into 2cm lengths

1 white-skinned onion, cut lengthways
  into eighths

1 celery stick, cut into 3cm lengths

1 large garlic clove, peeled

½ star anise, crushed

¼ tsp coriander seeds, crushed

large pinch of white peppercorns, crushed

few mixed sprigs of herbs (eg parsley, basil,
  chives and chervil)

lemon wedge

50ml dry white wine

SAUCE

100g dried white beans (haricots blancs),
  soaked in cold water overnight

300ml home-made chicken stock

¼ carrot

¼ celery stick

¼ white-skinned onion

1 garlic clove, peeled

50g piece of smoked bacon

250ml Madeira

500ml reduced home-made beef stock

10g fresh black truffles, chopped

white truffle oil to taste

1 First make the vegetable nage. Put the vegetables and garlic into a heavy saucepan and pour in cold water until it reaches the same level as the vegetables. Bring to the boil over a high heat. Skim, then simmer over a medium heat for 8 minutes.

2 Add the crushed spices with the herbs and lemon wedge. Simmer for a further 2 minutes, then take the pan off the heat and pour in the wine. Stir. Leave until cold, then refrigerate in a sealed glass or plastic container for 24 hours.

3 The next day, strain the liquid through a fine sieve. Keep, covered, in the fridge until ready to use. Discard the vegetables and flavourings.

4 To make the sauce, drain and rinse the beans, then put them in a pan of fresh water and bring to the boil. Drain and rinse under cold running water. Put the beans back into the pan and add the chicken stock, 200ml water, the carrot, celery, onion, garlic, bacon and a pinch of salt. Bring to the boil. Turn down to a simmer, then cover and cook for 15–20 minutes. The beans need to be tender, but should still have some

bite. Drain the beans in a colander. Remove the vegetables, garlic and bacon. Leave the beans to cool, then chop them roughly with a sharp knife.

5 Boil the Madeira in a pan until reduced to 100ml. Add the reduced beef stock with the chopped beans and truffles, and continue to cook over a low heat for 20 minutes. Add truffle oil to taste and season with salt if needed. Set aside.

6 Now cook the halibut. Measure 150ml vegetable nage into a saucepan and heat until hot, then set aside in a warm place. Heat the olive oil in a non-stick frying pan over a medium-high heat. Season the halibut with fine salt and place skinned-side down in the pan. Fry for 3–4 minutes or until nicely coloured, then gently turn the fish over with a palette knife and cook for 1 more minute. Take the pan off the heat. Cover the top of the fish with the chopped chervil, then put the butter in the pan followed by the hot vegetable nage. Cover the pan with baking parchment and return to the heat to cook for 2 minutes.

7 Remove the fish from the nage and set aside in a warm place. Leave the pan on the heat and boil the nage, stirring all the time, until it is reduced to a thick emulsion. At the same time, reheat the bean sauce.

8 To serve, cut each piece of fish in half with a sharp knife, then place the fish in bowls and spoon a little of the reduced nage over each piece to glaze. Spoon the bean sauce over and around, and drizzle with olive oil. If you want to be really extravagant, slice fresh black truffles over the top just before serving.

SMOKED EEL MOUSSE
WITH BOXTY PANCAKES, HORSERADISH AND MUSTARD GRAIN CREAM, AND FRESH HERB SALAD

SERVES 4

500g fresh eel fillet, skinned
1 medium egg white
olive oil
125ml chilled double cream
250g smoked eel fillet, preferably Lough Neagh, diced
small handful each of coriander, basil, chervil and rocket leaves
salt and pepper

BOXTY PANCAKES

125g raw peeled potato (a floury variety such as Dunbar Standard or Maris Piper), grated
125g mashed potato, made from 200g floury potatoes, peeled and cooked
125g plain flour, plus extra for dusting
½ tsp baking powder
½ tsp salt
large knob of salted butter, melted and cooled
a little milk if needed

HORSERADISH AND MUSTARD GRAIN CREAM

300ml whipping cream
1 tsp freshly grated horseradish
1 tsp wholegrain mustard, preferably Castle Leslie

1 First make the smoked eel mousse. Check the fresh eel for any stray bones or skin, then work the flesh to a fine purée in a blender. Add the egg white and a pinch of salt, and purée again. Press the mixture through a very fine sieve into a bowl, checking again that there are no bones. Place the bowl over a bowl of ice and put into the fridge to chill for 10–15 minutes.

2 Preheat the oven to 150°C/fan 130°C/gas 2. Lightly brush four 7.5–10cm non-stick moulds with olive oil (or use oiled ramekins lined with discs of baking parchment).

3 Remove the purée from the fridge and gradually mix in the cream using a rubber spatula. Do this very slowly or the mixture may curdle. Fold in the diced smoked eel and season. Spoon into the moulds. Cover them closely with cling film and then with foil. Set them in a roasting tin and pour enough warm water into the tin to come halfway up the sides of the moulds. Bake for 8 minutes or until a knife inserted in the centre comes out clean. Remove from the oven and leave to cool.

4 For the boxty pancakes, put the grated raw potato on a cloth and wring over a bowl, to catch the liquid. This will separate into a clear fluid with starch at the bottom. Pour off and discard the fluid. Add the grated and mashed potato to the starch left in the bowl and mix well. Sift the dry ingredients and mix into the potatoes along with the melted butter, adding a little milk if necessary to make a pliable dough.

5 Knead the dough lightly on a floured surface. Divide into four and form each portion into a flat round cake about 1cm larger than the moulds used for the eel mousse. With the back of a knife, mark each pancake into quarters without cutting right through.

6 Heat a large griddle or heavy frying pan until hot. Dust with flour, then place a pancake marked-side down on the griddle. Cook over a medium heat for 3–5 minutes or until browned. Turn the pancake over and repeat on the other side. Remove from the griddle and keep warm while you cook the remaining pancakes in the same way.

7 Meanwhile, make the horseradish cream. Whip the cream until it holds a peak, then fold in the horseradish, mustard, and salt and pepper to taste. Mix the herb leaves together, and season with sea salt and a small drop of olive oil.

8 To serve, put a pancake, marked-side up, on each plate, and unmould an eel mousse onto it. Garnish with the herb salad and a quenelle of horseradish cream.

JEREMY LEE

SALAD OF POTATOES, ARBROATH SMOKIE, AYRESHIRE BACON
AND A SOFT-BOILED EGG

SERVES 4
500g little new potatoes
5 tbsp olive oil
2 tsp red wine vinegar
4 fresh organic eggs

8 thin rashers of streaky bacon
a brace of Arbroath smokies
2 knobs of butter
1 tsp Dijon mustard
salt and pepper

1 Cook the potatoes in a pan of plenty of lightly salted water for 12–15 minutes or until tender. Drain and, while still hot, peel and toss them with 1 tbsp of the oil and 1 tsp of the vinegar. Keep warm.

2 Preheat the oven to 170°C/fan 150°C/gas 3.

3 Fill a small pan with water and set to a furious boil. Lay in the eggs with a spoon and cook for 4–4^1/$_2$ minutes. Remove the eggs swiftly and plunge into iced water to arrest the cooking. Peel and let sit in cold water until required.

4 Place the rashers of bacon on a wire rack and sit this on a baking sheet. Cook in the preheated oven for about 10 minutes or until the bacon is golden and crisp, cooking for longer if necessary.

5 Meanwhile, butter the smokies with a knob of the butter, then warm them briefly in a dish in the oven. Remove the skin and as many bones as possible. Flake the fish into a heatproof dish. Just before serving, lightly butter the flakes with the remaining knob of butter and warm gently in the oven.

6 Stir sea salt and freshly ground pepper into the remaining 1 tsp vinegar to dissolve, then add the mustard and whisk well. Gradually whisk in the remaining oil.

7 To serve, heap the potatoes onto plates. Scatter the warmed flaked smokies over. Cut the eggs in half and lay two halves on each serving. Lay the bacon rashers on top and spoon over the vinaigrette.

SOUSED MACKEREL
WITH POTATO SALAD

SERVES 4

4 mackerel fillets, each about 100g,
  as fresh as possible

35g fine sea salt

¼ cucumber

4 tsp freshly grated horseradish (or strong
  horseradish relish)

2 banana shallots, very finely sliced

MARINADE

400ml white wine vinegar

200g caster sugar

1 star anise

sprig of thyme

8 black peppercorns

POTATO SALAD

200g new potatoes, boiled in their skins
  until tender, then roughly chopped

3 tbsp mayonnaise

finely chopped chives

1 You need to start curing the mackerel 4–7 days ahead. First, check the fillets for pin bones with your fingertips and pull out any stray bones with tweezers. Lay the fish skin-side down in a shallow dish and sprinkle the salt liberally over the top. Cover and leave for about 6 hours or overnight in the fridge. You will find salty fish juices leach out and the flesh firms – this is all fine.

2 To make the marinade, pour the vinegar into a medium-sized pan. Put it over a low heat and add the sugar, star anise, thyme and peppercorns. Bring slowly to the boil, then take off the heat, cover and allow to cool.

3 Meanwhile, peel the piece of cucumber, halve lengthways and scoop out the seeds. Cut the cucumber into matchsticks and divide into four equal bundles.

4 Rinse the fish well in cold water, then pat dry with kitchen paper. Spread the horseradish thinly over the flesh side of the fillets. Lay a cucumber bundle at one end of each fillet and carefully roll up the fish around it. Secure the rolls with a wooden cocktail stick.

5 Take a smallish dish (not too shallow) that's just big enough to hold the mackerel side by side, and sprinkle some of the shallot slices over the bottom. Place the mackerel on top of the shallots, packing the fillets tightly together. Scatter the rest of the shallots on top, then pour the cooled vinegar marinade over the fish, making sure that the fillets are immersed. Cover tightly with cling film or with an airtight lid and refrigerate for at least 4 days, but no longer than 7 days.

6 When ready to serve, make up the potato salad by mixing all the ingredients together. Serve each mackerel fillet with a little pile of potato salad alongside.

DEVON CRAB AND GINGER DUMPLINGS
WITH A LEMON THYME AND GINGER SAUCE

SERVES 4

VEGETABLE STOCK

1 onion

1 leek

3 carrots

4 celery sticks

3 garlic cloves, unpeeled, lightly crushed

2 star anise

1 tsp white pepper

1 bay leaf

5 cloves

250ml white wine

sprig each of thyme, tarragon, chervil and coriander

SAFFRON DUMPLING DOUGH

1 (0.25g) packet saffron

2 tsp olive oil

1 egg

3 egg yolks

250g plain flour, sifted with 1 tsp salt

CRAB, SCALLOP AND GINGER MOUSSE

75g scallops

1 egg yolk

100ml double cream

75g brown crab meat, free of any cartilage or shell

20g very finely diced fresh ginger

250g white crab meat, free of any cartilage or shell

cayenne pepper

lemon juice

salt and pepper

LEMON THYME AND GINGER SAUCE

175g unsalted butter

75g shallots, sliced

25g fresh ginger, chopped

40g lemon thyme

1 tsp white peppercorns

1 tsp coriander seeds

75g brown crab meat, free of any cartilage or shell

250g crab shells

200ml fish stock

lemon juice

GARNISH

5cm piece of fresh ginger, peeled

squeeze of lemon juice

pink grapefruit segments, cut into small pieces

finely shredded coriander leaves

1 To make the stock, cut the vegetables into medium rough dice. Put them into a stainless steel saucepan with the garlic, star anise, pepper, bay leaf, cloves and enough water just to cover. Bring to the boil and cook until the vegetables are soft. Add the wine and bring back to the boil. Remove from the heat, add the herbs and leave too cool. Strain and reserve for the sauce.

2 To make the dumpling dough, put 1 tbsp water in a small saucepan with the saffron and olive oil, and bring to the boil. Leave to cool. Lightly beat the egg and egg yolks, and mix into the saffron liquid. Place the flour in a food processor. With the machine running, slowly add the egg mixture to make a dough with a grainy texture that just starts to cling together but is not too wet. The amount of liquid absorbed by the flour will vary, so be careful not to make the dough too dry or wet. Remove the dough and bring together into a ball. Wrap in cling film and leave to rest at room temperature for 30 minutes.

3 Meanwhile, make the mousse. Put the scallops, egg yolk, cream and brown crab meat in a blender and blend to a fine purée. Turn into a bowl and set in another bowl of iced water to cool. Put the diced ginger in a small pan of cold water, bring to the boil and boil for 1 minute, then refresh in cold water. Repeat this blanching twice. Add the ginger and white crab meat to the scallop purée, then season with a pinch of cayenne, a few drops of lemon juice, salt and pepper. Put the mousse mixture into a piping bag fitted with a small round nozzle (or keep in the bowl if you would prefer to spoon the mousse). Chill while you make the sauce.

4 Melt 75g of the butter in a stainless steel saucepan, add the shallots, ginger and lemon thyme, and sweat for 5 minutes, without colouring. Add the peppercorns and coriander seeds, and sweat for 2 more minutes. Add the brown crab meat and crab shells, and sweat for a further 5 minutes. Pour in 300ml of the vegetable stock and the fish stock and bring to the boil. Simmer for 20 minutes. Strain through a colander, then a fine sieve.

5 Measure 100ml of this flavoured stock (any remaining stock can be frozen) into a small pan, heat and then whisk in the remaining butter, a small piece at a time. Season with salt and pepper and a drop of lemon juice. This is the sauce for the dumplings. Set aside.

6 Using a mandolin, carefully cut the piece of ginger for garnishing into thin slices, then into fine strips. Put in a saucepan with a squeeze of lemon juice and enough water to cover. Bring to the boil, then refresh in cold water. Repeat this blanching three times. Set the ginger aside in a small pan of cold water.

7 Using a pasta machine (take it down to the last number), roll out the dumpling dough until it is smooth and fine. Using a 6–8cm round cutter, cut out discs of dough and place on a cling film-lined tray. You need 12 discs.

8 Make one dumpling at a time. Drop a disc of dumpling dough into boiling water and cook for 30 seconds, then refresh in iced water. Remove and dry on a towel, then place on a piece of cling film that is bigger than the disc. Pipe or spoon a ball of crab mousse into the middle. Lift up the cling film and mould the dough around the mousse into a ball. Twist the end of the film to seal like a money bag. Repeat to make 12 dumplings in all. (You may have extra mousse.)

9 Drop the wrapped dumplings into a pan of simmering water and cook them for 6 minutes. While they are cooking, reheat the dumpling sauce, the ginger garnish (in the water) and the pink grapefruit (in their own juice). Remove the dumplings from the water with a slotted spoon, then carefully unwrap them.

10 To serve, arrange three dumplings in each serving bowl, garnish with the ginger strips and the grapefruit, and pour in the sauce. Finish with a scattering of coriander.

PAN-ROASTED
DUBLIN BAY PRAWNS

SERVES 4

75g unsalted butter

good handful of wild garlic leaves

24 large raw Dublin Bay prawns
  (langoustines), in shell

200g organic green salad leaves

squeeze of lemon juice

salt and pepper

1 Heat the butter in a heavy pan until hot. Add the wild garlic leaves followed by the langoustines, and pan-roast over a high heat for 3–5 minutes. Season.

2 To serve, dress the salad leaves with the lemon juice and the juices from the pan. Serve immediately, with the cooked langoustines.

JEREMY LEE

A BROTH OF
SCOTTISH SHELLFISH

SERVES 4

2 live lobsters, each about 500g

at least 16 good-sized live langoustines
  in shell

4 big handfuls of fresh mussels in shell,
  about 800g total weight

4 smaller handfuls of fresh clams in shell

a few fresh razor clams in shell

50g unsalted butter

1 small onion, finely chopped

glass of white wine

squeeze of lemon juice

big handful of chopped parsley

salt and pepper

1 Fill a large saucepan with water and bring to a furious boil. Season with as much salt as needed to make the water taste of the sea. Drop in the lobsters, put the lid on the pan and bring back to the boil as quickly as possible. After 1–2 minutes, remove the lobsters to a tray and leave them to cool. Return the water to the boil, drop in the langoustines and cook for 45 seconds. Remove these to a tray.

2 Remove the beards from the mussels, then wash well under cold, running water. Wash the clams in a similar fashion.

3 Melt the butter in a large pan, add the onion and cook gently until softened but not coloured. Turn up the heat. Tip in the mussels, add the white wine and season with salt and pepper. Place the lid on the pan, shake gently and let the mussels steam open. Discard any that remain firmly shut. Once opened, remove the mussels with a slotted spoon to a bowl and cover with a damp cloth.

4 Place the clams in the liquid in the pot and steam open in the same way, then remove to a bowl and cover. Do the same with the razor clams.

5 Pour the cooking liquid from the mussels and clams into a medium pan, checking closely for any grit and straining if required. Add 150ml water and bring to the boil, then set aside. This is your broth.

6 Pull the claws from the lobsters and crack well to remove the meat. Split the tail lengthways and remove the meat from the shell. Remove the langoustines from their shells. Slice the lobster and langoustine meat. Take all the clams and mussels from their shells.

7 To serve, bring the broth to the boil and add a squeeze of lemon juice and the parsley. Check the seasoning, then stir in all the shelled shellfish. Ladle into bowls.

MARK BROADBENT

ROAST SCALLOPS
WITH ENGLISH PEAS, CRISP AIR-DRIED HAM AND PEA SHOOTS

SERVES 4
8 slices of air-dried ham, preferably
  Peter Gott's Cumbrian ham
12 diver-caught scallops
80g soft unsalted butter
vegetable oil
4 punnets of pea shoots (available from
  Chinese shops)
salt and pepper

PEA BLANCMANGE
1 tbsp caster sugar
20g mint leaves
650g freshly shelled peas
3 large gelatine leaves
200ml double cream
grated zest and juice of ¼ lemon

PEA DRESSING
2 tsp double cream
organic rapeseed oil
2 tbsp shredded mint

1 First make the pea blancmange. Bring a saucepan of salted water to the boil. Add the sugar and half the mint leaves, then the peas. Bring back to the boil and simmer for 1–1¹/₂ minutes or until the peas are soft. Drain and refresh the peas in iced water, then drain again. Set 50g peas aside for the dressing. Blitz the remaining peas in a food processor until just smooth.

2 Soften the gelatine in warm water for about 10 minutes. Lift the gelatine out, drop into a small heavy pan and add just enough water to cover the bottom of the pan. Heat very gently until the gelatine has melted, then stir into the cream. Strain the gelatine cream through a fine sieve into a large bowl, then whip to a soft peak.

3 Fold the cream and pea purée gently together. Fold in the remaining chopped mint and the lemon zest and juice. Season to taste. Transfer the blancmange to a smaller bowl, cover and chill in the fridge for about 3 hours or until set firm yet still delicate.

4 For the pea dressing, blend the reserved 50g peas with the cream and a splash each of rapeseed oil and water using a hand blender or small mixer. The dressing should be loose enough to drizzle but still retaining some texture. Season, then add the shredded mint. Set aside.

5 Preheat the oven to 140°C/fan 120°C/gas 1. Put the slices of ham on a baking sheet and set another baking sheet on top so the ham is kept flat. Roast for 20–30 minutes or until the ham is crisp.

6 Meanwhile, smear one face of each scallop with softened butter. Keep the scallops cool, not chilled, until ready to cook.

7 Heat a heavy frying pan until very hot, then add a splash of vegetable oil and put in the scallops butter-side down. Sear, without moving them, for 1 minute. Turn them over and sear the other side for 1 minute. Remove to kitchen paper to drain. Season with salt and pepper.

8 To serve, place a generous quenelle of pea blancmange in the middle of each plate. Arrange three scallops around, then place two pieces of ham in the pea blancmange. Spoon the pea shoots and pea dressing decoratively around the plate.

TOMATO AND FENNEL ESSENCE
WITH OYSTERS, DUBLIN BAY PRAWNS AND CRAB

SERVES 4

12 raw Dublin Bay prawns (langoustines) in their shells
4 fresh oysters in their shells
1 cooked crab
fresh soda bread to serve

ESSENCE

1.5kg dark red, over-ripe tomatoes, coarsely chopped
1 fennel bulb, chopped
5 celery sticks, chopped
2 large shallots, finely chopped
3 garlic cloves, thinly sliced
100g light soft brown sugar

1 tsp each chopped basil, chervil and coriander
50ml Pernod
1 tbsp Tabasco sauce
2 tsp Worcestershire sauce
salt
cayenne pepper

GARNISH

4 basil leaves
leaves of 1 sprig of coriander
1 ripe tomato, skinned, deseeded and diced

1 To make the essence, put all the ingredients in a blender with 1.5 litres cold water and a pinch each of salt and cayenne. Purée, then transfer to a chinois or very fine sieve placed over a bowl. Leave to strain overnight in the fridge.

2 When ready to serve the next day, preheat the oven to 150°C/fan 130°C/gas 2. Drop the prawns into a saucepan of boiling salted water. Return to the boil and cook for 2–3 minutes or until all the shells turn pink. Drain the prawns and leave them to cool, then peel off the shells.

3 Open the oysters using an oyster knife. Keep them refrigerated in their liquor in a covered container until required.

4 Remove the claws from the crab, crack open with a rolling pin or small hammer and remove the white meat. Remove the white meat from the body. Flake all the white meat (do not use any brown meat – save it for another dish).

5 Divide the white crab meat among four ovenproof bowls and top with the prawns followed by the drained oysters. Put the bowls in the oven and warm the shellfish through for 5–10 minutes. Meanwhile, pour the strained tomato essence into a saucepan and heat gently.

6 Ladle the hot essence over the warm shellfish, and garnish with the herb leaves and diced tomato. Serve immediately, with fresh soda bread.

SCALLOPS, LOBSTER AND SPIDER CRAB
WITH WILD SEASHORE VEGETABLES AND OYSTER BUTTER

SERVES 4

1 small cooked lobster

1 medium cooked spider crab

couple of handfuls of wild seashore
   vegetables, such as samphire, sea beet,
   rock samphire, sea purslane and sea peas,
   trimmed of any thick or woody stalks

4 scallops, with or without corals

good knob of unsalted butter

salt and pepper

OYSTER BUTTER

2 shallots, roughly chopped

½ glass English white wine

2 shucked oysters

150g cold unsalted butter, diced

juice of ½ lemon, or to taste

1 For the oyster butter, put the shallots in a saucepan with the wine and the same amount of water and simmer until reduced by two-thirds. Add the oysters, remove from the heat and whiz in a blender until smooth. Return to the pan over a low heat and whisk in the butter to form a smooth sauce. Add lemon juice, salt and pepper to taste. Remove from the heat, cover the surface of the oyster butter with cling film and keep in a warm place.

2 Preheat the oven to 160°C/fan 140°C/gas 3.

3 Remove the meat from the tail and claws of the lobster, and cut into 1cm-thick slices. Remove the white meat from the body and claws of the crab. (Don't throw the lobster and crab shells and the brown meat away – use them for a soup, stock or sauce.) Heat the lobster and crab meat in a covered dish in the oven for 6–7 minutes.

4 Meanwhile, bring a saucepan of water to the boil and quickly blanch the sea vegetables (except sea peas) for 10–15 seconds or until just tender. Keep the different types separate. Drain and keep warm.

5 Cut the scallops horizontally in half and season with salt and pepper. Melt the butter in a frying pan until almost browned, then quickly cook the scallops for just 10 seconds on each side.

6 To serve, arrange the blanched sea vegetables on plates with the scallops, lobster and crab on top, then spoon the oyster butter around. If you've got some sea peas, scatter them on raw at the end.

LANGOUSTINES
WITH SUMMER VEGETABLE STEW

SERVES 4
12 live langoustines
4 sticks of rosemary

VEGETABLE NAGE
1 large onion, chopped
1 leek, chopped
2 celery sticks, chopped
1 fennel bulb, chopped
4 large carrots, chopped
1 head of garlic, cut in half crossways
8 white peppercorns, crushed
1 tsp coriander seeds
1 star anise
1 bay leaf
40g mixed herbs, such as chervil,
  tarragon, parsley, chives and basil
300ml dry white wine

TOMATO WATER
1½ tsp white wine vinegar
1½ tsp caster sugar
10 ripe plum tomatoes, quartered

pinch of Maldon salt
¼ tsp Tabasco sauce
½ tsp Worcestershire sauce
8 basil leaves

VEGETABLE STEW
50g butter
2 small carrots, diced
⅓ garlic clove, very finely chopped
2 baby leeks, very finely sliced
1 small courgette, diced
75g mange tout, chopped
3 tbsp freshly shelled peas
2 tbsp finely chopped flat-leafed parsley
3 spring onions, sliced
12 cherry tomatoes, quartered
grated zest of ½ lemon

TO FINISH
4 chervil leaves
a few chives, sliced into big sticks
4 basil leaves, scrunched up and shredded
  finely into a chiffonade

1 To make the nage, put all the chopped vegetables into a large pan and cover with water (about 1 litre). Add the garlic, peppercorns, coriander seeds, star anise and bay leaf. Bring to the boil and simmer for about 8 minutes. Add the fresh herbs and simmer for a further 3 minutes. Now add the white wine, stir and remove from the heat. Cover and leave to infuse for 48 hours in a cool place.

2 For the tomato water, put the vinegar and sugar in a small saucepan and mix well. Simmer over a medium heat for 1½–2 minutes to produce a syrup. Remove from the heat and stir in 180ml water. Add the tomatoes, along with any tomato juice, and the remaining ingredients. Purée the mixture, in batches, in a blender, then pour into a colander lined with a sterilised linen cloth or muslin set over a bowl. Allow to drain in the fridge overnight. The next day, discard the solid material in the colander, and set the liquid aside.

3 Strain the nage through a fine sieve and discard the vegetables and herbs. Set the nage aside. (You don't need all the nage for this recipe; that left over can be frozen and used as a stock for sauces, soups and so on.)

4 Put a large pan of water on to boil over a high heat. Pull the heads off the langoustines. If the gut has remained in the body, find the middle segment of the tail and fold it backwards. Break it and pull away from the body. The gut should come away with it.

5 When the water is boiling, use a slotted spoon to lower in the langoustines, then blanch for 30 seconds. (Do this in two batches.) Lift them out and plunge straight into a bowl of iced water to stop them cooking further. Leave for a few seconds, then remove and drain. Crush each langoustine gently in your hand to break the shell. It should then peel off easily.

6 Strip the rosemary leaves off the sticks, retaining about 2cm at the top (growing) end. Skewer three langoustines onto each stick of rosemary and set aside.

7 To make the vegetable stew, place a large pan over a medium heat and add 30g of the butter and 300ml of the vegetable nage. Whisk together into an emulsion. Add the carrots and garlic and cook for $1^{1}/_{2}$ minutes. Add the baby leeks. You may need to add a little boiling water if the sauce has reduced right down – it should be like a soupy butter emulsion. Stir the leeks for a few seconds, then stir in the courgette. Add the mange tout and peas. Cook for about 30 seconds. Add the parsley, spring onions, cherry tomatoes and lemon zest. Stir, then take off the heat.

8 Melt the remaining 20g of butter in a large frying pan. Add 75ml of the tomato water and whisk to emulsify. (The remaining tomato water can be frozen, or used as the base for a savoury jelly.) Remove from the heat. Add the skewers of langoustine to the tomato emulsion and allow them to sit in it for a few minutes to take on the flavour, turning them once.

9 To serve, arrange the vegetables in shallow bowls and spoon over some of their saucy liquid. Remove the langoustine skewers from their emulsion, place a skewer in the centre of each bowl and sprinkle with the chervil, chives and basil.

106 ASSORTMENT OF CRAB

SERVES 4
2 carrots, roughly chopped
2 onions, roughly chopped
2 celery sticks, roughly chopped
1 live crab, about 2kg
1 tbsp olive oil
1 tbsp tomato purée
250ml brandy
bunch of basil, stalks reserved and
   leaves cut into julienne
3 tomatoes
1 shallot, diced
knob of butter
250ml double cream
squeeze of lemon juice
2 tsp rice wine vinegar
about 3 tbsp toasted sesame oil
squeeze of lime juice
salt and pepper

RAVIOLI
225g Italian '00' flour
2 eggs
1 tbsp saffron olive oil (steep a few strands
   of saffron in the oil, then strain)
bunch of basil, finely shredded
drop of lemon juice

CRAB TUILES
50g butter
50g plain flour
50g egg whites (about 2 medium
   egg whites)
sesame seeds

CRAB ROYALE
2 egg yolks
80ml double cream
freshly grated nutmeg

1 To cook the crab, put half the roughly chopped vegetables in a pan of salted water, bring to the boil and simmer for 5 minutes. Add the crab and cook for 9 minutes. When the crab is ready, lift it out and leave to cool. Discard the water and vegetables.
2 Preheat the oven to 140°C/fan 120°C/gas 1. Put a roasting tin in the oven to heat.
3 Crack the crab body and claw shells and pick out the meat, keeping the brown and white meat separate. Check through the white crab meat to ensure all of the shell and cartilage are taken out. Chill the crab meat until needed. Bash the crab shells, then place in the hot roasting tin. Cook in the oven for 10–15 minutes or until dry.
4 While the shells are in the oven, make the stock. Sauté the remaining chopped vegetables in the olive oil in a large saucepan over a high heat for about 5 minutes or until golden. Stir in the tomato purée and cook for 2 minutes, stirring. Pour in the brandy, stirring to deglaze the pan. Add the crab shells. Deglaze the roasting tin with a little water to catch up all the flavoursome bits, then pour into the saucepan. Top up with more water (about 1 litre) to cover the vegetables and crab shells. Bring to the boil, skimming frequently. Add the basil stalks and simmer for 40 minutes.
5 Strain the stock through a muslin-lined sieve into a clean pan. Reduce by half over a high heat. Take out 250ml of this stock and reduce in a small pan for 3–4 minutes, to a thick glaze. This will be used later for the dressing and in the crab tuiles. Set the rest of the stock and the glaze aside.

6 To make the crab sauce, blanch the tomatoes, then remove and reserve the skins and seeds. Set the tomatoes aside. Sweat the shallot in the butter in a medium saucepan until translucent. Add the tomato skins and seeds, and cook until they are soft. Pour in the cream and bring to the boil. Add enough of the crab stock to give a sauce consistency and bring back to the boil. Season with lemon juice, salt and pepper to taste. Pass the sauce through a fine sieve and set aside.

7 For the ravioli dough, sift the flour into a bowl. Add the eggs, saffron oil and a pinch of salt. Knead until the dough is smooth, then wrap and leave to rest in the fridge for 1 hour.

8 Meanwhile, to make the mixture for the crab tuiles, heat the butter until it starts to turn brown, then let it cool. Sift the flour into a bowl. Add the browned butter, then the egg whites. Finally, gently mix in enough of the cold crab glaze to bind to a paste. Cover and leave to rest for 1 hour.

9 Preheat the oven to 140°C/fan 120°C/gas 1.

10 Pass the reserved brown crab meat through a fine sieve. Weigh out 80g of this sieved meat into a separate bowl and set aside for the crab royale. To make the ravioli filling, mix 50g of the picked white crab meat with the remaining sieved brown crab meat. Add a handful of the shredded basil and season with salt, pepper and a drop of lemon juice. Set aside.

11 To finish the crab royale, add the egg yolks and cream to the 80g sieved brown crab meat. Season with salt, pepper and nutmeg. Mix well and pass through a fine sieve. Divide the mixture among four heatproof shot glasses and stand them in a small deep tin. Pour enough hot water into the tin to come halfway up the glasses. Bake for about 15 minutes or until set like a custard. Remove from the oven and set aside in the tin of hot water. Turn the oven up to 200°C/fan 180°C/gas 6.

12 Roll out the ravioli dough as thinly as possible using a pasta machine, then divide into two rectangles, each about 20cm long and 14cm wide. (Keep any remaining dough for another pasta dish.) Lay one rectangle flat on the work surface and mark it into quarters. Divide the ravioli filling into four and pile a portion in the middle of each quarter of the dough sheet, with equal spaces between. Brush the dough around the filling with water and place the second sheet of dough on top, gently pressing to seal. Cut to make four square ravioli. Cover and set aside.

13 Use a palette knife to spread the tuile mixture as thinly as possible into eight oval shapes on one or two baking sheets. Sprinkle with sesame seeds and bake for 5–8 minutes or until golden and crisp. Cool on a wire rack.

14 Add the rice wine vinegar and sesame oil to the remaining crab glaze. Season with salt and pepper and keep this dressing to one side. Finely chop the reserved tomatoes and add to the remaining white crab meat along with the julienned basil. Season with salt, pepper, lime juice and extra sesame oil if needed, and mix well.

15 Cook the ravioli in boiling salted water for 4 minutes; drain.

16 To serve, spoon the white crab meat salad into four 4cm rings set on four plates. Remove the rings. Position the crab tuiles on top. Season the ravioli with salt, place next to the crab salad and drizzle with some of the dressing. Lift the warm shot glasses of crab royale from the water, dry them and put one on each plate. Gently reheat the crab sauce, then foam it using a stick blender and spoon a little foam into each glass on top of the crab royale.

MICHAEL CAINES

PAN-ROASTED SCALLOPS
WITH CRISP SMOKED BELLY PORK,
PEA PURÉE AND A SHALLOT AND BACON FOAM

SERVES 4
8 large scallops
olive oil for frying
lemon juice
salt and pepper
pea shoots to serve

BRAISED BELLY PORK
1 onion, halved
6 cloves
1 piece of smoked, boned pork belly, about
    500g, preferably Gloucestershire Old Spot
    or another traditional breed
6 shallots, peeled
1 carrot, halved lengthways
4 garlic cloves, peeled
about 1 tbsp fresh ginger peelings
2 tsp black peppercorns
1 tsp chicken bouillon powder
1 star anise
10 juniper berries
1 strip of orange zest, oven-dried or fresh
bouquet garni

OLIVE OIL VINAIGRETTE
150ml olive oil
3 tbsp Champagne vinegar or white
    wine vinegar
1 small garlic clove, lightly crushed
small sprig of fresh thyme

SHALLOT AND BACON FOAM
200g smoked bacon, chopped
250ml milk
70g unsalted butter, plus a knob to finish
250g shallots, sliced
large sprig of thyme
1 bay leaf
300ml fish stock
3 tbsp double cream

PEA PURÉE
300g frozen peas
100g unsalted butter, cut into pieces

1 For the belly pork, stud each onion half with 3 cloves and place in a saucepan with the belly pork, the rest of the pork ingredients and 1.5 litres water. Bring to the boil, then immediately reduce the heat so the water is at 80–90°C (use a thermometer to check). The water must not boil while the belly cooks. Cook for 2–3 hours or until cooked and tender. Allow to cool in the liquid.

2 Remove the belly pork, place on a tray and set another tray on top. Wrap completely in cling film, ensuring the pork is pressed flat. Chill for 6 hours. Strain the cooking liquid and reserve.

3 Meanwhile, mix all the ingredients for the vinaigrette in a bowl. Pour into a bottle or plastic pourer and set aside. Shake well before using.

4 To make the shallot and bacon foam, place the chopped bacon and milk in a saucepan and bring to the boil. Set aside to infuse. Meanwhile, heat the 70g of butter in a pan, add the shallots and a pinch of salt, and sweat until softened but not coloured. Add the thyme and bay leaf, and continue to sweat for 2 minutes. Pour in the fish stock, cream and the infused milk with the bacon. Bring to the boil and simmer gently for 20 minutes. Remove the bacon, thyme and bay leaf, and pour the liquid and shallots into a blender. Blend until very smooth, then pass through fine sieve into a clean pan. Season with salt and pepper and set aside.

5 For the pea purée, cook the peas in boiling salted water until tender. Drain and refresh in iced water, then purée in a food processor. Pass the purée through a sieve into a heavy-based pan. Warm through, gradually adding the butter while stirring. Season with salt and pepper. Keep warm.

6 Remove the pressed pork from the fridge and cut into four 1cm-thick slices. Remove the thick rind. Cut the slices into 6cm lengths and put them in a pan with some of the reserved cooking liquid. Reheat, but be careful not to boil.

7 Meanwhile, season the scallops with salt and pepper. Heat a little olive oil in a non-stick pan. Add the scallops and cook until golden brown, then turn over and gently finish cooking until the centres are warm. Season with lemon juice and keep warm.

8 To serve, dress the pea shoots with a little of the vinaigrette (any extra can be used another time). Spoon the pea purée onto each plate, then drag a spoon across to create a tear shape. Place the pork in the middle and set two scallops on top of each serving. Gently reheat the shallot and bacon foam, add a knob of butter and blend with a hand blender to create a cappuccino effect. Spoon this over the scallops and top with the pea shoots.

CRAB AND WILD CRESS SALAD
WITH COCKLE DRESSING

SERVES 4
400g live cockles in their shells
dry white wine
400g fresh white crab meat
1 tbsp chopped chervil
1 tsp chopped tarragon
1 tsp extra virgin olive oil
4 handfuls of wild watercress
salt and white pepper

SAFFRON VINAIGRETTE
50ml white wine vinegar
pinch of saffron strands
200ml olive oil

1 To make the vinaigrette, warm the vinegar with 100ml water in a small pan. Drop in the saffron and leave to infuse off the heat for 30 minutes. Stir in the olive oil and season with a pinch each of salt and pepper. (This makes more than you need for this recipe, but it keeps well in a screw-top jar in the fridge.)

2 Put the cockles in a saucepan, splash in some wine and cover the pan. Cook over a strong heat for 1–2 minutes or until the shells open, shaking the pan from time to time. Pour the cockles into a colander to drain and leave until cool enough to handle, then pick out the cockle meat, reserving some cockles in their shells for the garnish.

3 Mix the crab meat with the chervil and tarragon, and season with a pinch each of salt and pepper. Add the olive oil.

4 To serve, pile a generous amount of crab meat on each plate and place some watercress alongside. In a small bowl, stir the shelled cockles with as much saffron vinaigrette as you like, then spoon over the watercress. Garnish with the reserved cockles in their shells.

CROMER CRAB TART

SERVES 6
300g shortcrust pastry
2 tbsp olive oil
2 small bunches of spring onions,
  finely sliced
450g white crab meat
40g Parmesan cheese, freshly grated
salt and pepper
lightly dressed salad leaves to serve

CUSTARD
3 medium eggs, plus 2 medium egg yolks
425ml double cream
pinch of freshly grated nutmeg

1 Preheat the oven to 180°C/fan 160°C/gas 4. Place a 23cm round, 4cm deep flan ring or loose-bottomed tart tin on a baking tray.

2 Roll out the pastry and use to line the flan ring or tin, then line the pastry case with baking parchment and fill with baking beans. Bake blind for about 25 minutes or until the pastry just starts to colour. Carefully remove the baking beans and parchment. If there are any cracks in the pastry, use leftover pieces of pastry or beaten egg to fill them. Return the pastry case to the oven to finish cooking the base for 3–5 minutes. Leave to cool.

3 Meanwhile, make the custard. Place the eggs, egg yolks and cream in a bowl and beat gently, seasoning with nutmeg and salt and pepper to taste. Pass through a sieve into a jug. (The pastry and custard can be prepared ahead to this stage. Keep the custard in the fridge.)

4 Heat the olive oil in a frying pan, then quickly fry the spring onions until just softened. Scatter them in the pastry case. Stir the white crab meat and Parmesan into the custard mixture and lightly season, then carefully pour it onto the spring onions.

5 Bake the tart for about 50 minutes or until the filling is just set. Leave to cool for a few minutes before serving, with some lightly dressed salad leaves.

HOT SPIDER CRAB PÂTÉ

SERVES 4-6
1 large cooked spider crab, 1.5–2kg
4 shallots, finely chopped
1 garlic clove, crushed
½ tsp cayenne pepper
100g unsalted butter
40ml dry sherry
100g brown crab meat
50g fresh white breadcrumbs
juice of ½ lemon, or to taste
salt and pepper
thin slices of toast to serve

1 To get the meat out of the crab, twist the legs and claws off, then crack them open and remove the white meat. Now turn the main body on its back and twist off the pointed flap. Push the tip of a table knife between the main shell and the part to which the legs were attached, twist the blade to separate the two, then push it up and remove. Scoop out the brown meat from the well of the shell and put with the leg and claw meat.

2 On the other part of the body, remove the dead man's fingers (the feather-like, grey gills attached to the body) and discard. Split the body in half with a heavy knife. Now you need to be patient and pick out the white meat from the little cavities in the body. Add this to the rest of the meat. Scrub and reserve the shell for serving, if you like.

3 Gently cook the shallots, garlic and cayenne pepper in the butter for 3–4 minutes or until soft. Add the sherry, 100ml water and 100g brown crab meat as well as the brown crab meat from the spider crab. Stir well, then add the breadcrumbs, half the lemon juice and seasoning to taste. Simmer for 7–8 minutes, stirring occasionally.

4 Whiz one-third of this mixture in a blender, then stir it back into the main mixture in the pan along with the white crab meat. Taste and add more lemon juice and seasoning, if necessary.

5 Spoon the mixture into the crab shell, if using, or into a serving dish. Serve hot, with thin slices of toast.

ROAST RIB OF WELSH BLACK BEEF
WITH ONION PURÉE

SERVES 4

1 rib-eye joint of Welsh Black beef,
  about 800g
olive oil for frying
300g white onions, very thinly sliced
butter for frying
300g fresh ceps, cut in half
100g green beans
1 small shallot, finely diced
salt and pepper

OXTAIL

300g oxtail, in one piece
500ml red wine
1 large onion, chopped
1 large carrot, chopped
1 bay leaf
50g plain flour
2–3 tbsp vegetable oil
2 litres chicken stock

BONE MARROW

4 pieces bone marrow, each 5cm thick
25g coarse dry breadcrumbs
25g dried onion
50g plain flour
2 eggs, beaten
oil for deep-frying

1 Put the oxtail in a glass dish, cover with the red wine and add the onion, carrot and bay leaf. Leave to marinate in a cool place for 24 hours.

2 Preheat the oven to 160°C/fan 140°C/gas 3.

3 Strain the red wine marinade from the oxtail and pour into a pan. Reserve the oxtail and vegetables. Bring the marinade to the boil and skim off any scum that rises to the surface. Remove from the heat and set aside.

4 Mix the flour with a little salt and pepper to season. Heat the vegetable oil in a flameproof casserole on a medium heat. Dust the oxtail in the seasoned flour, then add to the hot oil and fry until golden brown. Remove from the casserole and set aside. Add the marinated vegetables to the casserole and fry until golden brown. Deglaze with the reserved red wine marinade and reduce by half.

5 Return the oxtail to the casserole and pour in the chicken stock. Bring to the boil. Skim, then cover and transfer to the oven to cook for 2¹/₂ hours. Remove and leave to cool. (The oxtail can be cooked a day ahead and refrigerated overnight.)

6 When the oxtail has cooled, remove it from the liquid and pick the meat from the bones, keeping the meat in large pieces. Strain the liquid and reduce by half. Set the meat and liquid aside (this is the sauce).

7 Take the marrow out of the bones, either by pushing it through or breaking the bones. Rinse the marrow under cold water, then leave to soak for 30 minutes to remove all the blood. Drain and pat dry. Mix the breadcrumbs with the dried onion. Season the marrow and roll in the flour, then coat in the eggs and finish by rolling in the breadcrumbs. Keep chilled until ready to cook.

8 Turn the oven up to 190°C/fan 170°C/gas 5. Season the rib of beef with salt and pepper. Heat a heavy roasting tin with a little olive oil and sear the beef until golden brown on all sides. Transfer to the oven and roast for 25 minutes for medium rare, or 35 minutes for medium. Remove from the oven and leave to rest for 25 minutes.

9 While the beef is roasting and resting, make the onion purée. Cook the white onions in a heavy-bottomed pan over a low heat with a large knob of butter until translucent (this takes about 20 minutes). Season with salt and pepper, then blend in a food processor until smooth. Set aside.

10 Deep-fry the marrow in oil heated to 170°C for 45–60 seconds or until golden brown and crisp. Drain on kitchen paper and keep warm.

11 Season the ceps with salt and pepper. Heat a splash of olive oil and a knob of butter in a warm frying pan, add the ceps, placing them face down, and fry briefly until they are golden. Keep warm.

12 Cook the green beans in boiling salted water for 2–3 minutes. Remove from the pan with a slotted spoon and place in iced water to stop the cooking process, then drain. Cook the shallot with a small knob of butter in a frying pan until soft. Add the green beans, season with salt and pepper, and toss to warm through.

13 To serve, reheat the sauce, and the oxtail in a little of the sauce. Place the green beans to one side of each warmed plate. Carve the beef into slices of 1cm thickness and lay on top of the beans. Spoon the onion purée on one side of the beef, then arrange the bone marrow, oxtail and ceps on the other side. Drizzle over the sauce.

FILLET STEAK
PICKLED WALNUTS AND HORSERADISH

SERVES 4

4 fillet steaks, each 250g, trimmed
  of any sinew
4 tbsp groundnut oil
80ml Madeira
225ml good beef stock
9–12 pickled walnuts, plus 1 tbsp
  of the pickle
50g unsalted butter
salt and pepper

HORSERADISH CREAM

good-sized stick of fresh horseradish,
  about 1.5cm wide x 5cm long (make
  it longer if you like things hot)
2–3 tsp caster sugar
2 tbsp white wine vinegar
200ml double cream

1 To make the horseradish cream, peel the horseradish swiftly and then grate finely. The tears will flow, but grate with fury, so it will be done quickly. The heat of fresh horseradish is vital for this dish. Stir the sugar into the vinegar to dissolve, then heap in the horseradish. Let sit for half an hour or so. Very lightly whip the cream, then stir into the horseradish. Cover the bowl well – then dry your eyes. (The sauce can be made a few hours ahead and chilled, but not too far ahead or the horseradish flavour will fade dramatically.)

2 Place the steaks cut-side up and season liberally and evenly with sea salt and freshly ground pepper. Warm a heavy-bottomed frying pan, then pour in the oil. When gently smoking, carefully sit the steaks in the pan and do not touch – at all. Let the meat cook gently until the edges turn a good rich, dark brown, moving the pan if the steaks are cooking unevenly. After 7–8 minutes, turn the steaks onto the other side and you should reveal a splendid crust. Continue to cook for a few minutes further, then remove the steaks to warm plates and set aside.

3 Stir the Madeira into the pan and boil until only a teaspoonful remains. Add the stock and the spoonful of pickle from the walnuts, simmering gently until slightly thickened. Add the butter all at once. Return to the boil, then pour the sauce through a fine sieve into a small pan and keep warm.

4 To serve, slice the pickled walnuts in half and heap over the steaks. Pour the sauce over and add a dollop of horseradish cream alongside.

120

BRAISED FEATHERBLADE AND
PAN-ROASTED FILLET OF BEEF
WITH BROAD BEANS, PEAS
AND BABY SPINACH

SERVES 4

1 piece of boneless beef featherblade (shoulder), about 800g
vegetable oil
250g shallots, quartered
mirepoix of finely chopped vegetables (1 onion, 1 carrot, 2 celery sticks and ½ leek)
4 tbsp tomato purée
½ head of garlic, cut in half crossways
small bunch of thyme
75ml Port
500ml red wine
750ml home-made veal or beef stock

1 centre-cut piece of beef fillet, about 180g
50g salted butter
1 quantity mash (see Pan-fried John Dory on page 76; make without the lobster and herbs)
salt and pepper

VEGETABLE GARNISH

100g freshly shelled broad beans
100g freshly shelled peas
2 tbsp olive oil
250g baby spinach

1 Preheat the oven to 120°C/fan 110°C/gas ½.

2 If there is a lot of fat still attached to the beef shoulder, trim it off until the piece is just lightly covered all over in fat. Season the meat, then sear in a little hot vegetable oil in a large, heavy flameproof casserole over a high heat until coloured on all sides. Remove the meat from the pot and set aside.

3 Drain the fat from the casserole. Splash in a little more oil and heat until hot. Add the shallots and the mirepoix, and fry until lightly coloured. Stir in the tomato purée and cook for 2 minutes, then add the garlic, thyme, Port and wine. Bring to the boil. Pour in the stock and return the beef shoulder to the pot. Cover with greaseproof paper, then transfer the casserole to the oven to braise for 3–3½ hours or until the meat is tender. Remove the beef to a wire rack and set aside until cold. Strain the sauce into a clean pan and boil until reduced by half. When the beef and sauce are cold, chill in the fridge overnight.

4 The next day, prepare the vegetable garnish. Blanch the broad beans in boiling salted water for 3–5 minutes or until tender. Drain and refresh in iced water, then drain again and peel off the thin skins. Blanch the peas for 1–2 minutes or until tender. Drain and refresh in iced water, then drain again.

5 Preheat the oven to 200°C/fan 180°C/gas 6.

6 Cut the chilled beef shoulder into four pieces, each weighing about 120g. Place the pieces in a heavy pan, pour over enough of the reduced sauce to half cover the meat and add 50ml water. Cover and bring slowly to the boil, then transfer to the oven to heat for 15 minutes. At the end of this time the beef should be hot and tender, and the sauce should have reduced by half again and be thick enough to coat and glaze

the beef. If the sauce is too thin, pour half of it into another pan and boil it until reduced, then return to the pan of beef. Set aside in a warm place.

7 Stand the fillet of beef on one of its cut ends and slice downwards with the grain into four equal pieces. Season the pieces on all sides. Heat a large, heavy frying pan until hot. Add the butter and melt until the foam starts to turn golden brown, then add the pieces of fillet and sear over a high heat for about 3 minutes or until evenly coloured on all sides. Baste constantly during cooking, watching that the butter remains golden – if it gets too hot and starts to turn dark, remove the pan from the heat to cool. Transfer the pieces of fillet to a wire rack and leave to rest while you finish the vegetables.

8 Heat the olive oil in a saucepan, add the beans and peas, and warm through gently for 1 minute. Add the spinach, mix well and season lightly, then remove from the heat and let the spinach wilt, stirring occasionally. Reheat the mash, and the glazed beef if necessary.

9 To serve, put a piece of glazed braised beef on each plate and top with an upturned piece of fillet, which has been cut in half at a 45° angle. Put a quenelle of mash next to the meat with a spoonful of green vegetables. Spoon some of the sauce over the meat and serve the rest separately.

NOEL MCMEEL

FILLET OF BEEF
WITH TRADITIONAL CHAMP, SLOW-ROASTED MUSHROOMS, AND CABBAGE AND BACON, SERVED WITH STOUT GRAVY

SERVES 4

1 tightly packed Savoy cabbage, about 600g
rapeseed oil
4 rashers of back bacon, preferably
  Pat O'Doherty's black bacon, rinds
  removed, cut into lardons
4 fillet steaks, preferably Kettyle Northern
  Irish, each 150–200g
salt and pepper

SLOW-ROASTED MUSHROOMS

50ml rapeseed oil
4 garlic cloves, crushed
leaves of 1 sprig of rosemary, finely chopped
leaves of 3 sprigs of thyme, finely chopped

4 flat cap mushrooms, stems removed
  and caps peeled

CHAMP

1.5kg potatoes, preferably British Queens,
  peeled
100ml whipping cream
4 spring onions, chopped
50g salted butter

GRAVY

350ml Irish stout
3 tbsp redcurrant jelly
sprig each of rosemary and thyme
2 garlic cloves, roughly chopped

1 Preheat the oven to 130°C/fan 110°C/gas ¹/₂.

2 First prepare the mushrooms. Mix together the oil, garlic, rosemary and thyme. Arrange the mushrooms gill-side up on a non-stick baking tray, pour over the oil and herb mixture, and season with sea salt and freshly cracked black pepper. Roast the mushrooms for 1 hour.

3 Meanwhile, cook the potatoes for the champ in boiling salted water for about 20 minutes until soft, then drain and mash until all lumps are eliminated. Bring the cream and spring onions to the boil in the pan, add the mash and beat until smooth. Season and add the butter. Set aside in a warm place.

4 Cut the cabbage into six or eight wedges. Discard the thickest part of the core, but leave a little to help hold the leaves together. Heat a little oil in a frying pan until it is very hot and fry the bacon until crisp. Add the cabbage and mix with the bacon, then reduce the heat, cover the pan with a lid and cook slowly for 5–10 minutes or until the cabbage is tender. Season and set aside in a warm place.

5 Remove the mushrooms from the oven and keep warm. Increase the oven temperature to 200°C/fan 180°C/gas 6 and place a baking tray inside to heat up.

6 Season the steaks all over. Heat a heavy frying pan until red hot, then add a little oil. Place the steaks in the pan and sear all over (top, bottom and sides). Transfer the steaks to the hot tray and finish cooking in the oven, allowing 4–5 minutes for medium-rare meat. Remove the steaks from the oven and leave to rest in a warm place while you make the gravy.

7 Deglaze the steak juices in the frying pan with the stout, then boil to reduce by about three-quarters. Add the redcurrant jelly, rosemary, thyme and garlic, and simmer for 5 minutes. Strain and season, then keep hot.

8 To serve, put a mushroom in the middle of each warmed plate. Top with cabbage and bacon, and then a steak. Spoon a quenelle of champ on top of each steak, and drizzle the gravy around the plate.

124

POACHED FILLET
OF WELSH BLACK BEEF WITH SAUTÉED SNAILS
AND ASPARAGUS ON CAULIFLOWER PURÉE

SERVES 4
24 spears of young asparagus
1 litre beef consommé or beef stock
olive oil
4 fillet steaks, preferably Welsh Black
   beef, each about 250g
knob of unsalted butter
salt and pepper

CAULIFLOWER PURÉE
1 large white onion, sliced
50g unsalted butter
1 large or 2 small heads of cauliflower,
   trimmed and chopped
about 250ml full-fat milk

SNAILS
20 ready prepared snails (see note below)
knob of unsalted butter
100g fresh wild garlic leaves, or 1 wild garlic
   root, chopped, or 1 garlic clove, chopped
25g finely chopped shallots
leaves ripped from a few sprigs of thyme
1 tbsp chopped flat-leaf parsley

1 First make the cauliflower purée. Sweat the onion in half the butter until soft. Add
the cauliflower and stir briefly, then cover the pan and cook gently for 20–25 minutes
or until the cauliflower is soft but not brown. Add the milk and bring back to the boil.
Purée in a food processor with the remaining butter, which should be cold. Push the
purée through a fine sieve into a bowl. Check the consistency – it should just hold
its shape. If it is too stiff, let it down with a little milk. Set aside in a warm place.
2 Plunge the asparagus spears into a pan of boiling salted water and blanch for
1–2 minutes, then drain and refresh in iced water. Drain again and set aside.
3 Bring the consommé to a gentle simmer in a wide pan. Meanwhile, heat a little
olive oil in a large heavy frying pan until very hot, and sear the steaks over a high heat
until nicely coloured on all sides. Transfer the steaks to the consommé, reserving the
meat juices in the frying pan. Simmer gently for 8 minutes for rare beef. Do not let
the liquid boil. Remove the steaks from the consommé and let rest for 5 minutes.
4 While the steaks are resting, add a ladleful of the consommé and a knob of butter
to the meat juices in the frying pan and simmer until reduced. At the same time,
sauté the snails in a knob of butter in another frying pan with the garlic leaves,
shallots and thyme leaves. Throw in the blanched asparagus spears and parsley,
and season to taste. Reheat the cauliflower purée, if necessary.
5 To serve, spoon some cauliflower purée onto each plate and place a steak on top.
Garnish with snails, garlic and asparagus, and drizzle over the reduced sauce.
Note: Buy ready prepared frozen snails in bags and thaw them before use. Or use
canned snails: drain and rinse, then blanch briefly by dipping in boiling water.

DRY-AGED BEEF
WITH TEXTURES OF THE ONION FAMILY

SERVES 4

15 large banana shallots
olive oil
few sprigs of thyme and rosemary
100g salted butter
500ml good chicken stock, plus extra
  for the sauce
2kg chicken wings, each chopped into thirds
groundnut oil
200g firm, small button mushrooms,
  very thinly sliced
2 bay leaves
2 very ripe plum tomatoes, halved

1 garlic clove, squashed
150g small baby onions
1 piece boned well-aged beef sirloin, such
  as Dexter or other rare breed, about 800g
about 100ml milk
20 spring onions, trimmed
1 white onion, thinly sliced in rings
soy sauce
1 egg, beaten with salt and pepper for
  an egg wash
about 100g fresh white breadcrumbs
salt and crushed white pepper

1 Preheat the oven to 160°C/fan 140°C/gas 3. Set 2 of the shallots (skin on) on a
sheet of foil. Drizzle with olive oil, then scatter over a thyme sprig and some salt.
Wrap up in the foil and bake for 45 minutes or until soft. Leave to cool, still wrapped.
2 Peel and very thinly slice 8 more of the shallots. Melt 75g of the butter in a pan,
add the sliced shallots and fry over a low to medium heat for about 1 hour or until
well caramelised. Pour in the 500ml chicken stock, scrape the bottom of the pan to
deglaze it and simmer for 2 minutes. Pour everything into a blender and blend to a
purée, which will be like a thick soup. Sieve the purée into a clean pan and set aside.
3 To make the sauce, lay the chopped chicken wings in a large roasting tin and roast
for 1–1½ hours or until golden brown and well caramelised, turning them every
10 minutes so they don't catch. Meanwhile, heat a little groundnut oil in a small
pan with the remaining 25g of butter, add the sliced mushrooms and another 3 thinly
sliced shallots, and cook over a low heat for about 45 minutes or until softened and
caramelised. Drain on kitchen paper.
4 Tip the chicken wings into a large colander set over a bowl. Reserve the fat and
juices that drain into the bowl. Put the chicken wings and the caramelised
mushrooms and shallots into a pressure cooker. Add a sprig each of rosemary and
thyme, the bay leaves, tomatoes, garlic and a pinch of salt. Pour in enough chicken
stock so the chicken wings are barely covered, then pressure cook for 45 minutes.
(If you don't have a pressure cooker, put everything into a large heavy pan instead,
wrap three layers of cling film over the top of the pan and place the lid on top. Bring
slowly to the boil, then simmer gently for 1½ hours.)
5 Meanwhile, bake the baby onions. Turn the oven temperature up to 200°C/fan
180°C/gas 6. Lay the baby onions (skins on) in a small casserole and add enough

salt to cover them. Cover with a lid and bake for 1 hour or until soft and the salt has created a crust. Remove and cool slightly, then peel off the skins and set aside.

6 While the baby onions are cooking, cook the beef (see note on page 136). Heat a little groundnut oil in a pan, add the beef and sear to caramelise it the outside. Transfer the beef to a vacuum-sealed, airtight bag. Heat a pan of water to 58°C. Put the beef in the pan and poach, uncovered, for 1¼ hours, keeping the water at a constant 58°C. Remove the beef from the water and leave to rest in the bag.

7 Peel and very thinly slice another of the shallots, preferably using a mandolin. Put in a shallow dish and pour over enough milk to cover. Leave to soak for about 1 hour.

8 When the pressure cooking is done, allow everything to cool, then strain the stock through muslin into a clean saucepan. Reduce over a high heat to a light sauce consistency, not too thick.

9 Finely chop the remaining shallot. Whisk 1 tbsp of the reserved fat and juices from the chicken into the reduced stock and stir in the shallot. Set the sauce aside.

10 Drop the spring onions into a pan of boiling salted water to blanch for 2 minutes, then remove with a slotted spoon into a bowl of seasoned iced water. Dress the white onion slices with a little olive oil, soy sauce and salt. Set aside.

11 Drain the milk-soaked shallots and pat them dry, then dip in the beaten egg. Season the breadcrumbs with salt and pepper and use to coat the onions. Heat oil in a deep-fat fryer to 140°C, add the breaded shallots and fry for 4–5 minutes or until golden and bubbles stop coming to the surface of the oil. Drain the shallots on kitchen paper and keep hot.

12 Take the shallots from the foil parcel and split down the middle (skin still on). Heat a splash of olive oil in a non-stick frying pan and lay the shallots in the pan, cut-side down. Fry for about 4 minutes or until caramelised. Keep warm. Drain the spring onions well, then fry in a little hot oil for 2–3 minutes. Keep warm.

13 Remove the beef from its bag. Heat a little olive oil in a large frying pan, add the beef and cook for no more than 1 minute, rolling it around in the hot fat. It should be well caramelised on the outside but still pink all through.

14 To serve, season the beef with salt and pepper, then carve into four slices and lay a slice on each serving plate. Scatter the dressed white onion slices over the beef. Arrange the 'textures of the onion' around the plate – the caramelised shallots, fried spring onions, deep-fried shallots, baked baby onions and a dollop of the warmed shallot purée. Reheat the sauce gently, then drizzle over and around the whole dish.

RACK OF LAMB, SAUTÉED TONGUE AND SWEETBREADS
WITH SAMPHIRE AND BROAD BEANS

SERVES 4
2 lambs' tongues
700g lambs' sweetbreads
white wine vinegar
1 rack of lamb with 8 rib bones, chined
150g freshly podded young broad beans
seasoned plain flour for dusting
50g unsalted butter

150g samphire
300ml lamb stock
salt and pepper

GARNISH
mint leaves
flat-leaf parsley leaves

1 Put the tongues in a pan of cold water and bring to the boil. Simmer, uncovered, for $1^{1}/_{2}$–2 hours or until tender. Remove from the heat and set the tongues aside in the cooking liquid.

2 To prepare the sweetbreads, put them in a large bucket or bowl filled with cold water and leave to soak in the fridge for at least 2 hours. Bring a saucepan of water to the boil with a splash of vinegar and a little salt. Drain the sweetbreads, put them in the boiling water and bring back to the boil. Remove and refresh in iced water. Take off the tough outer coating and fatty membrane from the sweetbreads, leaving them clean. Refrigerate in a covered container until ready to cook.

3 Preheat the oven to 200°C/fan 180°C/gas 6.

4 Set the rack of lamb in a roasting tin and roast for 15–20 minutes (for rare to medium-rare meat). Remove from the oven, cover loosely with foil and leave to rest in a warm place.

5 While the lamb is roasting, blanch the broad beans in rapidly boiling salted water for 1 minute. Drain, refresh in iced water and drain again. Set aside.

6 Dust the sweetbreads with seasoned flour. Heat 30g of the butter in a frying pan until foaming, then sauté the sweetbreads over a medium heat for 2–3 minutes on each side or until nicely coloured. Remove with a slotted spoon and set aside.

7 Drain the tongues and cut them in half lengthways. Sauté them in the same pan for 2–3 minutes on each side or until nicely coloured. Throw in the broad beans and samphire, return the sweetbreads to the pan and add the stock. Simmer together for 2–3 minutes. Add the rest of the butter to glaze, and season to taste.

8 To serve, divide the sweetbreads, tongues and vegetables among warmed large bowls and spoon the sauce around. Cut the rack into cutlets and put two on each serving. Garnish with mint and parsley leaves. Accompany with potatoes and butter.

128

LAMB RACK AND PAN-FRIED LAMB PATTIES
FLAVOURED WITH ROSE PETALS

SERVES 4

2 racks of lamb, each with 4 rib bones, chined and excess fat removed
plain yoghurt to serve
salt and pepper

MARINADE

1 tbsp very finely chopped raw papaya
1 tbsp very finely chopped garlic
1 tsp very finely chopped green chillies
1 tsp ground fennel
1 tsp black pepper
1 tsp sweet paprika
3 tbsp mustard oil
100ml single cream
3 tbsp double cream
2 tbsp gram flour
2 tbsp Pernod or Ricard
pinch of grated nutmeg

MINT CHUTNEY

200g mint leaves
2 tbsp roughly chopped red onion
2 tbsp lemon juice
1 green chilli
2 tsp vegetable oil
4 tbsp thick, full-fat plain yoghurt

TAMARIND VINAIGRETTE

4 tbsp fresh tamarind extract (made by soaking tamarind slab in water and passing through a sieve)
1 tbsp finely chopped red onion
½ tbsp each finely chopped red and green pepper
5 tbsp olive or vegetable oil

LAMB PATTIES

1 tbsp finely chopped raw papaya
15g fried brown onions
¼ tsp Kashmiri red chilli powder
¼ tsp garam masala powder
small pinch of ground cardamom
½ tsp each ginger and garlic pastes, mixed
1 tsp finely chopped fresh ginger
1 green chilli, finely chopped
1 tbsp finely chopped coriander leaves
1 tbsp finely chopped mint leaves
1 tbsp gram flour, toasted in a pan until lightly browned
1 tsp dried rose petals
1 tbsp toasted pine nuts
2 tbsp thick, full-fat plain yoghurt
2 tbsp single cream
pinch of saffron strands
250g boned leg of lamb, finely minced
about 4 tbsp vegetable oil for shallow-frying

GARNISH

a few lightly sautéed slices of baby fennel bulb
fresh rose petals
mint leaves
sprigs of coriander
finely sliced red onions
olive oil for drizzling

1 Whisk all the marinade ingredients together and leave at room temperature for 30 minutes. Then rub the marinade all over the lamb racks. Set aside in the fridge to marinate for at least 2 hours before cooking.

2 Meanwhile, to make the mint chutney, drop the mint leaves into boiling water, lift out immediately with a slotted spoon and refresh in iced water. Drain well. Finely chop the mint in a food processor with rest of the chutney ingredients to make a very smooth consistency. Chill until required.

3 Combine the ingredients for the vinaigrette and whisk together with a little salt. Set aside until required.

4 To make the lamb patties, put all the ingredients except the minced lamb and oil for frying in a food processor. Blend to make a paste. Mix the lamb with the paste. Leave at room temperature for 30 minutes.

5 Preheat the oven to 200°C/fan 180°C/gas 6.

6 Shape the mince mixture into six 5–6cm patties (you will have two left over, which can be frozen). Heat a non-stick frying pan and add a little of the vegetable oil. Fry the patties in batches over a medium heat until cooked and light golden on both sides. As they are cooked, remove and keep warm. Add more oil as needed.

7 Meanwhile, remove the lamb racks from the marinade, shake off the excess marinade and place the lamb in a roasting tin. Roast for 5–7 minutes for rare meat, basting with the excess marinade or juices from the meat halfway through. For medium meat, roast for a further 2–3 minutes, or 5 minutes more for well done. Remove the racks, baste with more of the juices and let rest in a warm place.

8 Toss all the garnish ingredients together, dressing them with a drizzle of olive oil. Carve the racks into 8 cutlets.

9 To serve, spoon a large dot of mint chutney and tamarind vinaigrette in the centre of each warmed plate, side by side. With the back of spoon, stretch them into a straight line in opposite directions. Place two cutlets on one side of the plate, one leaning on the other. Place a lamb patty at the top of the plate. Arrange the garnish on top of the patty. Serve with yoghurt.

130

ROAST BEST END OF DEVONSHIRE LAMB
WITH PAN-ROASTED POTATOES, SPINACH, TOMATO FONDUE AND A LIGHT LAMB JUS

SERVES 4

1 best end (rack) of lamb with 8 rib bones, French trimmed
olive oil
knob of butter
large sprig of rosemary
200g young spinach
salt and pepper

TOMATO FONDUE

1 small onion, chopped
2 garlic cloves, crushed
3 tbsp olive oil
300g whole plum tomatoes (about 4), skinned, deseeded and halved
3 sprigs of thyme, leaves stripped and finely chopped
4 small tomatoes, preferably 'English Breakfast' variety, blanched and skinned

ONION PURÉE

2 large onions, peeled and quartered
1 tbsp white breadcrumbs
15g butter
½ tsp chopped thyme leaves

LAMB SAUCE

800g lamb bones, chopped small
about 100ml olive oil
2 small onions, chopped small
1 head of garlic, cut crossways in half
1 carrot, chopped small
1 leek, chopped small
large sprig of thyme
large sprig of rosemary
1 tsp cumin seeds
½ cinnamon stick
200g ripe plum tomatoes, roughly chopped
2 tbsp tomato purée
400ml chicken stock
100ml veal glacé (optional)

BASIL AND MUSTARD PURÉE

10g basil leaves
½ tsp thyme leaves
1 tbsp olive oil
1 tsp Dijon mustard

ROAST POTATOES

4 large baking potatoes such as King Edward (6cm deep and 5cm wide)
about 200g butter
2 garlic cloves
sprig of thyme

1 Preheat the oven to 200°C/fan 180°C/gas 6.

2 To make the tomato fondue, sweat the onion and garlic with the olive oil in a heavy-based ovenproof pan until soft; do not colour. Add the plum tomatoes and thyme, season lightly and stir together. Transfer to the oven and roast for 15 minutes. Stir, then roast for another 15 minutes. Repeat until the tomatoes are dried out and thick in texture. You should have enough fondue to fill the small tomatoes. Set aside.

3 Lower the oven to 180°C/fan 160°C/gas 4. Cut the tops off the small tomatoes and, using a teaspoon, remove and discard the seeds. Fill with the tomato fondue. Place on a baking tray, season and brush with olive oil. Roast for 10–15 minutes, then set aside.

4 For the onion purée, put the onions in a saucepan and cover with water. Bring to the boil and add a pinch of salt. Reduce to a simmer and cook for about 25 minutes or until soft and translucent. Drain in a colander, then purée in a blender. Pass through a sieve into a clean heavy-based pan. Add the breadcrumbs and butter, and cook, stirring from time to time, for 10–15 minutes, adding a little water if necessary to make a thin purée. Add the chopped thyme and season. Set aside.

5 For the sauce, put the lamb bones in a roasting tin and roast for 20 minutes or until golden, stirring occasionally. Meanwhile, heat some of the oil in a large saucepan, add the onions, garlic, carrot and leek, and fry until soft but not coloured. Add the thyme, rosemary, cumin seeds and cinnamon, and sweat for 5 minutes. Stir in the tomatoes and tomato purée, and cook for a further 10 minutes.

6 Transfer the roasted bones to the saucepan and add 100ml water, the chicken stock and veal glacé, if using. Bring to the boil, then reduce to a gentle simmer and cook for 30 minutes. Pass through colander or sieve, then through a fine sieve into a clean pan. Simmer for about 5 minutes or until reduced to a sauce consistency. Set aside.

7 Place all the ingredients for the basil purée in a small blender and blend to a fine purée. Set aside.

8 To make the roast potatoes, use a deep 6cm round cutter to cut a big round chunk from each potato. Melt 150g of the butter in a small, heavy-based pan with the garlic and thyme. Add the potatoes (the butter should come about halfway up the side of the potatoes, so add more butter if necessary). Season with salt and pepper. When the potatoes are starting to colour underneath, turn them over. Fry for 20 minutes or until tender and golden. Remove from the heat and set aside in the pan.

9 Raise the oven temperature to 220°C/fan 200°C/ gas 7.

10 Season the lamb joint with salt and pepper. Put a little olive oil in a small, heavy roasting tin and put into the oven to heat. Remove from the oven, add a little butter and place the lamb fat-side down in the tin. Add the rosemary. Return to the oven and roast for 5 minutes. Turn the lamb over and roast for another 5 minutes, for medium rare. For medium-well done, roast for a further 5 minutes. Brush the lamb with the basil paste and leave to rest in a warm place for 15 minutes.

11 Meanwhile, put the potatoes and tomatoes in the oven to warm through while you cook the spinach. Heat a little olive oil in a large pan, then add the spinach and cook briefly until it just wilts. Season with salt and pepper. Reheat the lamb sauce and onion purée.

12 For each serving, place a 6cm round cutter in the centre of the plate. Spoon some of the spinach into the cutter. Place a roasted potato on top and remove the cutter. Set a stuffed tomato on top of the potato to create a tower. Carve the lamb into eight cutlets and serve two per serving leaning against the spinach, on either side of it. Drizzle the sauce around and spoon the onion purée to the side or serve it in a separate dish. Serve immediately.

ROAST SADDLE AND SLOWLY BRAISED
SHOULDER OF SPRING LAMB
WITH FRIED NEW POTATOES,
NORFOLK ASPARAGUS AND YOUNG CARROTS

SERVES 8

BRAISED SHOULDER OF LAMB

1 tbsp olive oil

25g butter

1 shoulder of spring lamb, blade end,
  about 900g

about 800g duck or goose fat

salt and pepper

CHICKEN MOUSSE

110g skinless boneless chicken breast, diced

½ egg white, lightly beaten

140ml double cream

SADDLE OF LAMB

1 saddle of lamb on the bone, with fillet
  underneath and without the chump ends,
  about 1.25kg (ask the butcher to remove
  the tough outer skin)

225–250g large leaf spinach, picked from
  the stalks

3 tbsp sunflower oil

25g butter

GRAVY

1 large onion, chopped

6 garlic cloves, chopped

2 carrots, chopped

2 celery sticks, chopped

2 large glasses of white wine

chicken stock

redcurrant jelly (optional)

VEGETABLES

2 tbsp olive oil

40g butter, plus a large knob

275g new potatoes, peeled and cut
  into small even-sized dice

2 garlic cloves, roughly chopped

sprig of mint

about 16 young carrots, scraped

16–24 asparagus spears

1 This recipe needs to be started well in advance. Preheat the oven to 140°C/fan 120°C/gas 1.

2 Start by braising the shoulder of lamb. Heat a frying pan over a high heat, then add the olive oil and butter. Add the lamb and turn to sear and lightly brown all over, seasoning with salt and pepper as you do so. Transfer the lamb to a deep saucepan and add enough duck or goose fat just to cover. Bring up to a gentle tremble on a medium heat, then cover the pan with a lid or foil. Transfer to the oven and cook for 1½ hours. Lower the oven temperature to 120°C/fan 100°C/gas ½ and cook for another 1½ hours. The lamb should be meltingly tender.

3 Carefully lift the lamb out of the fat and set it on a trivet to drain. When the lamb is cool enough to handle, shred about 275g of the meat with your fingers into a bowl, discarding any fat or gristle; cover and set aside in the fridge. (The rest of the meat can be frozen and used for other dishes, such as the base of a cottage pie; the duck or goose fat can also be used again.)

4 To make the chicken mousse, purée the chicken breast in a food processor. With a spatula, push the mixture back towards the blades, then add the egg white and process again. Remove the puréed chicken from the food processor. If you want a finer mixture, push the purée through a sieve into a bowl (this is best done a little at a time using the back of a ladle). Don't use too fine a sieve or it will take a long time.

5 Slowly pour the double cream into the chicken purée, beating carefully with a spatula to reach a dropping consistency. Add the shredded braised lamb, season with salt and pepper, and mix thoroughly. Cover and set aside in the fridge.

6 To prepare the saddle of lamb, use a sharp filleting knife to very carefully remove the whole central bone from the saddle (your butcher can do this for you, but you must emphasise to him that you want it with no holes through the middle of the saddle). Take off the little 'under' fillets of lamb. Set these aside to use later when assembling the dish.

7 Lay the saddle on your worktop, fat side down, and very carefully ease the loins away from the fat, leaving on the work surface a rectangular piece of lamb fat all in one piece. Working really carefully, using a very sharp knife, remove layers from the fat to leave as thin a layer as you can. The aim is to end up with a really, really thin layer of fat measuring about 32.5 x 23cm. Trim off any fat or sinew from the loins, then lay them lengthways, side by side, in the centre of the piece of fat.

8 Quickly blanch the spinach in boiling salted water for 2 minutes. Drain in a colander and refresh immediately under cold running water. Pat dry, spreading out the leaves on a clean tea towel. Lay the spinach leaves over the loins to cover them both completely. In the gap between the two loins, put the lamb and chicken mousse mixture. Place the 'under' fillets of lamb on top of this. Roll up the whole joint in the thin layer of fat and tie very tightly at 2.5cm intervals with butcher's string. Keep in the fridge until about 30 minutes before you are ready to cook.

9 Roughly chop the bones from the saddle of lamb and put them in a large saucepan with the vegetables, wine and enough stock to cover everything. Bring to the boil, then lower the heat and simmer very gently for about 4 hours, skimming off any scum as it comes to the surface. Strain through a sieve into a clean saucepan and boil to reduce by at least two-thirds, tasting until the gravy reaches the required depth of flavour. Pass through a very fine sieve and set aside. Stir in a little redcurrant jelly to sweeten when reheating, if wished.

10 Preheat the oven to 190°C/fan 170°C/gas 5.

11 Heat a very large, heavy-based frying pan until hot. Add the sunflower oil and butter and allow to foam, then put the saddle in the pan and turn to brown all over. Lift the saddle onto a rack set in a roasting tin and season well. Roast for 25–35 minutes, depending on the thickness of the meat. When the lamb has finished cooking, remove from the oven and leave to rest for about 10 minutes.

12 Cook the vegetables while the meat rests. Heat the oil and the 40g butter in a frying pan over a medium heat, add the potatoes, garlic and mint, and season. Fry the potatoes, keeping them moving in the pan as they start to colour. When the potatoes are tender, drain in a sieve or on kitchen paper.

13 Meanwhile, plunge the carrots and asparagus into boiling salted water and cook for 2–3 minutes, then drain well and toss with a knob of butter and salt and pepper to taste. Reheat the gravy.

14 To serve, snip the string off the lamb and carve into 2.5cm-thick slices. (When carved the meat should be perfectly pink inside.) Arrange on the plates surrounded with the vegetables and add a drizzle of gravy.

SAT BAINS

RUMP OF LAMB 'SOUS-VIDE'
GOAT'S CHEESE, DEHYDRATED TOMATOES, DRIED SEEDS AND YOUNG SALAD SHOOTS

SERVES 4

2 rumps of lamb, each 250g (ask your
   butcher to trim and clean, and give
   you the trimmings)
100ml olive oil, plus extra for frying
   and drizzling
pared zest of 1 lemon
pared zest of 1 orange
5 sprigs of lemon thyme, coarsely chopped
2 sprigs of rosemary, coarsely chopped
4 bay leaves, coarsely chopped
250ml chicken stock
salt and white pepper

TOMATOES

8 very ripe, medium-sized vine tomatoes
sea salt
1 garlic clove, crushed
25g lemon thyme
3 tbsp extra virgin olive oil

TO SERVE

25g each pumpkin, sesame and
   sunflower seeds
50g pine nuts
200g young salad shoots or salad leaves
100g goat's cheese (log-shaped and
   ash-coated is good), left at room
   temperature for 2 hours

1 Season the lamb rumps with salt and white pepper. Heat a little oil in a frying pan, add the lamb and fry over a high heat for about 1 minute on each side to caramelise the surface of the meat. Leave to rest and cool.

2 Mix the 100ml olive oil with the lemon and orange zests and the chopped herbs in a large glass bowl. Put the lamb in and roll it around in the marinade, then cover and leave to marinate in the fridge for 24 hours.

3 Meanwhile, prepare the tomatoes. Preheat the oven to its lowest temperature. Make 2–3 slits in the skin of each tomato, being careful not to go through to the flesh. Halve the tomatoes widthways. Crush a generous sprinkling of sea salt with the garlic and thyme using a pestle and mortar. Roll the tomatoes in the mix. Lay the tomatoes cut-side up on a baking tray lined with baking parchment and drizzle with the oil to coat, then bake for 4–6 hours. The tomatoes will become dense and a bit wrinkly, but should still be softish inside and have a vibrant colour.

4 Transfer the lamb with its marinade to an airtight vacuum-sealed bag (see note below). Fill a large pan with water and heat it to 62°C. Put the bag in the water and cook the lamb for 1^1/$_2$ hours, keeping the water temperature at a steady 62°C. The meat should now be really tender and pink inside.

5 While the lamb cooks, put the reserved lamb trimmings in a dry frying pan and fry over a high heat until caramelised. Drain, pat dry and transfer to a small pan. Pour over the chicken stock, cover with a lid and simmer gently for 45 minutes, to extract all the flavour from the lamb. Strain and keep this gravy warm.

6 Meanwhile, toast all the seeds and pine nuts in a dry frying pan on top of the stove. Set aside.

7 When the lamb is cooked, open the bag carefully, remove the lamb and pat it dry with kitchen paper. (Discard the marinade.) Heat a little oil in a non-stick frying pan. Season the fat side of the lamb with salt, then put the lamb in the pan and fry over a high heat to add colour only and caramelise the fat – it doesn't need more cooking. Remove and leave it to rest on a board for 30 seconds.

8 To serve, mix the seeds and nuts with the salad shoots. Sprinkle over a little salt and a drizzle of olive oil, then toss gently together with enough of the warm gravy to moisten. Put 2 tomatoes on each plate. Cut the goat's cheese into 1cm slices and put two slices on each plate. Carve each rump of lamb into four to give you eight slices in total. For each serving arrange one slice of lamb on the goat's cheese and another on the plate. Scatter the dressed salad shoots over the lamb.

Note: Sous-vide, which means 'under vacuum', is a great technique for cooking meat as well as fish and vegetables, and is widely used in restaurants. The meat is slowly poached in a sealed bag at an exact temperature so texture, moisture and flavour are kept intact. I shrink-wrap the meat using a vacuum-sealing machine, then poach in a Clifton water bath, both of which are specially designed for the professional kitchen.

SLOW-COOKED SHOULDER OF MOUNTAIN LAMB
WITH LEEK-WRAPPED LOIN AND CHAMP

SERVES 4

1 shoulder of lamb on the bone, about 1.5kg, trimmed of excess fat and sinew, and bone fully cleaned
few sprigs each of rosemary and thyme
olive oil
mirepoix of finely diced vegetables (2 carrots, 2 celery sticks and 1 large onion)
½ bottle (75cl) dry white wine
200ml white wine vinegar
1 best end (rack) of lamb, meat removed from the bones in one piece and bones reserved
½ onion, finely chopped
2 garlic cloves, roughly chopped
250g button mushrooms, sliced
1 large leek, leaves separated
knob of unsalted butter
salt and pepper

ONION SOUBISE

2 onions, finely sliced
2 shallots, finely sliced
1 garlic clove, chopped
½ tsp thyme leaves
olive oil
knob of unsalted butter

CHAMP

1kg floury potatoes, such as Kerr's Pink, King Edward or Desirée
300ml full-fat milk
60g unsalted butter
6 spring onions, finely chopped
2 tbsp chopped chives
1 banana shallot, finely chopped

GARNISH

1kg broad beans in their pods, shelled
500g peas in their pods, shelled
50g unsalted butter

1 Prick the shoulder of lamb all over with the rosemary and thyme sprigs, then coat lightly in olive oil. Leave to marinate in the fridge for 24 hours.

2 The next day, preheat the oven to 190°C/fan 170°C/gas 5.

3 Season the lamb and sear in hot olive oil in a heavy frying pan until well coloured on all sides. Meanwhile, heat a little olive oil in a large flameproof casserole that has a tight-fitting lid. Add the vegetable mirepoix and sweat over a low to medium heat for 8–9 minutes or until softened but not coloured, stirring frequently.

4 Sit the lamb on the mirepoix. Pour over the wine and wine vinegar, and bring just to the boil. Cover the casserole with two layers of foil and tie with string, then put on the lid. Transfer to the oven to cook for 1 hour. Lower the temperature to 130°C/fan 110°C/gas ½ and cook for a further 3 hours, removing the lid and foil for the last 30 minutes. When cooked, remove from the oven and set aside.

5 While the lamb shoulder is in the oven, season the loin from the best end of lamb, then sear on all sides in a little hot olive oil in a heavy frying pan. Remove from the pan and set aside to rest.

6 Clean the pan, then heat a little more olive oil and sweat the onion until softened but not coloured. Add the garlic and soften briefly, then add the mushrooms and cook for 2–3 minutes. Tip into a blender and blitz until finely chopped.

7 Blanch 4 large leek leaves in boiling water for 10 seconds. Drain and refresh in iced water, then drain and dry. Lay two large (catering-size) sheets of cling film on top of each other on a board and smooth out any wrinkles. Lay the leek leaves next to each other on the cling film, overlapping them slightly so they form a rectangular sheet of leaves. Spread the mushroom stuffing evenly over the leeks. Place the seared loin of lamb at one of the narrow ends and roll up to encase the meat in the sheet of leeks. Now roll the parcel in the cling film and tie the ends tightly with string. Keep in a cool place until ready to cook.

8 To make the onion soubise, sweat the onions, shallots, garlic and thyme in a little olive oil in a heavy pan for 8–9 minutes, stirring frequently. When the mix is soft and juicy but not coloured, remove the pan from the heat, cover and leave to cool slightly. Blitz in a blender with the knob of butter, then pass through a fine sieve into a clean pan. Set aside.

9 Next, make the champ. Cook the potatoes in their skins in a pan of simmering salted water for 20–30 minutes or until just tender (the flesh should offer no resistance when pierced in the centre with the tip of a small, sharp knife). Drain the potatoes and remove the skins, then lightly mash the flesh. In a small pan, combine the milk and butter, and bring to the boil. Add the spring onions, chives and shallot, remove from the heat and allow to infuse for about 1 minute. Stir this into the mashed potatoes and season. Keep warm.

10 While the potatoes are simmering, prepare the garnish and sauce. Blanch the broad beans and peas in separate pans of boiling salted water until tender. The beans should take 3–4 minutes, the peas 1–2 minutes. Drain and refresh both vegetables in iced water, then drain again. Remove the outer skins from the beans. Set the garnish vegetables aside.

11 Lift the shoulder of lamb off the mirepoix, cover and keep warm. Tip the contents of the casserole into a fine sieve and strain the liquid into a bowl; discard the solids. Deglaze the casserole with enough water to cover the bottom, then add this liquid to the strained cooking liquid in the bowl.

12 Heat a little olive oil in a frying pan until almost smoking. Add the bones and any trimmings from the best end of lamb, season and fry for 3–4 minutes or until well coloured and almost caramelised. Add the liquid from the lamb shoulder and reduce by half, then pass through a sieve lined with wet muslin into a clean pan. Add a knob of butter, season to taste and set aside.

13 Steam the lamb parcels above boiling water for 3 minutes. Reheat the broad beans with the butter and a spoonful of water for 1–2 minutes, then add the peas and toss with the beans until hot. Reheat the onion soubise and champ, if necessary.

14 To serve, cut the lamb parcels into portions and carefully remove the cling film. Divide the shoulder of lamb into chunks with a spoon and put some chunks on top of the peas and beans on one side of each warmed plate. Put a spoonful of onion soubise on the opposite side and top with the leek-wrapped loin of lamb. Spoon the champ in quenelles on the plates, then drizzle a little sauce over both types of lamb and around the plate.

BRYN WILLIAMS

WELSH LAMB STEW

SERVES 4-6
1kg boned shoulder of lamb, diced
about 2 tbsp olive oil
1.25-1.5 litres lamb stock
1 large potato, about 350g
1 medium leek
1 medium carrot
½ swede
salt and pepper
crusty bread to serve

1 Season the diced lamb with salt and pepper. Heat the olive oil in a heavy-based pan and brown the meat, stirring occasionally, for about 10 minutes. Cover with the stock, bring to the boil and skim off any surface scum if necessary. Simmer very gently for 40–45 minutes or until the meat is almost tender.
2 While the meat is cooking, cut all the vegetables into rough dice.
3 Stir the potatoes into the stew and cook for 5 minutes. Add all the remaining vegetables and cook for a further 20–30 minutes. When the vegetables are tender, the stock should be reduced to a thickened gravy.
4 Serve the stew with fresh crusty bread.

CANON OF LAMB
WITH BLACK PUDDING, MINTED PEA PURÉE, AND WILD GARLIC POTATO CAKES, GARNISHED WITH LAMB SWEETBREADS AND ROSEMARY GRAVY

SERVES 4

4 boneless loins of lamb, each about 150g

about 6 tbsp rapeseed oil

200g black pudding, preferably Pat O'Doherty's

100g caul fat, soaked in salted water for 4 hours, rinsed and dried

800g floury potatoes, such as Dunbar Standards, peeled

100g wild garlic leaves, finely chopped (see note on page 142)

200g freshly shelled peas

leaves of 4 sprigs of mint

200g lamb sweetbreads

salt and pepper

GRAVY

300ml red wine

1 tbsp roughly chopped rosemary leaves

1 tbsp roughly chopped thyme leaves

2 garlic cloves, roughly chopped

300ml brown beef stock

4 tbsp redcurrant jelly

60g chilled salted butter, diced

1 Season the lamb. Heat 2 tbsp oil in a heavy frying pan until very hot. Add the lamb and sear over a high heat for about 2 minutes until browned on all sides. The meat should still be very rare inside. Place the loins on a wire rack and allow them to cool to room temperature.

2 Remove the skin from the black pudding. Soften the pudding in a bowl, then spread a thin layer on top of each lamb loin. Wrap each loin in caul fat, then in cling film, and put in the fridge to firm up.

3 To make the potato cakes, finely grate the potatoes into a bowl. Season and add the chopped garlic leaves. In a heavy frying pan, heat 1 tbsp oil until it is just beginning to smoke. Press one-quarter of the potato mixture into a 10cm round, add to the hot pan and cook over a medium heat until golden brown on each side. This should take 8–10 minutes in total. Repeat with remaining mixture to make four cakes altogether, adding more oil as needed, and placing them on a baking tray as they are cooked.

4 Meanwhile, cook the peas in boiling salted water for about 5 minutes or until soft but still vibrant green. Drain and purée in a blender until smooth. Add the mint and purée a little more. Rub the purée through a very fine sieve into a clean saucepan, to remove the pea skins. Set the potato cakes and pea purée aside in a warm place.

5 For the gravy, pour the red wine into a pan and add the rosemary, thyme and garlic. Bring to the boil and reduce by two-thirds. Pour in the stock, bring back to the boil and reduce by three-quarters. Add the redcurrant jelly and stir until melted, then strain the gravy into a clean pan. Finish by whisking in the chilled butter, a piece at a time, for a high gloss. Set the gravy aside.

6 Blanch the sweetbreads in boiling salted water for 2 minutes. Drain and refresh in iced water, then lift the sweetbreads out and remove the outer skin with a very sharp knife. Set the sweetbreads aside in the iced water.

7 When you are ready to serve, preheat the oven to 200°C/fan 180°C/gas 6.

8 Remove the cling film from the lamb and sear the loins in a very hot pan, rolling them over, for about 2 minutes or until the caul fat is browned on all sides. Transfer the loins to a baking tray and roast on the top shelf of the oven for 5–8 minutes, according to how well done you like your lamb. Remove and allow to rest for 2–3 minutes. Turn the oven temperature down to 160°C/fan 140°C/gas 3.

9 While the lamb is roasting and resting, heat 2 tbsp oil in a heavy frying pan. Drain, dry and season the sweetbreads, then pan-fry over a medium heat for 3–5 minutes or until lightly browned. At the same time, quickly reheat the potato cakes in the oven, and the pea purée and gravy on top of the stove.

10 To serve, carve the lamb into neat slices. Put a potato cake on each plate and top with slices of lamb. Garnish with the sweetbreads and pea purée, and pool the gravy on the side of the pancake.

Note: When wild garlic is out of season, you can use 100g sorrel or spinach leaves with 2 crushed garlic cloves.

STUART GILLIES

ROASTED LOIN OF SUCKLING PIG WITH MUSTARD SAUCE

SERVES 8-10

1 boneless loin from a 10-12 week old suckling pig, about 3kg, flap removed and trimmed
about 450g sea salt (150g per kg of pork)
bunch of flat-leaf parsley, roughly torn
bunch of basil, roughly torn
150g wild garlic leaves, roughly torn
50ml olive oil
salt and pepper

VEGETABLE GARNISH
16 baby carrots, peeled
caster sugar

about 300g unsalted butter
10 Charlotte potatoes, about 7.5cm each, peeled
½ head of garlic, cut in half crossways
2 tbsp olive oil
500g baby spinach leaves
bunch of flat-leaf parsley, coarsely chopped

MUSTARD SAUCE
500ml home-made chicken stock
2 shallots, shredded or finely sliced
200ml double cream
25g coarse grain mustard
30g Dijon mustard

1 Weigh the loin and the amount of salt you need, then spread the salt out on a tray. Press the loin skin-side down into the salt. Cover with cling film and leave in the fridge for 12 hours.

2 Carefully rinse off all the salt and pat thoroughly dry. Lay the loin, skin-side up, on a board. Using a razor-sharp knife, Stanley knife or scalpel, score the skin carefully all the way along at 5mm intervals. Turn the loin over and stuff with the parsley, basil and wild garlic, then roll up tightly and tie with string. Place the loin skin-side up on a rack in a roasting tin and return, uncovered, to the fridge.

3 Cook the carrots in boiling salted water with a pinch of sugar for about 5 minutes or until just tender. Drain, refresh in iced water and drain again. Set aside.

4 To make the mustard sauce, boil the stock with the shallots until reduced by half, then pass through a fine sieve into a clean pan and bring to the boil again. Whisk in the cream and bring back to the boil, then reduce the heat and whisk in both of the mustards. Cook over a low heat until reduced to a pouring consistency, then remove from the heat. Cover and keep warm, stirring now and again.

5 Melt the butter in a wide, shallow, heavy saucepan. Add the potatoes. They should all be immersed in the butter, so add more butter if necessary. Add the garlic and seasoning, and bring the butter up to a brown foam. Cook the potatoes in the foam for about 25 minutes or until they are a deep golden brown and tender in the middle, shaking the pan gently every few minutes. Remove the pan from the heat and keep the potatoes warm in the butter.

6 Preheat the oven to 220°C/fan 200°C/gas 7.

7 Drizzle the pork with the olive oil, then sprinkle with fine salt and rub well into the skin. Roast for 25–30 minutes or until the skin starts to firm and blister. Remove from the oven and leave to rest somewhere warm. Leave the oven on.

8 While the meat is resting, reheat the carrots in the olive oil without colouring, then add the spinach and chopped parsley, and toss until hot. Lift the potatoes out of the butter with a slotted spoon and put them in a small, heavy pan. Pour over 2 tbsp of the butter they were cooked in and put the potatoes into the oven to reheat for about 2 minutes. Gently reheat the mustard sauce without boiling.

9 Remove the string from the pork and carve the meat into equal slices, allowing two per person. Reheat in the oven on a non-stick mat or foil for 2 minutes.

10 To serve, check the potatoes for seasoning, then place on the side of the warmed plates. Put the other vegetables next to them, then place the pork in the middle, resting the slices on the potatoes. Pour over a little of the mustard sauce, and serve the rest on the side.

144

PLATE OF AGED MUTTON
POTATOES AND BROAD BEANS, WITH
CAPER AND HERB RELISH

SERVES 4

RACKS OF MUTTON

2 racks of mutton, preferably aged
  Herdwick, each with 6 rib bones, chined
  and trimmed of all fat
large sprig each of thyme and rosemary
4 garlic cloves, sliced
about 450ml organic rapeseed oil
salt and pepper

MUTTON 'PARK RAILINGS'

100ml organic rapeseed oil
2 onions, very finely diced
2 carrots, very finely diced
1/2 head of celery, very finely diced
2 leeks, very finely diced
1 head of garlic, smashed
1/2 bottle (75cl) dry white wine,
  preferably English
1 breast of mutton, preferably aged
  Herdwick, trimmed of all skin
plain flour for coating
3 medium eggs, beaten
200g home-made fresh white breadcrumbs,
  seasoned with salt and pepper
vegetable oil for frying

RELISH

75g can anchovies, chopped
2 tbsp extra-fine capers, plus a little
  of their vinegar
150ml organic rapeseed oil
1/2–3/4 tsp English mustard powder
squeeze of lemon juice
2 tbsp each very finely shredded flat-leaf
  parsley, basil and mint

TO SERVE

12–16 small new potatoes, preferably
  Maris Bard, scraped
few sprigs of mint
750g fresh broad beans, podded
butter
100ml mutton jus, made as duck jus
  (page 46), but using mutton bones and
  white wine, or 100ml gravy leftover from
  a lamb roast, warmed for serving

1 Put the racks of mutton in a strong plastic bag with the herbs and sliced garlic. Add enough rapeseed oil (about 400ml) to cover the meat. Seal and shake the bag, then leave in the fridge overnight. The next day, cut each rack in half so you have 4 racks, each with 4 bones.

2 Preheat the oven to 180°C/fan 160°C/gas 4.

3 Heat 100ml rapeseed oil in a large, heavy flameproof casserole until hot. Add the diced vegetables and the smashed garlic, and brown over a medium to high heat. Pour in the wine and stir well, then place the breast of mutton on the vegetables. Add enough cold water to cover the meat. Bring to a simmer, then cover the casserole and transfer to the oven. Braise for 2 hours or until the meat is meltingly tender.

4 Take the breast out of the liquid, and twist and pull out the bones while the meat is still warm. Put the meat between two sheets of greaseproof paper, put heavy weights on top to flatten it and leave for 3–5 hours. After pressing, cut the meat into eight long strips (traditionally called park railings), each about 12cm long and 1.5cm wide.

5 Make the relish by stirring together all the ingredients except the herbs.

6 Cook the potatoes with the mint in a pan of gently simmering salted water for 10–12 minutes or until tender. Drain and set aside. Plunge the broad beans into well-salted boiling water to blanch for 2 minutes. Drain and refresh in iced water, then drain again and peel off the skins. Set aside.

7 Preheat the oven to 220–230°C/fan 200–210°C/gas 7–8.

8 Season the racks of mutton. Heat a heavy ovenproof frying pan until hot, add a splash of oil and caramelise the racks quickly and evenly all over. Transfer to the oven to finish cooking for 8–10 minutes. Remove the racks from the oven, cover them loosely with foil and leave to rest in a warm place for 10–15 minutes so they will be evenly pink.

9 Meanwhile, coat the park railings in flour, beaten egg and breadcrumbs. Pour vegetable oil into a deep frying pan to a depth of 2.5–5cm (enough to cover the railings). Heat the oil until hot, then fry the railings for 2–3 minutes or until crisp and golden. At the same time, reheat the potatoes and broad beans together in a pan with a little butter, a drop of water and seasoning to taste. Mix the herbs into the relish and taste for seasoning.

10 To serve, carve one rack into three double cutlets and the other rack into one double cutlet and four single cutlets. Slot the bones of each double cutlet with a single cutlet on each plate, then criss-cross two park railings in front. Spoon the broad beans and potatoes on the left, and the caper relish on the right. Finish with a cordon of warm mutton jus.

146

PORK CUTLETS
WITH CELERIAC AND APPLE MASH

SERVES 4

4 thick pork cutlets, preferably organic
   Saddleback, with bone and untrimmed
25g unsalted butter, melted
8 sage leaves
salt and pepper

MASH

1 celeriac, 500–700g, peeled and cut
   into cubes
sprig of thyme
150ml full-fat milk
3 Bramley's cooking apples, peeled and
   cut into cubes
unsalted butter

1 To make the mash, put the celeriac in a heavy saucepan with 150ml water, the thyme, milk and seasoning. Cook for 20–30 minutes or until tender. At the same time, cook the apples with a little butter in a separate pan over a gentle heat for about 20 minutes or until soft, then blitz to a purée in a blender.

2 Drain the celeriac, return to the hot pan and mash roughly. Immediately add the apple purée and toss together. Cover the pan and leave in a warm place while you cook the pork cutlets.

3 Brush the cutlets well with melted butter. Place a sage leaf on both sides of each cutlet and brush with more butter so the sage leaves stick to the meat, then season with salt and pepper. Pan-roast in a heavy pan over a high heat until the internal temperature of the pork reaches 70°C when tested with a meat thermometer. Cooking should take 5–6 minutes in total, turning the cutlets halfway. At the end of cooking the meat should be coloured on the outside but pink inside. Strain the pan juices and reserve, then let the meat rest in the pan in a warm place for 10 minutes.

4 To serve, place a pork cutlet on each plate, spoon the mash alongside and drizzle over the strained juices from the pork.

POT ROAST PORK BELLY COOKED IN CIDER
SERVED WITH ITS OFFAL AND CRACKLING, WITH SUMMER VEGETABLES

148

SERVES 4

1 piece of pork belly on the bone, with skin,
   1.5–2kg
1 large onion, roughly chopped
2 celery sticks, roughly chopped
2 carrots, roughly chopped
3 garlic cloves, halved
few sprigs of thyme
500ml dry cider
½ tbsp plain flour
1 litre hot beef or chicken stock
2 shallots, roughly chopped
about 100g unsalted butter
vegetable oil
1 pig's kidney, about 150g, cored and cut
   into rough 1cm dice
250–300g runner beans, very thinly sliced
   on the diagonal
500g fresh young broad beans, podded
   (about 200g podded weight)
salt and pepper

1 Preheat the oven to 180°C/fan 160°C/gas 4.

2 Cut the bones out of the pork belly and place them in a flameproof casserole with the onion, celery, carrots, garlic and thyme.

3 Cut the meat into four equal servings. Remove the skin from each one using a razor-sharp knife or a Stanley knife. Score parallel lines in the skin, keeping them as close together as possible and cutting right through into the fat beneath. Blanch the skin in boiling water for 3–4 minutes, then drain and dry well. Set aside.

4 Score the fat on the pieces of pork in a criss-cross pattern, then season. Heat a heavy frying pan and cook the pieces of pork on a fairly high heat for 3–4 minutes on each side until nicely coloured. Place the pork fat-side up on top of the vegetables and bones in the casserole and pour in half the cider. Cover with a lid and cook in the oven for 1 hour, basting the meat every so often.

5 Season the blanched pork skin with salt, place on a baking tray and roast in the oven with the pork.

6 Remove the lid from the pork and drain off about two-thirds of the cooking liquid. Continue cooking the pork, uncovered, for a further 30 minutes or until the liquid has evaporated and the pork is crisping up. Check the crackling on the baking tray and continue cooking if it isn't yet crisp.

7 Lift the pork from the casserole and keep hot. Drain off all the fat from the pot, leaving behind the vegetables and bones. Place the pot over a low heat. Dust the vegetables and bones with the flour and stir well. Gradually stir in the rest of the cider and the stock, then bring to the boil and simmer for 15–20 minutes. Strain into a saucepan. Skim off any fat, and simmer until the sauce has reduced to about 250ml. Remove from the heat.

8 Gently cook the shallots in another saucepan with 50g butter for 1–2 minutes, then pour in the reduced sauce and stir to mix. Heat a little vegetable oil in a frying pan, season the kidney and fry for 2–3 minutes or until nicely coloured. Drain the kidney on kitchen paper and add to the sauce. Taste for seasoning and keep hot.

9 Cook the runner beans in boiling salted water for 3–4 minutes or until just tender. Drain, toss in a little butter and season to taste. Now cook the broad beans in boiling salted water for 3–4 minutes or until tender; drain and cool a little, then remove the outer skins if they are tough. Toss the beans in a little butter and season to taste.

10 To serve, place the runner beans in the centre of four plates. Slice each piece of pork into four or five pieces and place on the beans. Drizzle the sauce over, and scatter the broad beans around the edge. Break the crackling into shreds where it has been scored, and pile on top of the sliced pork.

SLOWLY BRAISED BELLY AND ROASTED LOIN CHOP OF PORK
WITH CRACKLING

SERVES 8

½ boned short pork belly, skin on, trimmed
   to weigh about 1.5kg
300ml vegetable oil
2 carrots, cut into 2cm pieces
4 celery sticks, cut into 2cm pieces
1 white onion, cut lengthways into eighths
1 head of garlic, cut crossways in half
1 leek, cut into 2cm pieces
6 ripe tomatoes, halved
small bunch of thyme
small bunch of rosemary
1 bay leaf
2.2 litres hot home-made chicken stock
20g salted butter

2 pork loins, each with 4 rib bones,
   preferably Middle White or another
   traditional English breed, chined and
   fully trimmed
40g unsalted butter
1 Duchy cabbage, leaves cut into forty eight
   6cm squares
salt and pepper

1 Soak the pork belly in cold water for about 1 hour. Remove and dry very well, then season all over with salt. Heat 150ml of the oil in a large, heavy roasting tin over a medium-high heat until you can see a light haze rising. Gently place the pork belly skin-side down in the pan, taking care because the oil may spit a little. Cook for 5–8 minutes or until the skin has a nice colour, then turn the joint over and cook for another 5 minutes or until the meat is golden brown. Transfer the joint to a wire rack, placing it skin-side up.

2 Keep the roasting tin on the stove over a medium heat, and add the carrots, celery, onion, garlic and leek. Cook until well coloured, then add the tomatoes and cook until soft. Place the pork belly skin-side up on the vegetables. Add the herbs and 2 litres chicken stock, and bring to the boil. Turn the heat down to a very gentle murmer (almost not moving), cover the tin with a lid and cook for 3–3½ hours. Check the meat is done by piercing it in the middle with the tip of a sharp knife – it should slide in effortlessly. Remove the meat from the tin and leave to cool, then keep covered in the fridge.

3 Strain the cooking liquid through a fine sieve lined with muslin into a heavy saucepan. Simmer until reduced to about 500ml, skimming frequently. Season this sauce with salt if necessary, and set aside.

4 Preheat the oven to 190°C/fan 170°C/gas 5.

5 Heat 50ml of the remaining oil in a clean, heavy roasting tin over a medium heat. Add the salted butter and heat until it starts to foam. Season the loins of pork well with salt, then sear until golden brown on all sides, turning regularly. Transfer the tin to the oven and roast for about 35 minutes or until the loins are glazed and moist. Turn them every 8 minutes or so, and baste with a spoonful or two of the remaining hot chicken stock. Remove from the oven and allow to rest in warm place.

6 Turn the oven up to 210°C/fan 190°C/gas 6^1/$_2$. Remove the skin from the pork belly, taking a little of the fat beneath, and leaving a 2mm-thick layer of fat attached to the meat. Cut the skin into 2 x 4cm rectangles using a razor-sharp knife or a Stanley knife and set aside.

7 Cut the belly into eight 7 x 4cm rectangles. Heat 50ml of the remaining oil in a heavy frying pan until you can see a light haze rising. Carefully place the belly fat-side down in the pan and cook over a medium-high heat for about 5 minutes or until a deep golden colour. Place fat-side up on a tray and transfer to the oven to cook for 6 minutes.

8 Meanwhile, heat the remaining oil in a heavy frying pan. Season the pork skin, then put it skin-side down in the hot oil and fry over a medium-high heat until crisp. This will take 4–5 minutes, turning halfway. Remove the crackling with a slotted spoon, drain on kitchen paper and keep hot.

9 Heat the unsalted butter in another pan until it melts and starts to bubble. Add the 48 cabbage leaf squares, season with salt and cook for 2–3 minutes or until tender. Season with a good few twists of pepper, then transfer to kitchen paper using a slotted spoon and keep hot.

10 Reheat the sauce. Cut each piece of pork belly in half widthways. Carve the loins into single chops, and season the cut flesh with a little sea salt.

11 To serve, sit two pieces of pork belly on each plate and arrange six squares of cabbage in front. Rest a chop against the cabbage and garnish with the crackling, either left as it is or cut into pieces. Spoon a little of the sauce over and around, and serve the rest in a jug.

ROAST RACK OF PORK
WITH CRACKLING, ROSEMARY AND GARLIC, GOOSEBERRY PURÉE, WILTED SPROUTING BROCCOLI AND OLIVE OIL MASHED POTATOES

SERVES 6-8

1 rack of pork with at least 3 rib bones, about 1.5kg, chined and rind finely scored

2–3 garlic cloves, thinly sliced

sprigs of rosemary

450g purple sprouting broccoli, preferably Norfolk-grown

salt and pepper

GOOSEBERRY PURÉE

250g gooseberries, topped and tailed

about 50g caster sugar

2 elderflower blossoms (if available)

OLIVE OIL MASH

200ml milk

2 garlic cloves, finely chopped

2 sprigs of thyme

sprig of rosemary

1kg floury potatoes such as Desirée, peeled and chopped

about 175ml olive oil

1 Preheat the oven to 220°C/fan 200°C/gas 7. Weigh the pork and calculate the cooking time, allowing 45 minutes per kg, then adding 20 minutes extra.

2 Make incisions about 2.5cm apart through the rind and into the flesh of the pork using a sharp knife, then push a slice of garlic and a small sprig of rosemary into each cut. Place the pork in a roasting tin and splash the rind with cold water before liberally sprinkling with salt.

3 Roast the pork, without opening the oven door, for 25 minutes. During this time, the crackling should start to bubble. Turn the oven down to 190°C/fan 170°C/gas 5 and continue to roast for the remainder of the calculated cooking time. You should have good crackling and moist succulent meat. Check with a skewer to be sure the meat is cooked properly – the juices should run pink but not bloody. Remove the pork from the oven and allow to rest for 5 minutes in a warm place before carving.

4 While the pork is roasting, prepare the accompaniments. To make the gooseberry purée, put the gooseberries in a saucepan and add enough caster sugar just to cover and the elderflower blossoms, if using. Pour in enough cold water just to cover the gooseberries and sugar. Cover the pan and cook over a moderate heat for about 15 minutes or until the gooseberries are soft. Remove the elderflower blossoms and blitz the cooked gooseberries in a blender. Pass the purée through a fine sieve into a clean pan. Taste and add more sugar if needed. Set aside (reheat gently to serve).

5 For the olive oil mash, pour the milk into a saucepan, add the garlic, thyme and rosemary, and bring to the boil. Remove from the heat, cover and leave to infuse while you cook the potatoes.

6 Put the potatoes in a saucepan of salted water, bring to the boil and cook for about 15 minutes or until soft. Drain in a colander, then return to the pan and dry out by shaking the pan over a low heat. Push the potatoes through a sieve with the back of a ladle into a bowl, or use a potato ricer.

7 Strain the milk into another pan, add 100ml of the olive oil and slowly bring to the boil. Vigorously whisk the hot milk and olive oil into the potatoes to create a mash with a fairly runny consistency. (You can use an electric mixer, but not a food processor as this will make the potatoes too sticky and glutinous.) Adjust the consistency by adding more warm olive oil or milk, or both. Taste and season, and keep hot. (If preparing ahead, allow to cool, then gently reheat by stirring in a saucepan over a low heat.)

8 To prepare the broccoli, trim any tough stalks, much as if you were preparing asparagus. Bring a large saucepan of salted water to the boil and drop in the broccoli. Cook for a few minutes only, until the stalks are just tender (test with the point of a knife). Drain the broccoli immediately and give it a good grinding of salt and pepper.

9 To serve, carve the rack of pork and serve with the slightly warmed gooseberry purée, olive oil mash and sprouting broccoli.

MARK BROADBENT

CRACKLED PORK
WITH BEETROOT, CELERY LEAF AND HORSERADISH

SERVES 4

½ pork belly on the bone, preferably Middle
  White, skin scored
250g Maldon sea salt
2kg goose fat, duck fat or lard, or 2 litres
  grapeseed oil
6 small, raw beetroots
red wine vinegar
250g unsalted butter
150g celery leaves
200ml pork jus, made as duck jus (page 46),
  but using pork trimmings and bones and
  white wine, or 200ml gravy leftover from
  a pork roast, warmed for serving
salt and pepper

HORSERADISH SAUCE

100g fresh horseradish, peeled and
  finely grated
½ tbsp Dijon mustard
juice of ½ lemon
2 generous tbsp crème fraîche

1 Rub the skin of the pork belly with the sea salt, working it into the scored cuts. Leave uncovered in the fridge for 8 hours or overnight.

2 The next day, preheat the oven to 120°C/fan 100°C/gas ¼.

3 Rinse the salt off the pork. Bring the fat to the boil in a large flameproof casserole. Lower the pork into it until submerged, then cover the pot and place in the oven to braise for 2½–3 hours or until tender.

4 Remove from the oven. Leave the pork belly in the fat until lukewarm, then lift out and place skin-side down on a board. Twist and pull out all the bones, then cut away any gristle and excess fat. Now turn the pork skin-side up and sandwich between two sheets of greaseproof paper. Place a chopping board on top and press down lightly, then chill in the fridge overnight. Strain the fat and reserve.

5 The next day, put the beetroots in a saucepan of cold salted water, add a healthy splash of wine vinegar and bring to the boil. Simmer for up to 1 hour or until just cooked. Allow the beetroots to cool in the liquid, then lift out and peel with a vegetable peeler. Strain and reserve the cooking liquid.

6 Make the horseradish sauce by mixing all the ingredients together with salt and pepper to taste. Cover and chill for at least 2 hours before serving.

7 Preheat the oven to 230°C/fan 210°C/gas 8.

8 Cut the pressed pork into four neat rectangular blocks, about 8.5 x 6.5cm (leftover pork can be immersed in goose or duck fat and kept as 'confit' in the fridge for up to a month). Heat a flameproof casserole or heavy ovenproof frying pan until hot. Add enough of the reserved strained fat to cover the bottom and heat until the fat is hot, then put in the pork skin-side down. Transfer to the oven and roast for 20 minutes or until the skin is crackled. Remove the pork and drain on kitchen paper. Keep hot.

9 Cut the beetroots in half lengthways. Heat through in a pan with a spoonful of the reserved cooking liquid, half the butter, and salt and pepper to taste.

10 Blanch the celery leaves in boiling salted water for 1–1½ minutes. Drain and refresh in iced water, then drain again and squeeze out the excess water. Reheat the leaves with the remaining butter and seasoning.

11 To serve, put the celery leaves in the middle of each large bowl or plate. Set the pork on top to one side and place the beetroot halves next to it. Drizzle over a little jus, and top the beetroot with a quenelle of horseradish cream.

156

A PLATE OF SCOTTISH PORK

SERVES 6-8

PORK BELLY
1 large onion, sliced
250g salt
200g golden caster sugar
8 juniper berries
1 bay leaf
1 tbsp black peppercorns
4 cloves
1 small piece of nutmeg
4 sprigs of thyme
1 Lombok chilli, slit lengthways in half
1 piece of pork belly on the bone,
   about 1.5kg, skin on
1 onion, chopped
4 celery sticks, chopped
2 carrots, chopped
2.5 litres chicken stock

GLAZE FOR BELLY
4 tbsp dark muscovado sugar
good pinch of ground cloves
1 tsp picked thyme leaves

PORK LOIN
1 tbsp olive oil
1 boned pork loin, about 650g, trimmed
salt and pepper
1 banana shallot, diced
½ fennel bulb, diced
2 celery sticks, diced
1 medium carrot, diced
250ml dry cider
200ml chicken stock
½ Granny Smith apple, peeled and diced

1 To prepare the pork belly, take a pan that's big enough to hold the pork and put in 2 litres of water, the sliced onion, salt and sugar. Bring to the boil and stir until the salt and sugar have dissolved. Take off the heat and add all the spices (except the chilli) and thyme, then allow to cool. When completely cold, add the chilli.
2 Immerse the pork belly in the spiced brine, making sure that it is completely submerged. Cover and keep in the fridge for 10 hours. Then remove the pork and place on a wire rack to drip dry.
3 Preheat the oven to 180°C/fan 160°C/gas 4. Set the pork in a flameproof casserole. Place over a medium heat and add the chopped onion, celery, carrots and chicken stock. Bring to the boil, then transfer to the oven. Braise for 2 hours.
4 Take the casserole out of the oven, remove the pork and allow to cool slightly. Turn the oven up to 200°C/fan 180°C/gas 6.
5 Combine all the ingredients for the glaze. Remove the skin from the pork and score the remaining fat in a criss-cross pattern. Press on the glaze. Place the pork glazed-side up in a roasting tin and add about 200ml of the stock from the casserole. Put the tin in the oven and roast for about 20 minutes, basting frequently, until the glaze is dark and sticky. When the belly has finished cooking, remove from the oven and keep warm. Lower the oven to 180°C/fan 160°C/gas 4.

6 While the belly is cooking, prepare the loin (if you have a double oven, you can cook it while the belly cooks). Take an ovenproof pan that's big enough to hold the pork loin and set over a high heat. Add the olive oil. Season the pork loin and place it in the pan. Fry until golden brown on all sides. Remove from the pan and keep in a warm place.

7 Turn the heat down and allow the pan to cool slightly, then add the diced vegetables. Sweat in the juices left by the pork, but do not allow to colour. Add the cider and pull all the vegetables into the centre of the pan. Place the pork on top of the vegetables (so that it doesn't stew). Cover the pan with a lid and transfer to the oven. Cook for 30–35 minutes or until the pork reaches a core temperature of 52°C. Take the pan out of the oven, remove the pork and allow to rest somewhere warm for about 10 minutes.

8 Meanwhile, place the pan with the vegetables on the heat and add the stock. Reduce by about half until an intense flavour is achieved, then strain the liquid into a clean pan, pressing down on the vegetables in the sieve with the back of a spoon. Add the apple to the liquid and cook for about 1 minute.

9 To serve, slice the pork loin and divide among the warmed plates. Slice the belly pork into large chunks and add to the plates. Drizzle round the apple 'sauce'. Accompany with mashed potatoes.

JEREMY LEE

GROUSE AND ACCOMPANIMENTS

SERVES 4
4 grouse (ask the butcher to remove the intestines but leave the liver and heart)
75–90g unsalted butter
4 discs of white bread, about 4cm in diameter and 6mm thick
Madeira (optional)
salt and pepper

BREAD SAUCE
200ml full-fat milk
½ small onion, sliced
1 bay leaf
2 cloves
3 white peppercorns
5–6 scrapes of nutmeg
60g fresh, soft white breadcrumbs

FRIED BREADCRUMBS
40g unsalted butter
125g coarse breadcrumbs

GAME CHIPS
2–3 large potatoes (a good frying variety such as King Edward or Maris Piper), peeled
groundnut oil for deep-frying

TO SERVE
watercress
redcurrant jelly

1 To make the bread sauce, tip the milk into a saucepan and add the onion, bay leaf, cloves, white peppercorns and nutmeg. Heat the milk to just below boiling point. Remove from the heat, cover with a lid and let it sit quietly – the longer the better. Half an hour or so before serving, warm the infused milk, then strain it over the breadcrumbs. Stir gently, then cover and let sit for 10 minutes. Check the sauce for seasoning and consistency, adding a splash of milk if too thick or a few more breadcrumbs if too thin. Set aside.

2 Preheat the oven to 240°C/fan 220°C/gas 7.

3 Liberally cover the grouse with butter and lightly salt them evenly all over. Heat a roasting tin in the oven, then add the birds and roast for 15 minutes. Remove from the oven and leave to rest for at least 15 minutes.

4 While the grouse roast and rest, prepare the rest of the accompaniments. For the fried breadcrumbs, melt the butter in a frying pan over a gentle heat. Add the breadcrumbs and fry gently until they are a golden brown colour and crisp. Season with salt and pepper, then tip into a dish. Keep warm.

5 To make the game chips, slice the potatoes very thinly and rinse thoroughly until all trace of starch has vanished. Drain well, then dry the slices in a cloth. Heat the oil in a deep-fat fryer. Tip in a handful of the slices and fry until golden brown, stirring now and again to ensure they do not clump together. Remove and drain on kitchen paper. Add a little salt. Keep frying the game chips, then keep warm.

6 When the accompaniments are ready, remove the birds from the roasting tin and set aside. Set the tin over a gentle heat, add a little knob of butter and drop in the discs of bread. Fry gently, pushing the discs around the tin to pick up all residual grouse juices, until golden brown and crisp.

7 Remove the livers and hearts from inside the cooked birds and break them with a fork into a coarse paste. Season with a little salt and pepper. If a bottle of Madeira is handy, a spoonful would be very welcome. Spread this paste over the toasts and sit the birds on top.

8 Warm the bread sauce. Place the grouse, on their toasts, on individual warmed plates or all together on a big serving dish. Pile a big clump of watercress alongside the birds. Heap the game chips, fried breadcrumbs, redcurrant jelly and bread sauce in pretty bowls, and serve swiftly.

GLAZED BREAST OF DUCK
WITH CRISP SKIN, FENNEL PURÉE AND
BRAISED BABY FENNEL

160

SERVES 6

1 whole duck and 4 duck breasts,
  preferably Goosnargh duck
225ml duck fat
75g unsalted butter
18 baby fennel, trimmed
1 star anise, cracked
salt and white pepper

STOCK

150ml duck fat
1 carrot, cut into 2cm dice
4 celery sticks, cut into 2cm dice
1 onion, quartered
1 head of garlic, cut in half crossways
bunch of thyme
2 bay leaves
good pinch of rock salt
10 white peppercorns
20 coriander seeds
2 tbsp tomato purée
2 litres hot chicken stock

FENNEL PURÉE

75g unsalted butter
1 large fennel bulb, very finely sliced
hot chicken stock
50ml Pernod
100ml double cream
1 tbsp olive oil
1 tsp Dijon mustard

1 Remove the breasts from the whole duck and set aside with the other breasts.
Pull the legs off the carcass and chop them into 3cm pieces (including the bones).
Roughly chop the carcass and wings. Set all the chopped bones aside for the stock.

2 Carefully remove the skin from the duck breasts using a sharp knife, and remove
any sinews from the flesh. Set the breasts aside. Lay the skin flat on a tray and freeze
until completely solid, then cut into 2cm squares.

3 Melt 150ml duck fat in a pan, add the diced skin and cook over a medium heat,
stirring occasionally, for about 20 minutes or until the skin is crisp. Remove the
skin with a slotted spoon and drain on kitchen paper.

4 Warm the remaining 75ml duck fat in a bowl until it is the consistency of softened
butter. Season with a pinch of salt and a few twists of white pepper. Brush each duck
breast well with the duck fat on both sides, then roll into a sausage and wrap tightly
in cling film. Twist the ends of the film and tie tightly in a knot, as close to the duck
as possible. Keep in the fridge until needed.

5 Preheat the oven to 200°C/fan 180°C/gas 6.

6 To make the stock, spread the chopped duck carcass and wings (not the legs) in a large tray and roast for about 20 minutes or until a deep golden brown, turning frequently. Set aside. Heat the 150ml duck fat in a large, heavy saucepan on top of the stove and sear the chopped legs until nicely browned on all sides. Add the carrot, celery, onion, garlic and herbs. Season with the salt, peppercorns and coriander seeds, and cook until the vegetables are deep brown. Add the tomato purée and cook for 5 minutes, stirring regularly, then add the roasted bones followed by the hot chicken stock. Bring to the boil and skim off any froth, then turn the heat down to a gentle simmer. Cook for 1^1/$_2$ hours, skimming regularly.

7 Strain the stock through a colander, then strain again through a muslin-lined fine sieve into a clean pan. Bring to the boil and boil rapidly until reduced by about two-thirds. Remove 100ml of this reduced stock and reserve for the sauce, then continue to reduce the rest until you have a nice glaze that coats the back of a spoon. Remove from the heat and keep warm.

8 Next make the fennel purée. Melt the butter in a heavy pan, add the fennel and season with salt. Add the Pernod and reduce until all the liquid has gone. Continue cooking over a medium to high heat for about 10 minutes or until the fennel is very soft, keeping it moist by occasionally stirring in a spoonful or two of hot chicken stock. Add the cream and boil until reduced by two-thirds. Purée in a blender until very smooth. Keep the purée warm.

9 To cook the baby fennel, melt the 75g butter until it starts to foam. Quickly colour the fennel over a medium to high heat, then season with salt and add the star anise. Cook for about 7 minutes, gradually adding the reserved 100ml reduced stock. When the fennel is tender, lift it out and keep both the sauce and the fennel warm.

10 Heat a pan of water to 63°C. Drop in the duck breasts (still in the cling film) and cook for 26 minutes for medium rare, gently turning the duck and pushing it under the water. Use a thermometer to check that the temperature of the water stays constant throughout. If you like your duck more cooked, increase the cooking time by 8 minutes for each extra stage of doneness.

11 To serve, reheat the reserved glaze. Unwrap the duck breasts and slice each into four pieces. Brush the duck with the warm glaze and sprinkle with the crisp skin. Spoon the fennel purée on each plate and lay the slices of duck across it, then make a neat pile of baby fennel on top. Drizzle a little sauce over and around, and serve the rest separately in a jug.

HONEY ROAST CORNISH DUCKLING
WITH CABBAGE AND SMOKED BACON

SERVES 4

4 Gressingham duck breasts, each 180g
vegetable oil for frying
100g clear honey
1 tsp Chinese five spice powder
salt and pepper

DUCK SAUCE

1kg duck carcasses, chopped small
1 tsp Chinese five spice powder
1 large onion, cut into thick rings
½ head of garlic, cut in half crossways
15g thyme plus 5 large sprigs
700ml chicken stock
100g clear honey
3 tbsp sherry vinegar
300ml veal glacé
1 tsp white peppercorns
3 tbsp double cream

CABBAGE

350g Savoy cabbage, cut into strips,
  not too fine
1 shallot, chopped
20g unsalted butter
40g smoked back bacon slices, cut into
  fine strips
20g garlic purée

GARNISH

20 celeriac slices, cut into 1.5cm dice,
  blanched and deep-fried
20 garlic cloves, blanched and roasted

1 Preheat the oven to 220°C/fan 200°C/gas 7.

2 To make the duck sauce, put the duck carcasses in a roasting tin and roast lightly for 20 minutes. Just before they finish roasting, sprinkle the bones with the Chinese five spice. Remove the tin from the oven and place on top of the stove. Add the onion and garlic, and fry to very lightly colour the onion. Add the 15g thyme. Remove from the heat and leave to cool slightly. Pour the chicken stock into the roasting tin and stir well to deglaze.

3 Heat the honey in a large saucepan and bring to a rolling boil. Cook for 3 minutes over a high heat, but be careful not to burn the honey or the sauce will be bitter. Add the vinegar and reduce to nothing. Add the contents of the roasting tin, together with the veal glacé, peppercorns, remaining sprigs of thyme and the cream. Bring to the boil and skim off the scum. Reduce the heat to a simmer and cook for 30 minutes. Strain through a colander into a bowl, then pass through a fine sieve into a clean saucepan. Simmer to reduce to a sauce consistency, then taste and adjust the seasoning and acidity. Set aside.

4 Before cooking the duck breasts, put them in the freezer for a few minutes to make it easier to score the skins. Then, using a very sharp knife, score the fatty skin in a criss-cross pattern, being careful not to cut into the meat. Season the meat side with salt and pepper. Heat a little vegetable oil a heavy-based frying pan. Place the breasts skin-side down in the hot oil and cook over a fairly high heat so the fat is rendered; be careful not to burn the skin. Once the skin is golden brown and crisp, turn the breasts over and sear the other side for 1 minute. Turn the breasts over again and crisp the skin a little more. Then turn each breast once more and finish cooking to your desired degree.

5 Mix together the honey and five spice. Remove the breasts from the pan, brush the honey over the crisp skin and leave to rest.

6 Meanwhile, cook the cabbage in boiling salted water for a few minutes, then drain and refresh in iced water. Drain again well and pat dry. Soften the shallot in the butter. Add the bacon. Tip in the cooked cabbage and let it dry out briefly in the pan. Add the garlic purée and cook for a minute. Season with salt and pepper to taste.

7 To serve, reheat the sauce. Spoon the cabbage down the centre of each plate. Cut the duck breasts into thin slices and lay them on the cabbage. Arrange the garlic and celeriac all around and drizzle with the sauce. (Any extra sauce can be frozen.)

MARK HIX

RABBIT AND CRAYFISH STARGAZY PIE

SERVES 4

back and front legs from 4 wild rabbits
  (reserve the saddles for another dish,
  such as a salad)
3 tbsp plain flour
2–3 tbsp vegetable oil
2 onions, finely chopped
good knob of unsalted butter
1 glass of English white wine or cider
2 litres hot chicken stock
500g good-quality puff pastry
  made with butter
beaten egg
salt and pepper

CRAYFISH

1 tsp fennel seeds
12 black peppercorns
few sprigs of thyme
2 star anise
1 bay leaf
24 live freshwater crayfish
1 litre chicken stock

1 Season the rabbit legs and dust them with 1 tbsp of the flour. Heat the oil in a heavy frying pan until hot, then lightly colour the rabbit legs over a medium heat for 3–4 minutes on each side. Remove and drain on kitchen paper.

2 In a large saucepan, gently cook the onions in the butter for 2–3 minutes without colouring. Dust with the remaining flour and stir well over a low heat for a minute, then gradually add the wine and the hot stock, stirring to prevent lumps from forming. Bring to the boil.

3 Add the rabbit legs and season lightly. Cover with the lid. Simmer gently for about 1 hour or until the rabbit is tender. Remove the rabbit legs and leave to cool. The sauce should be fairly thick – if it's not, continue simmering for a while until it has reduced down by half.

4 To cook the crayfish, bring a large saucepan of water to the boil with the fennel seeds, peppercorns, thyme, star anise, bay leaf, and 1 tbsp salt. Simmer for about 5 minutes. Plunge the crayfish into the liquid, bring the water quickly back to the boil and simmer for $1^1/2$ minutes. Drain and leave to cool.

5 Pick out 4 similar-sized crayfish for the garnish and set aside. Peel the rest, including the large claws, first removing the head and then squeezing the shell between thumb and forefinger to crack it. Set the meat aside. Crush the shells a little, put them in a saucepan with the stock and simmer for 30 minutes. Strain the stock through a sieve into a clean pan. Boil to reduce to 4–5 tbsp. Mix into the rabbit sauce.

6 Once the rabbit legs are cool, remove the meat from the bones. Mix into the sauce with the crayfish meat. Spoon into a large pie dish or four individual dishes.

7 Preheat the oven to 200°C/fan 180°C/gas 6.

8 Roll out the pastry on a floured surface until about 3mm thick. Cut out a lid that is about 2cm larger all round than the top of the pie dish. (Or, if you are using individual dishes, cut the pastry into quarters, roll out and cut out four lids.) Brush the edge of the pastry lid with a little beaten egg, then lay it on top of the dish, egg-washed side against the rim. Trim the edge and press down to seal. Cut four small slits in the pastry lid (or a small slit in the centre of each of the individual ones) and insert the whole crayfish, keeping the top half of the body above the pastry lid. Brush the pastry with more beaten egg.

9 Bake the pie for 30–35 minutes or until the pastry is golden (small pies will take about 25 minutes); cover the crayfish with foil if they start to colour too much. Serve with greens or mashed root vegetables such as celeriac or parsnip and/or small boiled potatoes with chopped herbs.

166

SADDLE OF RABBIT IN SAVOY CABBAGE
WITH MILD PISTACHIO KORMA SAUCE

SERVES 4

3 long, boned saddles of rabbit, with livers

about 100g spinach leaves

butter for greasing

1 small Savoy cabbage, leaves lightly
   blanched

salt and pepper

mixed micro leaves, or mustard cress mixed
   with coriander leaves, to garnish

MARINADE

3 tbsp thick, full-fat plain yoghurt

2 tbsp double cream

pinch each of ground mace and ground
   cardamom

½ tsp garam masala powder

½ tsp finely chopped fresh ginger

½ tsp finely chopped, deseeded green chilli

tiny pinch of saffron stands

2 tbsp fried brown onions, blended to
   a paste with little plain yoghurt

PISTACHIO KORMA SAUCE

500g onions, diced

½ tsp each ginger and garlic pastes

5 green cardamom pods

1 small mace blade

1 green chilli, stalk removed

1 small bay leaf

4 black peppercorns

150g plain yoghurt

30g butter

25g toasted cashew nuts

3 tbsp single cream

½ tsp garam masala powder

2 tsp pistachio paste

pinch each of ground mace and
   ground cardamom

TOMATO RICE

4 large tomatoes

180g long-grain rice

1 tbsp vegetable oil or butter

½ tsp black or brown mustard seeds

1 tbsp unroasted peanuts

1 tbsp desiccated coconut

1 green chilli, deseeded and chopped

¼ tsp ground turmeric

¼ tsp ground coriander

1 Mix all the marinade ingredients together.

2 Split the two natural halves of the rabbit livers, still keeping them whole. Remove any sinew from the livers, and trim the excess fat from the rabbit belly (the meaty side of the boned saddle). Rub the marinade well onto the livers and belly of the rabbit, then set aside for 30 minutes.

3 Wrap the livers separately in enough of the spinach leaves to cover and protect them. Butter a 30cm square piece of foil. Place enough of the cabbage leaves on the foil to cover it, then place a marinated saddle on top. Put a spinach-wrapped liver in the cavity. Roll the saddle around the liver into a sausage shape and wrap in the foil, twisting the ends to ensure a tight parcel. Repeat with the remaining saddles and livers. Leave in the fridge overnight.

4 To make the pistachio korma sauce, pour 300ml water into a large pan and add the onions, ginger and garlic pastes, cardamoms, mace, green chilli, bay leaf and peppercorns. Bring to the boil, then simmer for 25–30 minutes or until the onions are soft and mushy. Remove and discard the bay leaf and chilli, and pour the rest of the ingredients into a blender. Blend to a smooth purée. Whisk in the yoghurt. Return to the pan and simmer for 10–15 minutes. Add the butter and simmer for a further 5 minutes.

5 Meanwhile, pound the cashew nuts to a fine paste using a pestle and mortar. Mix the cashew paste with the cream, garam masala, pistachio paste and ground spices. Add this mixture to the sauce in the pan and simmer for 5–10 minutes. Taste and adjust the seasoning, then set aside to cool.

6 Preheat the oven to 200°C/fan 180°C/gas 6.

7 Place the saddles of rabbit on a baking tray and roast them, turning a few times, for 12–15 minutes or until cooked (insert a small knife into the meat – the juices that run out should be clear). Remove the rabbit from the oven and let rest in the foil for 2–5 minutes before serving.

8 While the rabbit is roasting, make the tomato rice. Put the whole tomatoes in a blender and blitz, then strain the juice into a bowl. Boil the rice until cooked; drain if necessary. While the rice is cooking, heat the oil in a pan, add the mustard seeds and, when they crackle, add the peanuts and coconut. Sauté to colour lightly, then add the green chilli, turmeric and coriander. Add the strained tomato juice and cook for 10–15 minutes or until it thickens. Adjust the seasoning. Add the warm rice to the tomato mixture and mix lightly with a fork. Keep warm.

9 To serve, reheat the pistachio korma sauce. Set a 7.5cm metal ring on each warmed plate and spoon in the tomato rice, packing it in really tightly. Carefully remove the rings. Slice the saddles and arrange on the rice. Spoon the pistachio sauce around and garnish with the mixed leaves.

PIGEON WITH AYRSHIRE BACON
SERVED WITH CARROT AND CABBAGE AND CHANTERELLE MUSHROOMS

SERVES 4

4 wood pigeons, oven-ready
2 carrots, peeled or scraped
1 small Savoy cabbage
8 rashers Ayrshire streaky bacon, very
  thinly sliced
2 tbsp sunflower oil
150g chanterelle mushrooms
100ml Port
40ml double cream
25g butter

GAME STOCK

1 carrot, diced
1 onion, diced
2 celery sticks, diced
1 tbsp tomato purée
2 garlic cloves, halved

1 Preheat the oven to 220°C/fan 200°C/gas 7.

2 Remove the breasts from the pigeons, cover and place in the fridge. For the stock, pull the legs off the pigeon carcasses, and roughly chop up the legs and carcasses. Place in a roasting tin. Roast for 25–30 minutes to a golden brown; do not allow them to burn.

3 Remove the legs and carcasses and set aside. Add the diced carrot, onion and celery to the roasting tin and return to the oven to brown for 15–20 minutes. Stir the tomato purée into the vegetables. Cook for a few more minutes, then remove from the oven and deglaze the tin with a little water, mixing well and scraping the bottom of the tin with a wooden spatula.

4 Put the pigeon legs and carcasses in a large saucepan and add the liquid and vegetable mixture from the tin. Top up with enough water just to cover. Add the garlic. Bring to the boil, then simmer for about 50 minutes, skimming the surface occasionally. Strain the stock into a clean bowl and set aside.

5 Cut the carrots lengthways in half, then turn 90° and cut in half again. Turn 90° again and cut into matchsticks. Remove and discard the outer leaves of the cabbage; quarter the heart and cut out the stalk, then shred finely. Set the vegetables aside.

6 Remove the skin from the pigeon breasts, then wrap each breast in a rasher of bacon. Set a large frying pan over a high heat and add the sunflower oil. When it is hot, pan-fry the breasts for 2–3 minutes on each side or until coloured. Remove from the pan and allow to rest in a warm place.

7 Turn the heat down to medium and add the chanterelle mushrooms to the pan. Fry until golden. Remove and keep warm.

8 Add the Port to the pan and reduce to about half, scraping the bottom of the pan with a wooden spoon or spatula to pick up all the juices and caramelised pieces left by the pigeon and mushrooms. Pour in 150ml of the game stock, and again reduce by half. (Extra stock can be frozen.) Add the double cream. Toss the mushrooms back into the sauce and bring to the boil. Remove from the heat and keep warm.

9 Set a large saucepan over a medium heat and melt the butter with 4 tbsp water. Toss in the carrot matchsticks and the cabbage, and stir to coat with the buttery liquid. Put the lid on the pan and steam for about 5 minutes or until the cabbage and carrots are tender.

10 Meanwhile, warm the pigeon breasts in a hot oven for just a few minutes. (You don't want the meat to start cooking again, as pigeon is lean and should be pink.)

11 To serve, divide the carrot and cabbage mix among four warm plates. Carve each pigeon breast into two and lay two breasts on top of the carrot and cabbage on each plate. Spoon the mushrooms and sauce around. Accompany with mashed or fondant potatoes.

CHAPTER FOUR **DESSERTS**

172

SEASONAL BERRY CUSTARDS
WITH A BAKED OAT CRUMBLE AND
LAVENDER HONEY ICE CREAM

SERVES 4
9 medium egg yolks
250g caster sugar
1 vanilla pod, split lengthways
1 litre whipping cream
200g mixed seasonal berries
juice of ½ lemon
100ml lavender honey

CRUMBLE
100g plain flour
50g porridge oats
70g salted butter
50g caster sugar

1 Put the egg yolks and 200g of the caster sugar in a bowl. Scrape the vanilla seeds from the pod, add to the bowl and mix together with a whisk. Bring the cream to the boil with the empty vanilla pod. Add to the egg mixture and mix thoroughly. Discard the pieces of vanilla pod, then divide the custard equally between a bowl and a jug. Set the bowl of custard over another bowl of ice to cool rapidly, and chill in the fridge for 10–15 minutes. Set the jug of custard aside.

2 Preheat the oven to 170°C/fan 150°C/gas 3.

3 Combine the berries, remaining caster sugar and the lemon juice in a saucepan. Poach gently for 3–4 minutes. Spoon the berries into four 12cm moulds or cups and pour the unchilled custard from the jug on top. Set the moulds in a roasting tin and pour warm water into the tin to come halfway up the sides of the moulds. Bake for 30 minutes or until the custards are just set – they should wobble like a jelly when the mould is tapped. Remove the moulds from the tin of water and leave to cool, then put in the fridge. Keep the oven on.

4 To make the crumble, put all the ingredients into a food processor and blitz quickly. Spread the mixture on a baking sheet. Bake for 10–15 minutes or until golden. Leave to cool.

5 For the ice cream, mix the chilled custard with the lavender honey and churn in an ice cream machine until thickened. Decant into a container and freeze.

6 To serve, top the chilled berry custards with the crumble and ice cream.

ENGLISH TRIFLE
WITH A SORBET OF NORFOLK
RASPBERRIES AND SUGARED NUTS

SERVES 6

SUGARED NUTS
25g pine nuts
25g whole peeled almonds
25g whole peeled hazelnuts
25g pecan nuts, chopped
100g icing sugar, sifted
4 tbsp Grand Marnier

SPONGE
3 medium eggs
90g caster sugar
75g self-raising flour
1 tbsp cornflour
40g unsalted butter, melted and
  slightly cooled

SUGAR SYRUP
250g caster sugar
350ml sparkling rosé wine,
  preferably English

RASPBERRY SORBET
450g raspberries
juice of ½ lemon, strained

ROSE AND RASPBERRY JELLY
450g (hulled weight) really ripe raspberries
4 gelatine leaves
150ml sparkling rosé wine,
  preferably English

ENGLISH CUSTARD
300ml whipping cream
150ml full-fat milk
1 vanilla pod, split lengthways
4 medium egg yolks
100g caster sugar
2 tbsp cornflour

TO FINISH
about 5 tbsp Marsala
½ small jar of raspberry or strawberry jam,
  preferably home-made
425ml whipping cream

1 The sugared nuts, sponge, sorbet and jelly can all be made a day in advance (the nuts will keep for a few days in an airtight container). To make the sugared nuts, place all the ingredients in a large, heavy-based, non-stick frying pan and, over the lowest possible heat, gently melt the icing sugar. Stir occasionally, being very careful once the sugar starts to caramelise. Turn the mixture onto a very lightly oiled tray and allow to cool.

2 Preheat the oven to 180°C/fan 160°C/gas 4. Grease a deep, 20cm round cake tin and line the bottom with baking parchment.

3 To make the sponge, put the eggs and sugar into a large bowl set over a pan of hot water and beat with an electric mixer until the mixture becomes pale and creamy. The mixture will increase in volume considerably and should become thick enough to leave a trail on the surface when the beaters are lifted out. Remove the bowl from the pan and continue to whisk until the mixture is cold.

4 Mix the self-raising flour with the cornflour. Sift half of it onto the surface of the egg mixture and fold in with a metal spoon. Carefully pour half the cooled butter around the edge of the mixture and lightly fold in. Sift over the remaining sifted

flour mix and fold in, alternating with the remaining butter. Pour into the prepared tin. Bake for 20–30 minutes or until the sponge is well risen, firm to the touch and beginning to shrink away from the sides of the tin. Allow to cool in the tin for a few minutes before turning out onto a wire rack. Leave to cool completely.

5 For the sugar syrup, put the sugar and wine into a saucepan and heat to dissolve the sugar, then simmer gently for 2 minutes. Leave to get cold.

6 To make the sorbet, blitz the raspberries in a food processor or blender, then press the purée through a fine sieve into a jug. Stir in 150ml of the sugar syrup, tasting as you do so (you may not need to use this much, depending on the sweetness of the fruit). Finally, stir in the lemon juice. Churn in an ice cream machine until softly set, then transfer to a container and freeze.

7 To make the jelly, place the raspberries and 150ml of the sugar syrup in a saucepan and gently bring to the boil. Poach the fruit gently until really soft. Pass the mixture through a piece of muslin or jelly bag into a jug.

8 Soften the gelatine leaves in a dish of cold water for 5 minutes. Remove the softened leaves, squeezing out any excess water as you do so, then stir the gelatine into the still hot raspberry juice. Allow to cool at room temperature, still in the jug, until just about setting, then very slowly and gently stir in the wine, retaining as many bubbles as possible as you do so. (If you pour and stir too quickly, the mixture will get very frothy.) Chill for 3–4 hours or until set (you can leave it overnight).

9 Break up the sponge into pieces and place in the bottom of a large glass bowl, or divide among individual glasses. Douse with the Marsala, then spread over the jam and leave to soak. Carefully break up the jelly with a fork or whisk, then spoon it over the soaked sponge.

10 To make the custard, pour the cream and milk into a heavy-based saucepan. Scrape in the seeds from the vanilla pod and add the empty pod too. Bring slowly to the boil, then set aside to infuse. Whisk the egg yolks, sugar and cornflour together in a large bowl. Gently reheat the cream and milk mixture. As soon as it reaches boiling point, pour it onto the egg yolk mixture, whisking all the time. Pour back into the saucepan and stir over a low heat until the custard thickens enough to coat the back of the spoon. Immediately remove the pan from the heat and pass the custard through a fine sieve into a bowl. (If you are not using it immediately, push a piece of cling film tightly down on top of the custard, then place another piece over the top of the bowl; this will prevent a skin from forming.) Allow to cool and thicken a little before pouring over the jelly.

11 To finish, roughly chop the sugared nuts. Whip the whipping cream to very soft peaks and spread this over the top of the custard. Sprinkle over the sugared nuts (any left over will keep for another time). Serve with the raspberry sorbet.

176

VANILLA AND GINGERBREAD CHEESECAKES
WITH FRESH RASPBERRIES AND RASPBERRY SORBET

SERVES 8

250g full-fat soft cheese
250ml double cream
125g crème fraîche
125g caster sugar
seeds scraped from 1 split vanilla pod
300g English raspberries

GINGERBREAD

125g strong rye flour
125g plain flour
4 tsp baking powder
2 tsp ground mixed spice
2 tsp ground ginger
125ml full-fat milk
250g perfumed honey

3 medium eggs
50g light muscovado sugar
grated zest of 1 small lemon
grated zest of 1 small orange
seeds scraped from ½ split vanilla pod

STOCK SYRUP

1 thick slice of lemon
300g caster sugar
15g liquid glucose

RASPBERRY SORBET

500g English raspberries
caster sugar for sprinkling
¼ tsp liquid glucose
juice of ½ lemon

1 First make the gingerbread. Preheat the oven to 160°C/fan 140°C/gas 3. Grease and line a 900g loaf tin.

2 Sift the dry ingredients into a large bowl. Mix the milk, honey, eggs and sugar in another bowl with the citrus zest and vanilla seeds, then add to the dry ingredients and mix well until evenly combined. Spoon the mixture into the prepared tin. Bake for 45 minutes or until a skewer inserted in the centre comes out clean. Cool in the tin for about 30 minutes, then remove and leave to cool on a wire rack.

3 To make gingerbread crumbs (you need 100g), cut the gingerbread into 5mm-thick slices and leave to dry on a tray overnight. The next day, grind the slices to fine crumbs in a food processor. Store in a plastic container until ready to use. (The rest of the gingerbread can be eaten as a cake; wrapped in foil it will keep for a week.)

4 For the stock syrup, put the lemon slice in a heavy pan with the sugar, liquid glucose and 300ml water. Heat gently, stirring occasionally, until the sugar has dissolved, then bring to the boil and boil for 5 minutes. Cool. Remove the lemon slice, then pass the syrup through a fine sieve into a container. Cover and chill.

5 To make the sorbet, put the raspberries in a heavy pan, sprinkle lightly with caster sugar and 2 tbsp water, and cook over a low heat for about 5 minutes or until the raspberries soften down. Tip into a fine sieve set over a bowl and push the purée through to remove the seeds. Cover and chill in the fridge.

6 Set 100ml raspberry purée aside in the fridge for later. Combine the remaining purée with 250ml chilled stock syrup, the liquid glucose and lemon juice. Churn in an ice cream machine until thickened, then decant into a clean container and store in the freezer until ready to use.

7 For the cheesecakes, stand eight metal rings, each measuring 5.5cm tall and 4.5cm across, on a non-stick mat or baking sheet lined with cling film. Combine the cheese, cream, crème fraîche, sugar and vanilla seeds in a large bowl. Whisk together well until thick, then put the mixture in a plastic piping bag and pipe neatly into the rings. Make sure there are no gaps or air pockets and pipe right up to the tops, then smooth the tops with the back of a flat knife. Refrigerate for 2 hours or until set firm.

8 Meanwhile, make eight quenelles of sorbet using two spoons and place on a tray lined with baking parchment. Place in the freezer. Put the raspberries in a bowl with the reserved 100ml raspberry purée and 'muddle' with a fork. Set aside at room temperature.

9 About 5 minutes before serving, remove the cheesecakes from the fridge. One at a time, lift a cheesecake off the mat and dip both ends in gingerbread crumbs, then warm the ring in your hands for 30 seconds (or very quickly flash round the ring with a blowtorch). Now hold the ring over a plate and carefully lift it up so the cheesecake drops out onto the plate.

10 To finish, put a spoonful of muddled raspberries to the side of each plate and sprinkle a line of gingerbread crumbs between the cheesecake and the raspberries. Top each cheesecake with a quenelle of sorbet and serve immediately.

MARCUS WAREING

ALMOND PANNACOTTA
WITH POACHED PEARS AND TOASTED ALMONDS

SERVES 6

ALMOND PANNACOTTA
300ml full-fat milk
300ml whipping cream
60g demerara sugar
175g flaked almonds, chopped
3 large gelatine leaves, soaked in ice-cold
   water for 30 minutes

PEARS
250g caster sugar
pared zest of ½ lemon
½ cinnamon stick
3 William's pears

TO SERVE
125g flaked almonds
a little icing sugar

1 Take six metal rings, about 8cm in diameter and 1cm deep, and tightly cover one end of each ring with cling film like a drum skin. Stand the rings on their covered ends on a tray and chill in the fridge.

2 To make the pannacotta, mix the milk, cream and sugar in a saucepan and bring to the boil. At the same time, toast the almonds under a medium-hot grill until golden brown, turning them frequently to prevent them from burning. When the liquids have boiled, add the hot nuts and remove from the heat. Cover the pan tightly with cling film and leave to infuse until totally cold.

3 Strain the almond milk into a bowl through a very fine sieve (preferably lined with muslin). Discard the almonds, then weigh the liquid. If there is less than 460g, make up the difference with extra milk. If more, discard the excess.

4 Warm one-quarter of the almond milk in a clean saucepan. Remove the gelatine leaves from the water and squeeze out any excess water, then add to the warm almond milk and stir until melted. Strain through a fine sieve into the cold almond milk and stir until thoroughly mixed. Pour equal amounts of the almond milk into each of the prepared rings and return to the fridge to set. This should take 2–3 hours.

5 Meanwhile, prepare the pears. Mix the caster sugar in a saucepan with 500ml water, the lemon zest and cinnamon. Heat gently until the sugar has dissolved, then bring to the boil over a high heat. Quickly peel the pears and add to the pan, then cover the surface of the liquid with a sheet of baking parchment. Cook over a very low heat for about 20 minutes or until the pears feel quite soft when pierced with the tip of a sharp knife. Remove from the heat and leave the pears to cool in the syrup.

6 When the pears are cold, remove and drain. Cut each pear in half lengthways and carefully remove the core, then slice each half finely and fan out on a serving plate. Check that the pannacotta is set, then remove the cling film and stand each ring on a plate next to the fanned pears. Carefully release each ring by running a hot, sharp knife between the ring and the pannacotta, then gently lift off the ring.

7 To serve, lightly toast the flaked almonds under a medium-hot grill, turning them frequently to prevent them from burning. Sprinkle the hot almonds over the pears at the last minute, and dust lightly with icing sugar.

RICH CHOCOLATE MOUSSE
WITH BLOOD ORANGE SORBET

SERVES 8

BLOOD ORANGE SORBET
200g caster sugar
425ml freshly squeezed blood orange
  juice, strained
juice of 1 lemon

MOUSSE
2 medium eggs
100g caster sugar
175g bittersweet chocolate (minimum 64%
  cocoa solids), roughly broken in pieces
50g unsalted butter
freshly grated nutmeg
2 tbsp strong warm coffee (espresso is good)
175ml double cream

1 To make the sorbet, put the sugar and 275ml water in a saucepan and bring to the boil. When the sugar has dissolved, simmer for about 5 minutes to make a stock syrup. Remove from the heat and add the orange and lemon juices. Stir well, then strain through a sieve. Allow to cool completely before churning in an ice cream machine. Freeze in an airtight container.

2 To make the mousse, begin by making an Italian meringue. Separate the eggs and drop the whites into the bowl of an electric food mixer. (Keep the yolks for later.) Put the sugar and 2 tbsp water in a small saucepan and dissolve over a moderate heat, then bring to the boil. Put a sugar thermometer in the syrup. When the temperature reaches just below 110°C, turn on the food mixer and whisk the egg whites at high speed until stiff. When the syrup has reached 115°C, remove from the heat and pour it slowly and carefully over the egg whites while continuing to whisk. Keep whisking until the meringue has cooled a little, then turn the machine to its lowest speed.

3 Combine the chocolate, butter and a grating of nutmeg in a heatproof bowl set over a saucepan of hot water (make sure the base of the bowl does not touch the water and that the water does not boil). As soon as the chocolate and butter have melted, remove the bowl from the hot water and allow to cool a little, then beat in the egg yolks and coffee. Leave to cool a little more, then fold the meringue into the chocolate mixture.

4 Whip the cream until it reaches soft, floppy peaks. Fold into the chocolate and meringue mixture. Pour into small ramekins (6–7cm diameter) or a large dish (800–900ml capacity) and chill for about 1 hour.

5 Serve the chocolate mousse with the blood orange sorbet.

CARRAGEEN MOSS PUDDING
WITH APPLES, ROSEHIP SYRUP
AND OATCAKES

180

SERVES 6
25g dried carrageen moss, washed,
   plus extra to serve
100ml full-fat milk
250ml double cream
1 vanilla pod, split lengthways
6 egg yolks
100g caster sugar
3 large gelatine leaves, soaked in warm
   water for 10 minutes, then squeezed
10g agar-agar
250g buttermilk
170ml condensed milk

OATCAKES
75g dried dulse
250g plain white flour
2 tsp baking powder
1 tsp salt

250g jumbo oatmeal
100g ground almonds
100g demerara sugar
200g unsalted butter
6 large egg yolks

ROSEHIP SYRUP
200g dried rosehips
30g caster sugar

APPLE JELLY
300ml organic apple juice
2 Granny Smith apples, peeled and chopped
8g agar-agar

APPLE PURÉE
5 Granny Smith apples, peeled and sliced
5 Gala apples, peeled and sliced
25g caster sugar
organic apple juice

1 First make the dough for the oatcakes. Soak the dulse in cold water for about
10 minutes, then drain and chop finely. Sift the flour, baking powder and salt into
a bowl, then stir in the oatmeal, almonds and sugar. Rub in the butter, then mix in
the egg yolks and dulse. Divide the dough equally into four and form each quarter
into a log shape. Wrap each log in cling film and chill for 1 hour.
2 Meanwhile, make the rosehip syrup. Bring the rosehips and sugar to the boil
in a heavy pan with 100ml water. Cover and leave to infuse off the heat for 1 hour.
Blitz in a blender, then pass through a fine sieve and leave to cool.
3 Next, make the apple jelly. Bring the apple juice and apples to the boil in a heavy
pan. Simmer for 1 minute, then remove from the heat and leave to cool. Whisk in the
agar-agar. Pass through a fine sieve and pour into six serving glasses. Leave to set.
4 Preheat the oven to 200°C/fan 180°C/gas 6. Line a baking tray with baking
parchment. Unwrap the logs of oatcake dough and cut them into about 40 slices
that are eye-pleasingly thick. Place the slices on the baking parchment and bake
for 10–15 minutes or until golden brown. Transfer to a wire rack to cool.
5 For the apple purée, put the apples and sugar in a heavy pan with enough apple
juice to cover and cook over a low heat for 10 minutes. Blitz in a blender, then pass
through a fine sieve and leave to cool.

6 To make the pudding, wash the carrageen. Put it into a heavy pan with the milk, cream and vanilla, and simmer for 2–3 minutes. Meanwhile, whisk the egg yolks and sugar in a bowl. Tip the carrageen and liquid into a sieve held over the bowl and let the liquid strain through. Whisk this liquid into egg yolk mixture. Pour into a clean pan and stir over a very low heat until thickened. Remove from the heat and stir in the agar-agar and squeezed gelatine. Continue stirring until the gelatine has melted, then leave for 3–4 minutes to allow the agar-agar to soften. Pass the custard through a fine sieve (to remove the agar-agar) into a bowl, then add the buttermilk and condensed milk and stir well. Leave to cool. Put into a siphon (if using).

7 To serve, pour rosehip syrup over the set apple jelly, then cover with apple purée and syphon or spoon the pudding on top. Finish with some crushed dried carrageen moss. Serve the oatcakes on the side.

MARK HIX

DORSET BLUEBERRY TRIFLE

SERVES 4
100–125g sponge cake
4 tbsp Somerset Pomona (a blend of apple juice and cider brandy)
100–125g blueberries

JELLY
3 large gelatine leaves
100g caster sugar
150g blueberries

CUSTARD
300ml single cream
½ vanilla pod, split lengthways
5 medium egg yolks
60g caster sugar
2 tsp cornflour

TOPPING
250ml double cream
60g caster sugar, plus an extra 2–3 tbsp for frosting
2 tbsp dry English white wine, preferably Coddington Bacchus
juice of ½ lemon
pinch of freshly grated nutmeg
1 medium egg white
50g blueberries

1 First make the jelly. Immerse the gelatine leaves one at a time in a shallow bowl of cold water and leave for a minute or so until soft. Meanwhile, bring 220ml water to the boil in a saucepan. Add the sugar and stir until dissolved, then add the blueberries and simmer gently for 3–4 minutes. With a slotted spoon, take out about one-third of the blueberries and set aside for later. Strain the blueberry and syrup mixture through a fine-meshed sieve, pressing the berries lightly to extract their juice. Discard the berries in the sieve. Drain and squeeze the gelatine leaves. Add them to the blueberry syrup and stir the gelatine has until melted. Allow the jelly to cool, but do not let it set.

2 Break the sponge into pieces and put into four individual glass serving dishes or one large dish. Pour over the Pomona and scatter over the blueberries, then pour over the cooled jelly; it should just cover the berries. Chill for an hour or so to set.

3 Meanwhile, make the custard. Put the cream into a small saucepan. Scrape the seeds from the vanilla pod into the cream and add the pod too. Bring to the boil, then remove from the heat and leave to infuse for about 10 minutes. In a bowl, mix together the egg yolks, sugar and cornflour. Take out the vanilla pod and pour the cream onto the egg mixture, mixing well with a whisk. Pour back into the pan and cook gently over a low heat for a few minutes, stirring constantly with a wooden spoon until the custard thickens. Do not let it boil.

4 Remove the pan from the heat and give the custard a final mix with a whisk. Transfer to a bowl and lay cling film over the surface of the custard to prevent a skin from forming. Leave to cool for about 30 minutes.

5 Once the jelly has set, spoon the cooled custard over it. Leave to set for 30 minutes.

6 Now prepare the topping. Put the cream, sugar, wine, lemon juice and nutmeg into a bowl and carefully whisk until fairly firm (this won't take too long as the lemon juice will thicken the cream). Fold the reserved cooked blueberries through the cream, then keep in the fridge until the custard has set.

7 To frost the blueberries for decoration, lightly whisk the egg white just to break it up, then put the blueberries through it and shake off the excess. Now put the blueberries through the extra 2–3 tbsp caster sugar until well coated. Leave them on a plate to dry for about 15 minutes.

8 Just before serving, spoon the cream mixture on top of the trifle and decorate with the frosted blueberries.

184

RASPBERRY SHORTCAKE

SERVES 4

125g soft unsalted butter

40g caster sugar

1 tsp finely grated orange zest

170g plain flour

40g blanched best-quality almonds, such
  as Marcona, freshly ground (quite fine but
  still with some texture)

40g toasted white breadcrumbs
  (see note below)

250ml double cream

a great bowl of raspberries

a small bowl of caster sugar

a little icing sugar for sifting

1 Beat the butter and sugar together well until pale. Pop in the orange zest and beat very well. Add the flour, ground almonds and breadcrumbs, and mix thoroughly into a soft dough.

2 Cut a large piece of baking parchment. Place the dough at one end of the paper, then roll it in the paper to make a sausage shape roughly 5cm in diameter. Seal the sausage in the paper and chill overnight.

3 Preheat the oven to 170°C/fan 150°C/gas 3.

4 Line a large baking sheet with baking parchment. Cut the roll of shortcake dough into 3-mm thick slices (about the thickness of a £1 coin) and lay them on the baking parchment. Bake for 12–15 minutes or until golden brown. Let cool and become crisp. Choose the 12 best shortcakes and store the rest for another time.

5 When ready to serve, whip the cream to soft peaks. Apply a comma of cream onto each plate (this helps stop the shortcake sliding around) and sit a shortcake on top. Spoon on a generous spoonful of cream and heap with a few berries, then sprinkle a little caster sugar over. Apply another wee spoonful of cream and place another shortcake on it. Repeat with more cream, a few more raspberries and another little blob of cream, then place the last shortcake on top and add a dusting of icing sugar. (If your raspberries aren't quite sweet enough, layer the shortcakes with a mix of half cream and half custard instead of all cream, adding a touch of vanilla extract and a little lemon juice to taste.)

Note: For toasted breadcrumbs, chop up 70g bread (to include crusts) and spread on a baking sheet. Bake in a preheated 150°C/fan 130°C/ gas 2 oven for 30 minutes or until lightly toasted, then process to crumbs in a food processor.

186

STRAWBERRY SOUFFLÉ
WITH STRAWBERRY SORBET AND
WELSH SHORTBREAD

SERVES 4
500g strawberries, hulled
150g caster sugar, plus extra for dusting
1 vanilla pod, split lengthways
2½ tbsp cornflour
soft butter for the dishes
4 egg whites
sifted icing sugar to dust

SORBET
100g caster sugar
100ml boiling water
500g strawberries, hulled
SHORTBREAD
100g soft slightly salted butter
45g icing sugar, sifted
125g plain flour
pinch of salt

1 To make the jam base for the soufflé, blitz the strawberries and 100g sugar in a food processor to a purée. Rub through a fine sieve into a heavy-bottomed pan. Scrape in the vanilla seeds from the pod. Bring to the boil over a medium heat, whisking continuously. Stir the cornflour with about 60ml of water just to slacken, then whisk into the strawberry purée until the mixture thickens. Cool, then chill.

2 Brush the insides of four soufflé dishes that are 9cm diameter and 6cm deep with softened butter, then dust with caster sugar. Chill.

3 To make the sorbet, dissolve the sugar in the boiling water, then simmer for about 2 minutes to make a sugar syrup. Cool. Blitz the strawberries with the syrup to a purée, and rub through a fine sieve into a bowl. Cool, then chill. Place in an ice cream maker and churn for 15–20 minutes to a soft scoop texture. Scoop out four neat quenelles and freeze them on a plate. (The rest of the sorbet can be kept in the freezer for up to 2 weeks.)

4 To make the shortbread, beat the butter and icing sugar together, then gently mix in the flour and salt to make a dough. Roll into a cylinder about 5–6cm in diameter, wrap in cling film and chill for at least 2 hours.

5 Preheat the oven to 200°C/fan 180°C/gas 6. Cut the chilled dough into 5-mm thick slices (12–14 slices) and place on a baking sheet. Bake for 10–12 minutes or until golden round the edges. Slide onto a wire rack to cool and crisp. Leave the oven on.

6 To finish the soufflés, whisk the egg whites with the remaining 50g caster sugar to soft peaks. Fold into the soufflé jam base. Divide the mixture among the four dishes, filling them to the top, then level with the back of a knife. Bake for 9–11 minutes or until risen above the rim by half.

7 Remove from the oven and immediately dust the tops with icing sugar. Set each soufflé on a large plate. Put a frozen scoop of sorbet and a piece of shortbread to the side. Serve straightaway.

TRIO OF RHUBARB
RHUBARB AND GINGER MOUSSE,
RHUBARB ICE CREAM,
AND RHUBARB AND WHISKEY COMPOTE

SERVES 6
600g young, sweet rhubarb, chopped
325g caster sugar
50g fresh ginger, peeled and grated
2½ large gelatine leaves
100ml whipping cream
2 medium egg whites
6 sprigs of mint to finish

ICE CREAM
4 medium egg yolks
100g caster sugar
500ml whipping cream
½ vanilla pod, split lengthways

TUILE BASKETS
40g plain flour
40g icing sugar
2 medium egg whites, broken up with a fork
35g unsalted butter, melted and cooled

COMPOTE
15g salted butter
2 sticks of rhubarb, chopped
2 tbsp light soft brown sugar
3 tbsp whiskey, preferably Bushmills
1 tsp lemon juice

1 Put the rhubarb in a heavy pan with 200g of the sugar and 2 tbsp water. Cook gently for 8–10 minutes or until the rhubarb is soft and pulpy. Allow to cool.

2 Dissolve 25g sugar in 4 tbsp water in a heavy pan over a low heat. Add the grated fresh ginger and bring to the boil. Remove from the heat and leave to infuse until cold, then strain the syrup and discard the ginger. Set the ginger syrup aside.

3 To make the ice cream, mix the egg yolks and sugar in a bowl. Pour the cream into a heavy pan, scrape in the vanilla seeds and drop in the pod. Bring to the boil, then slowly pour onto the egg yolk mixture and stir together. Return to the pan and stir over a gentle heat until the custard coats the back of the spoon. Cool and chill, then mix with one-third of the rhubarb pulp and churn in an ice cream machine. Once softly set, store in the freezer.

4 Preheat the oven to 150°C/fan 130°C/gas 2.

5 For the tuile baskets, sift the flour and icing sugar into a bowl. Slowly add the egg whites, then the butter, and mix until evenly incorporated. Drop six spoonfuls of the mixture slightly apart on one or two baking sheets lined with a non-stick mat or baking parchment. Flatten with the back of the spoon to make six discs, each about 12cm in diameter. Bake for 5–6 minutes or until lightly browned. Remove from the oven. Lift each disc off the baking sheet and immediately mould around a ramekin. Leave until cold.

6 To finish the mousse, let the gelatine leaves soak in a bowl of cold water for about 10 minutes. Meanwhile, add the ginger syrup to the remaining rhubarb pulp, then

purée in a blender. Turn the purée into a pan and heat until hot, then remove from the heat. Drain and squeeze the gelatine, then stir into the rhubarb until melted.

7 Whip the cream in a bowl until it holds a soft peak. Whisk the egg whites in another bowl until they hold a soft peak, then slowly add the remaining 100g sugar and keep whisking until the sugar is dissolved and the mixture is thick and glossy. Fold the cream into the cold rhubarb and ginger purée followed by the egg whites. When all is incorporated, spoon into six 7.5–10cm non-stick moulds. Chill for about 4 hours or until set.

8 To make the compote, gently melt the butter in a pan and sauté the rhubarb for 5–6 minutes or until soft. Add the sugar, whiskey and lemon juice, and heat for a few minutes. If you would like a smoother texture, purée the compote in a mini-food processor or with a stick blender.

9 To serve, warm the mousse moulds by holding them in a hot cloth, then turn each mousse out onto a plate. Lift the tuile baskets off the ramekins and set them on the plates. Put a scoop of ice cream in each basket. Add a spoonful of compote on the side of the plate. Top each scoop of ice cream with a sprig of mint.

RICHARD CORRIGAN

CRANBERRY AND CLEMENTINE CRUMBLE
WITH STEM GINGER ICE CREAM

SERVES 4

250g cranberries
grated zest and juice of 8 clementines
150g caster sugar
100g preserving sugar with pectin added
12 clementine segments, all skin and
  pith removed
icing sugar for dusting
chopped dried cranberries and pistachios
  for decoration

LEMON CURD CREAM

100g caster sugar
125ml lemon juice
3 large egg yolks
50g unsalted butter, diced
125ml double cream

ICE CREAM

400ml double cream
200ml full-fat milk
1 vanilla pod, split lengthways
150g stem ginger with its syrup, grated
100g caster sugar
3 large egg yolks

CRUMBLE

75g ground almonds
75g plain flour
50g large jumbo oats
50g chopped walnuts
50g stem ginger with its syrup, grated
125g clear honey
75g unsalted butter, melted

1 First make the lemon curd cream. In a heatproof bowl, whisk the sugar, lemon juice and egg yolks until combined. Set the bowl over a pan of gently simmering water and whisk to the thick ribbon stage. Take the bowl off the pan and whisk in the butter a little at a time. Leave the lemon curd to cool, then chill for about 30 minutes. Whip the cream to the ribbon stage. Fold into the lemon curd and keep in the fridge.

2 Mix the cranberries in a large heavy pan with half the clementine zest and juice. Add both types of sugar and 50ml water, and stir over a very low heat until the sugar has dissolved. Cook very gently, stirring once or twice, for 40–45 minutes or until the consistency of jam. Leave to cool.

3 For the ice cream, bring the cream and milk to the boil in a heavy pan with the vanilla pod, half the ginger and syrup, and half the sugar. Put the egg yolks in a bowl with the remaining sugar and beat to the thick ribbon stage. Strain the hot liquid into the egg yolk mixture, whisking continuously, then pour back into the pan and cook over a low heat for 5 minutes, stirring all the time, until the custard is thick enough to coat the back of a spoon. Leave to cool, then churn in an ice cream machine, adding the remaining ginger and syrup just before the ice cream is ready. Continue churning until the ice cream has thickened, then decant into a clean container and place in the freezer.

4 Preheat the oven to 160°C/fan 140°C/gas 3.

5 To make the crumble, combine all the dry ingredients, then mix in the ginger and syrup, honey and melted butter. Spread the mixture out as flat as possible on a baking tray. Bake for 20–25 minutes or until light golden in colour. Scrape the hot crumble onto a cold tray (it will break into pieces), spread out flat and leave at room temperature to dry out and cool.

6 Put the remaining clementine zest and juice in a heavy pan. Reduce to a syrup, then add the clementine segments and warm through.

7 To serve, place a spoonful of cranberry jam in the bottom of each of four dessert glasses, then add a spoonful of lemon curd cream, a clementine segment and a light sprinkling of crumble. Repeat these layers twice, finishing with crumble dusted with icing sugar. Place a large quenelle of ice cream on top and sprinkle with chopped cranberries and pistachios to decorate.

190

RHUBARB AND GINGER POLENTA CRUMBLE
WITH SOURED VANILLA ICE CREAM

SERVES 4
200ml ginger wine
75g light soft brown sugar
strip of pared orange zest
250g young pink rhubarb, cut
  into 2.5cm bâtons

ICE CREAM
3 medium egg yolks
85g caster sugar
250ml full-fat milk
1 vanilla pod, split lengthways
200ml double cream
100ml crème fraîche

CRUMBLE TOPPING
50g blanched almonds
60g plain flour
40g polenta (medium ground)
50g caster sugar
pinch of salt
2 drops of pure vanilla extract
75g chilled unsalted butter, chopped

1 First make the ice cream. Mix the egg yolks and sugar in a bowl and set aside. Pour the milk into a saucepan, scrape in the vanilla seeds and drop in the pods. Infuse the milk with the vanilla by warming gently. Scald the cream in another pan.
2 Add the milk and cream to the egg yolks and sugar. Pour this mixture into a clean saucepan, place over a gentle heat and stir constantly until thickened. Remove from the heat, stir in the crème fraîche and pass through a sieve. Leave to cool, then churn in an ice cream machine until thickened. Decant the ice cream into a clean container and place in the freezer.
3 For the crumble topping, toast the almonds by tossing them in a heavy pan over a medium heat. Chop finely and mix with the flour, polenta, sugar, salt and vanilla extract. Rub in the butter. Spread out the crumble on a baking tray and chill for about 30 minutes. (This will firm up the crumble so that it will be more crisp when baked.)
4 Preheat the oven to 140°C/fan 120°C/gas 1.
5 Bake the crumble for 40 minutes. Allow to cool, then crumble into pieces with your hands. Set aside.
6 Gently heat the ginger wine with the sugar and orange zest in a large, shallow pan until the sugar has dissolved. Add the rhubarb and poach gently for 3–4 minutes or until soft. Leave the rhubarb to cool in the liquid, then drain the rhubarb really well.
7 To serve, for each crumble stand an individual metal ring (about 7.5cm in diameter and 3.5cm deep) on a plate or in a wide, rimmed bowl. Pack in pieces of rhubarb until the mould is nearly full. Add a generous sprinkling of crumble, then remove the ring. Top each serving with a spoonful of ice cream, or place it alongside.

APPLE TASTING
OF THE SOUTH EAST

SERVES 4

APPLE-BASIL GRANITA

100g caster sugar
leaves of 3 sprigs of basil
450ml freshly pressed Granny Smith apple
 juice, or other bottled apple juice

GINGER ICE CREAM

300ml full-fat milk
300ml double cream
2 tbsp chopped candied stem ginger
1 tbsp finely chopped fresh ginger
60g granulated sugar
5 medium egg yolks
pinch of salt

APPLE CONFIT

60g unsalted butter, melted
2 tbsp granulated sugar
¼ tsp ground cinnamon
¼ tsp ground star anise
2 Gala apples, peeled and thinly sliced
2 Cox's apples, peeled and thinly sliced
finely grated zest of 1 orange

APPLE CHARLOTTE

25g unsalted butter
2 Queen Cox, Royal Snow or Jupiter apples,
 peeled and chopped
½ vanilla pod, split lengthways
1 tbsp apple brandy
2 brioches, cut into 1 x 1 x 2.5cm sticks

CRUMB TOPPING

120g plain flour
60g soft unsalted butter
2 tbsp light muscovado sugar
60g pecan nuts, chopped
pinch of ground cinnamon
pinch of grated nutmeg
1 tsp vanilla extract

TO SERVE

apricot sauce
whipped crème fraîche
lavender flowers
custard sauce
raspberry sauce
4 shards of cinnamon sticks
Queen Cox cider, mulled with cloves
 and cinnamon

1 The granita, ice cream and apple confit all need to be made ahead. For the granita, put the sugar in a heavy-based saucepan with enough water (about 100ml) to cover. Bring to the boil and boil for a few minutes until syrupy. Measure and reserve 60ml of the sugar syrup (the rest can be used for another occasion). Drop the basil leaves into boiling water, lift out immediately and put into iced water. Drain, then purée with 3 tbsp of the measured sugar syrup in a small blender until smooth. Strain through a fine wire sieve or muslin. Reserve a spoonful of this basil syrup for later, and combine the remainder with the rest of the measured sugar syrup and the apple juice. Pour into a freezer container and freeze for 3–4 hours. Scrape the surface into shavings using a metal spoon or fork, then return the granita to the freezer. (The granita can be kept for about 1 week.)

2 To make the ice cream, boil the milk and cream with the stem and fresh ginger in a heavy-based pan. In a bowl whisk together the sugar, egg yolks and a pinch of salt until smooth. Slacken the yolk mixture with one-third of the hot milk mixture, whisking constantly. Whisk this back into the rest of the hot milk and cook over a low heat, stirring constantly, until thick enough to coat the back of a wooden spoon. Strain through a fine wire sieve into a bowl. Set the bowl over a bowl of iced water to chill. Pour into an ice cream machine and churn, then freeze until required.

3 Preheat the oven to 140°C/fan 120°C/gas 1.

4 To make the apple confit, lightly brush the inside of a 500g loaf tin or similar-sized small ceramic terrine mould with a little of the melted butter. Mix the sugar with the ground spices. Place a layer of sliced apples on the bottom of the tin, brush with some of the butter and sprinkle with some of the spiced sugar and orange zest. Repeat the layers until the tin is full. Lay a piece of baking parchment on the top layer and place a foil-wrapped heavy weight (such as a brick) on top. Bake for 8–10 hours or until the liquid has lightly caramelised and the height of the apple confit has significantly reduced. Remove the confit from the tin and cool, then wrap in cling film and chill overnight.

5 Turn up the oven temperature to 200°C/fan 180°C/gas 6.

6 For the apple charlottes, heat the butter in a frying pan, add the apples and vanilla, and sauté for 2–3 minutes. Pour in the brandy and remove from the heat. Remove the vanilla pod. Butter four 5cm-diameter dariole moulds. Line the moulds with overlapping slices of brioche sticks, then fill with the sautéed apples. Bake for 5–8 minutes or until the brioche is lightly coloured. Cool.

7 Reduce the oven temperature to 180°C/fan 160°C/gas 4. To make the topping, in a bowl rub the flour and butter together to coarse crumbs. Stir in the remaining topping ingredients to make a rough dough. Break into small pieces onto a baking sheet and bake for 3–5 minutes or until just golden brown. Cool.

8 Turn the apple charlottes our of their moulds, upside down. Finish the charlottes with the crumb topping. Cut the apple confit into 4cm squares.

9 To serve, spoon a little apricot sauce on each rectangular serving plate and place a square of apple confit on top. (Any extra confit will keep, wrapped in the fridge, for up to 2 days.) Garnish with crème fraîche topped with a lavender flower. Dot a little custard and raspberry sauces around. Add another small spoonful of apricot sauce and place a charlotte on top. Add a scoop of ginger ice cream. Scoop the granita into four shot glasses and add a shard of cinnamon stick to each as a stirrer. Sit this on the plates along with a glass of warm mulled cider.

RASPBERRY TRIFLE

SERVES 8

4 great big handfuls of raspberries

handful of slivered or flaked almonds,
  lightly toasted

icing sugar for dusting (optional)

LITTLE SPONGE CAKES

4 large organic eggs, separated

125g caster sugar, plus 2 tbsp

225g plain flour, sifted

50g unsalted butter, melted and cooled

SYLLABUB

thinly pared zest and juice of 1 lemon

1 glass of white wine

2 tbsp dry sherry, plus extra for soaking
  the sponge

60g caster sugar

300ml double cream

CUSTARD

500ml full-fat milk

5 large organic eggs

50g caster sugar

1 Start the trifle 1–2 days ahead. Preheat the oven to 170°C/fan 150°C/gas 3. Line two baking sheets with baking parchment.

2 To make the sponge cakes, put the egg yolks and 125g caster sugar into a bowl and beat with an electric mixer until thickened and pale, and the mixture will form a ribbon trail on its surface when the beaters are lifted out.

3 In a separate bowl, whisk the egg whites until stiff. Add the remaining 2 tbsp caster sugar and whisk until stiff peaks are formed again. Fold a spoonful of the whisked egg white into the egg yolk mixture, followed by a spoonful of flour and a little of the butter. Continue like this until all the egg white, flour and butter have been added. Heap little spoonfuls of the batter onto the lined baking sheets and bake for 15–20 minutes or until firm to the touch and golden brown (you'll make about 2 dozen sponges). Let cool. (The sponges can be very happily stored for several days in an airtight tin.)

4 The syllabub should be started a day ahead. Put the lemon zest and juice into a bowl with the wine and sherry. Cover and refrigerate overnight.

5 To make the custard (preferably also a day ahead), bring the milk to the boil in a good-sized pan. Stir the eggs and sugar together in a bowl. Pour the heated milk over the egg mix, stirring all the while, then pour back into the pan. Return the pan to a low heat and cook gently, stirring, until the custard is thickened and fully cooked. Take care that the custard doesn't get too hot or it could curdle. When done, strain and put to one side.

6 Now start to layer everything up (preferably the day before serving): place half the sponges in the bottom of a handsome bowl and liberally anoint with sherry. (The leftover sponges can be frozen or stored for another time.) Once happily plumped with the good stuff, tip in heaps of raspberries (keeping a few back). Pour over the custard, then cover with cling film and refrigerate.

7 Finish the syllabub just before serving. Stir the sugar into the chilled syllabub mixture until dissolved, then discard the lemon zest. Add the cream and beat gently to mix, then with vigour until soft peaks are achieved. Heap onto the custard and tumble the remaining raspberries on top. Scatter on the almonds and dust with icing sugar if you wish. Serve immediately.

MICHAEL CAINES

POACHED PEAR
IN MULLED RED WINE
WITH GINGERBREAD ICE CREAM AND CLOTTED CREAM

SERVES 4
GINGERBREAD ICE CREAM
600ml milk
25g milk powder
250g gingerbread, broken up

POACHED PEARS
1.5 litres red wine, such as Pinot Noir
300g caster sugar
1 strip of orange zest
1 tsp Chinese five spice powder
4 ripe pears, such as William's

TO SERVE
clotted cream

1 To make the gingerbread ice cream, pour the milk into a saucepan, stir in the milk powder and bring to the boil. Pour this onto the gingerbread in a bowl and leave to soak for 30 minutes. Blitz in a blender or food processor to a fine purée. Cool, then chill. Churn in an ice cream machine until softly set. Remove from the machine and place in a container in the freezer.
2 For the poached pears, pour the red wine into a saucepan and bring to the boil. Remove from the heat. Set the wine alight and allow the flames to die down. Add the sugar, orange zest and spice, and bring back to the boil. Leave to cool.
3 Peel the pears, leaving the stalks on, and place them in the cooled red wine syrup. (If you have time, leave the pears in the red wine syrup for 8 hours before cooking, as they will take on more colour.) Bring the syrup to a slow simmer and cook the pears for about 20 minutes or until soft through to the centre. Remove the pears from the syrup and set aside.
4 Strain 1 litre of the red wine syrup through a sieve into a clean saucepan. Bring to the boil, then simmer for 30–40 minutes to reduce to a syrupy consistency.
5 To serve, cut the pears in half and remove the cores. Place the pears on plates with some of the reduced syrup and serve with a scoop of the ice cream and clotted cream.

196

ICED WHISKY CREAMS
WITH PRUNES AND TEA SYRUP

SERVES 6
handful of prunes
vegetable oil
5 egg yolks
85g caster sugar
300ml double cream
3 tbsp Glengoyne whisky

TEA SYRUP
250g granulated sugar
1 Scottish blend tea bag
2 tsp lemon juice, strained
1 vanilla pod, split lengthways
1 tbsp Glengoyne whisky

1 You need to start this recipe a good day ahead. To make the tea syrup, put a saucepan over a medium heat. Add the sugar and 250ml water, and stir until the sugar has dissolved. Bring to the boil. Add the tea bag and boil for 5–6 minutes.
2 Strain the mixture through a fine sieve into a bowl. (Be careful to avoid splashing, as the syrup will be very hot.) Add the lemon juice, vanilla pod (scraping out some of the seeds into the syrup as you do) and whisky, then the prunes. Cool, then cover and chill. Keep for at least 24 hours before using. The flavour will improve over time. (You will only need about 150ml syrup, so save the rest in an airtight jar for another time, such as for mixing with fruit salad.)
3 For the whisky creams, lightly grease a small terrine or loaf tin with vegetable oil. Place the egg yolks in a heatproof bowl set over a pan of simmering water and beat with an electric mixer for about 5 minutes or until thick and pale. Remove from the pan and cool while you make the syrup.
4 Heat the sugar with 3 tbsp water in a small pan until dissolved, then boil the syrup for about 5 minutes or until it reaches the softball stage (116–118°C). To check without a sugar thermometer, tip a drop of hot syrup into a glass of cold water; if the syrup is ready, you should be able to roll it into a soft ball.
5 Beat the egg yolks on full speed as you slowly pour on the syrup in a continuous stream, then reduce the speed by half and beat for a further 5 minutes or until thickened. Set aside to cool to room temperature.
6 In a clean bowl, whip the cream with the whisky until it starts to thicken; don't over-whip. Combine the egg mix and whipped cream, then pour into the terrine or loaf tin. Freeze for about 12 hours.
7 When ready to serve, remove the vanilla pod from the tea syrup, then gently reheat the syrup. Remove the whisky cream from the freezer. Dip the terrine briefly into warm water to help release the contents. Dry the terrine, then invert and tip out the whisky cream onto a board. Cut into slices.
8 Place one or two slices of whisky cream on each plate and add a few prunes. Drizzle the hot syrup over and around. Serve at once, before the whisky cream melts.

198 # LEMON MERINGUE PIE

SERVES 6

SWEET PASTRY
140g plain flour
60g chilled butter, diced
30g caster sugar
1 egg yolk

LEMON CURD
1 tbsp cornflour
finely grated zest and juice of 2 medium
  lemons

150g butter
120g caster sugar
3 egg yolks
1 egg

MERINGUE
3 egg whites
90g caster sugar

1 Prepare the sweet pastry by rubbing together the flour, butter and sugar until the mixture looks like fine breadcrumbs. Mix in the egg yolk, then slowly add enough cold water to make a smooth dough. Wrap the dough and chill for about 30 minutes.

2 Preheat the oven to 190°C/fan 170°C/gas 5.

3 Roll out the pastry dough on a lightly floured surface so it is big enough to line a 23cm flan ring or loose-bottomed flan tin that is 2.5cm deep. Place the ring or tin on a baking sheet and line with the pastry. Trim the edges. Line the pastry case with a piece of greaseproof paper, then tip in some dried baking beans. Bake blind for 15 minutes or until the pastry is cooked and the edges are lightly coloured, removing the paper and beans for the last few minutes of baking.

4 Reduce the oven to 160°C/fan 140°C/gas 3.

5 To make the lemon curd, blend the cornflour with the lemon juice. Melt the butter in a saucepan. Add the lemon zest and sugar, and bring to the boil. Whisk in the cornflour mixture and cook, stirring, for 1–2 minutes to cook the cornflour. Remove from the heat and allow the mixture to cool slightly. Beat in the egg yolks and the whole egg. Return the pan to a very low heat to thicken the curd, stirring occasionally – if the heat is too high the eggs will scramble. Spoon the lemon curd into the pastry case while it is still warm, then leave to cool while you make the meringue.

6 Whisk the egg whites in a very clean bowl. Just before they reach soft peak stage, gradually add the caster sugar, whisking between each addition, and whisk until soft peaks are formed.

7 Spoon the meringue over the cooled lemon curd, making sure you completely cover the surface. Bake for 20–30 minutes or until the meringue is set and slightly coloured. Serve the pie warm.

ALMOND AND RASPBERRY TART
WITH CLOTTED CREAM

SERVES 6-8
500g English raspberries
25g caster sugar
clotted cream to serve
PASTRY
120g soft unsalted butter
60g icing sugar, sifted
60g caster sugar
300g plain flour, sifted
1 large egg, beaten

ALMOND CREAM
100g unsalted butter
100g icing sugar, sifted
1 large egg, beaten
25g plain flour, sifted
100g ground almonds

1 Put 200g of the raspberries in a heavy pan, sprinkle lightly with the caster sugar and 1 tbsp water, and cook over a low heat for 3–5 minutes or until the raspberries soften down. Tip into a fine sieve set over a bowl and push the purée through to remove the seeds. Cover and chill.

2 To make the pastry, soften the butter in a bowl and beat in both types of sugar until smooth and creamy. Work in half the flour, then repeat with the other half. Gradually add the egg, then turn the dough out of the bowl and knead lightly. Wrap and chill for about 30 minutes.

3 Preheat the oven to 180°C/fan 160°C/gas 4.

4 Roll out the pastry dough on a floured surface and use to line a fluted 23cm flan ring set on a baking sheet (or a loose-bottomed tart tin), leaving a 3cm overhang. Line with greaseproof paper and fill with baking beans, then bake blind for 12–15 minutes or until the pastry is crisp and golden. Remove from the oven, take out the paper and beans, and allow the tart case to cool. Leave the oven on.

5 Muddle the remaining raspberries with the raspberry purée by mixing them gently together with a fork, then spread evenly over the bottom of the pastry case.

6 For the almond cream, cream the butter and icing sugar together until light and fluffy. Beat in the egg, then fold in the flour mixed with the almonds. Pipe the almond cream on top of the raspberries, taking it right up to the rim. Bake for about 30 minutes or until just golden, then allow to cool.

7 To serve, trim off the overhanging pastry edge and cut the tart into wedges. Serve with clotted cream.

TOFFEE APPLE SUNDAES

SERVES 6

CARAMEL ICE CREAM
250g caster sugar
1 vanilla pod, split lengthways
200ml double cream
8 medium egg yolks
350ml full-fat milk

BUTTERSCOTCH SAUCE
400g light soft brown sugar
1 vanilla pod, split lengthways and seeds
  scraped out
500ml double cream
140g chilled unsalted butter, diced
4 tbsp liquid glucose

APPLE COMPOTE
1kg Bramley's apples, peeled and cut
  into large segments
juice of ½ lemon
100g caster sugar

TOFFEE APPLE SLICES
350g caster sugar
2 dessert apples, cut lengthways
  into 8 thin slices

TO SERVE
500ml plain yoghurt, preferably Ann
  Forshaw's Goosnargh yoghurt

1 First make the ice cream. Put the sugar in a heavy pan and heat gently, without stirring, until melted and golden brown. Scrape the seeds from the vanilla pods into the pan. Cut the pod into small pieces and add them too. Stir gently with a wooden spoon until the caramel is a deep mahogany colour. Wait a moment longer, until you think the caramel smells slightly burnt, then stir in the cream with a long-handled wooden spoon. Take care, as the mix will bubble furiously. Lower the heat and stir quickly to quell the bubbles. Remove from the heat.

2 Beat the egg yolks in a heatproof bowl. Heat the milk in a pan, then beat into the egg yolks. Stir this into the caramel-cream mixture. Cook gently as if making a custard sauce, until just below boiling point, then strain through a fine sieve into a cold bowl. Cover the surface with cling film to prevent a skin from forming and leave to cool. When cold, churn in an ice cream maker until thickened. Decant into a clean container and place in the freezer.

3 Next make the butterscotch sauce. Put the sugar in a heavy pan and heat gently, without stirring, until melted and golden brown. Add the vanilla pod and seeds, and stir gently with a long-handled wooden spoon until you have a deep mahogany coloured caramel. Wait a moment longer, or until you think the caramel smells slightly burnt, then stir in the cream. Take care, as it will bubble furiously. Lower the heat and stir quickly to quell the bubbles. When all the cream has been incorporated, stir in the diced butter a little at a time until you have a smooth, creamy sauce, then stir in the liquid glucose. Remove from the heat and cover the surface of the sauce with cling film to prevent a skin from forming. Leave to cool, then keep in the fridge.

4 Put the apples, lemon juice and sugar for the compote in a heavy saucepan. Cover and cook over a medium heat, stirring occasionally, until the apples soften but still

retain some shape and texture. The compote should be slightly tart, not sweet. Leave the compote to cool, then chill.

5 For the toffee apple slices, line a baking sheet with baking parchment and have ready two bowls of iced water. Dissolve the sugar in 350ml water over a low heat in a heavy pan. Bring to the boil and boil until the caramel reaches the hard-crack stage (145°C on a sugar thermometer). Remove from the heat and stop the cooking by immersing the base of the pan in one of the bowls of iced water. Remove the pan immediately or the caramel will set solid. Using a fork, dip the apple slices one at a time into the caramel, then lift out and plunge into the second bowl of iced water to set the caramel. Remove and leave to set on the parchment. If the caramel sets before you've dipped all the apple slices, return the pan to a gentle heat to loosen it.

6 Chill six large 'old-fashioned' glasses or sundae coupes in the freezer until ice-cold.

7 To serve, gently reheat the butterscotch sauce. In each glass, make alternate layers of apple compote, butterscotch sauce and yoghurt. Repeat the layers, then top with ice cream and toffee apple slices.

SAT BAINS

RASPBERRY SPONGE
WITH RASPBERRIES, GOAT'S MILK ICE CREAM AND BLACK OLIVE AND HONEY

SERVES 8

RASPBERRY OIL
150ml light olive oil
50g freeze-dried raspberries

BLACK OLIVE AND HONEY TUILE
50g pitted black olives, rinsed
50ml clear honey, warmed

GOAT'S MILK ICE CREAM
500ml goat's milk
100g clean, fresh hay, well washed (optional)
5 egg yolks
40g caster sugar

SPONGE
3 organic eggs
160g golden caster sugar
125ml semi-skimmed milk
160g plain flour, sifted
20g baking powder
60g ground almonds
20 raspberries

RASPBERRY JELLY
400g raspberries
50g caster sugar
1½ gelatine leaves

TO SERVE
about 2 tbsp raspberry vinegar
raspberry jam
about 150g raspberries
lemon curd
3–4 sprigs of mint

1 The raspberry oil is best made a week ahead (freeze-dried raspberries are available in healthfood shops). Blitz the olive oil and raspberries in a blender to extract the maximum flavour, then strain through a sieve and set aside.

2 Preheat the oven to the lowest setting. Lay a non-stick mat on a baking sheet, or line the sheet with baking parchment.

3 For the black olive tuile, blend the olives and honey in a small blender to a paste, then sieve if you like, pressing all the paste through. Spread the paste very thinly on the mat or parchment. Leave in the oven to dry out for 5–6 hours. The tuile will seem slightly soft and pliable, but will become very brittle when it cools.

4 Meanwhile, make the ice cream. Heat the milk in a large pan. If using the hay, throw it in, then remove from the heat and leave to infuse at room temperature for 1 hour; strain. Whisk the egg yolks and sugar in a bowl until the mixture leaves a ribbon trail when you lift the beaters. Add the milk, whisking it in, then pour into a saucepan. Heat slowly, stirring all the time and without allowing it to boil, to 86°C (check with a digital thermometer). The custard will be smooth and thickly coat the back of a wooden spoon. Strain into a bowl and chill. When cold, churn in an ice cream machine to the soft scoop stage. Transfer to a container and freeze overnight.

5 Preheat the oven to 190°C /fan 170°C/gas 5.

6 To make the sponge, whisk the eggs and sugar with an electric mixer until the mixture leaves a ribbon trail when you lift the beaters. With the machine running, pour in the milk, then add the combined sifted flour, baking powder and ground almonds. Slowly pour in the raspberry oil. The mixture will be like a soft batter.

7 Pour the mixture into a 20cm square cake tin that is 4cm deep (it's only necessary to line the tin if it isn't non-stick). Drop the whole raspberries all over so they softly sink into the sponge. Bake for 35–40 minutes or until firm to the touch. Cool for a few minutes in the tin, then turn out onto a wire rack to cool completely.

8 To make the raspberry jelly, tip the raspberries and sugar into a bowl, cover with cling film and set over a pan of gently simmering water. Poach the raspberries with the sugar for 20 minutes or until the raspberries have collapsed. Strain the juice through a piece of muslin into a bowl. You should have 300ml raspberry juice. Soak the gelatine in cold water, then squeeze and stir into the warm juice until melted. Leave at room temperature for about 1 hour or until softly set but still runny.

9 Cut the sponge into eight squares. Dip the sponge squares into the jelly and leave for a few minutes to absorb it, then set the sponge on a tray. Chill for 2 hours.

10 To serve, sit the cake squares on serving plates. Drizzle all over with the raspberry vinegar (or spray on using an atomiser), then lightly spread a little raspberry jam on the tops. Fill half of the raspberries with raspberry jam and half with lemon curd, then equally dot the raspberries around each plate. Tear up the sprigs of mint and scatter them over. Add quenelles of the ice cream on the side. To finish, crack the tuile sheet into pieces and lay them on top of the ice cream.

204

ANGLO-INDIAN APPLE CRUMBLE

SERVES 6
2 tbsp raisins
1 tbsp apple brandy
450g Granny Smith apples, peeled and
    cut into 1cm chunks
2 tbsp toasted slivered or flaked almonds
50g dark muscovado sugar
1 tbsp plain flour
pinch of ground cinnamon
pinch of crushed black pepper

CRUMBLE
300g plain flour, sifted
pinch of salt
175g dark muscovado sugar
200g unsalted butter, at room temperature,
    cubed, plus knob of butter for greasing

TO SERVE
thick cream, custard or vanilla ice cream

1 Soak the raisins in the apple brandy in a large bowl for 30 minutes (or overnight).
2 Preheat the oven to 200°C/fan 180°C/gas 6. Butter a 23–24cm round ovenproof dish.
3 To make the crumble, mix the flour, salt and sugar in another large bowl. Rub in the butter, adding a few cubes at a time, until the mixture resembles fine crumbs.
4 Add the apples and toasted almonds to the raisins and sprinkle over the sugar, flour, cinnamon and black pepper. Stir well, being careful not to break up the fruit.
5 Spoon the fruit filling into the buttered dish and sprinkle the crumble mixture on top. Bake for 35–40 minutes or until the crumble is browned and the filling is bubbling. Serve hot, with thick cream, custard or vanilla ice cream.

MARCUS WAREING

EARL GREY TEA CREAM
AND ECCLES CAKES

SERVES 6

ECCLES CAKES
225g plain flour
pinch of salt
160g chilled unsalted butter, plus 25g soft
    unsalted butter
100g caster sugar
200g currants
50g chopped candied peel
freshly grated nutmeg
milk and granulated sugar, to finish

EARL GREY TEA CREAM
95g egg yolks, from 5–6 large eggs
80g caster sugar
260ml full-fat milk
260ml double or whipping cream
7 Earl Grey tea bags

MILK FOAM
600ml full-fat milk
100ml condensed milk
100ml whipping cream

1 First make the pastry for the Eccles cakes. Sift the flour and salt into a bowl. Dice half the chilled butter and rub into the flour, then add just enough cold water (about 4–5 tbsp) to bring everything together into a soft dough. Cover the bowl with cling film and chill for 30 minutes.

2 On a lightly floured surface, roll out the dough into a rectangle measuring about 20 x 10cm. Cut the remaining chilled butter into thin slices. Cover the middle third of the dough with one-third of the butter slices, then fold the unbuttered thirds of dough over the buttered third, first one and then the other, making a square. Wrap and refrigerate for 15 minutes.

3 Repeat step 2 twice more, turning the block of dough 90° each time, and chilling between each rolling. Repeat two more times, but without any butter, then chill again for at least 30 minutes.

4 Make the Earl Grey tea creams while the pastry is chilling. Preheat the oven to 150°C/fan 130°C/gas 2. Set six shallow 150ml teacups or ramekins in a roasting tin.

5 Whisk the egg yolks and half the sugar in a large bowl. Put the milk, cream and tea bags in a heavy saucepan with the remaining sugar and bring just to the boil over a medium-high heat, stirring occasionally. Immediately the liquid reaches the boil, strain it slowly through a fine sieve over the egg yolks and sugar. (Don't let the liquid boil or leave the bags to steep, or the creams will taste like stewed tea.) Whisk well until evenly combined, then strain the mixture slowly through the sieve into a large measuring jug. Skim to remove any foamy bubbles.

6 Pour the mixture slowly into the cups so that each one is two-thirds full. Skim off any more bubbles. Pour hot water into the roasting tin to come halfway up the sides of the cups. Bake for 25–30 minutes. The creams should be only just set, with a slight wobble in the centre. Remove the cups from the water and leave to cool, then cover and refrigerate for at least 4 hours or overnight.

7 Boil the milk for the foam until reduced to 200ml. Pour into a bowl and leave until cold. Whisk the reduced milk with the condensed milk and cream, then pour into the siphon (see note on page 206). Charge the siphon with two cartridges and release a little gas, then shake well. Keep the siphon in a bowl of iced water until ready to use.

8 Finish making the Eccles cakes about an hour or so before serving, because they are best served warm. Preheat the oven to 240°C/fan 220°C/gas 8. Line a baking tray with baking parchment,

9 For the filling, cream together the 25g soft butter and the caster sugar, then add the currants, candied peel and nutmeg. Roll out the pastry on a lightly floured surface until 4mm thick. Cut out twelve 7cm discs. Spoon a little of the filling in the centre of each disc. Brush the edges with a little water, then pull the edges into the centre and pinch them together to seal.

10 Turn the cakes over, place on the prepared tray and push down lightly with the palm of your hand to flatten a little. With a small sharp knife, make three short

incisions in the top of each cake. Brush with a little milk and sprinkle liberally with granulated sugar. Bake for 10–12 minutes or until the edges have turned golden brown. Remove from the oven and leave to cool for a few minutes.

11 To serve, cover the top of each Earl Grey tea cream with milk foam, and place a warm Eccles cake on the saucer.

Note: You need a whipped cream dispenser (an iSi siphon) and two N2O cartridges.

MARK BROADBENT

STRAWBERRY KNICKERBOCKER GLORY

SERVES 4

CANDIED AND DRIED STRAWBERRIES
20 strawberries, hulled and thinly sliced
100–200g icing sugar, sifted

STRAWBERRY WAFERS
2 sheets of rice paper
200g caster sugar

SPICED STRAWBERRY COMPOTE
750ml raspberry liqueur (crème de framboise)
2 vanilla pods, split lengthways
pared zest of 1 orange, cut into julienne
pared zest of 1 lemon, cut into julienne
8 black peppercorns

750ml freshly squeezed orange juice, preferably from blood oranges
25 strawberries, hulled

VANILLA ICE CREAM
600ml full-fat milk
750ml double cream
1 vanilla pod, split lengthways
7 medium free-range egg yolks
250g caster sugar

TO FINISH
strawberry confetti (see method below)
500ml double cream

1 Preheat the oven to 85°C/fan 65°C/the lowest possible setting on a gas oven.

2 To make the candied and dried strawberries, lay half of the strawberry slices in a single layer on a non-stick mat, non-stick baking sheet or baking parchment. Dust with icing sugar. Dry the strawberries in the oven overnight until they are crisp and candied. Dry the remaining strawberries in the oven in the same way, but without dusting them with icing sugar.

3 The next day make the wafers, with the oven at the same temperature. Cut each sheet of rice paper into three or four pieces, or simply tear them to give a more natural look. Dissolve the sugar in 200ml water over a low heat, then increase the heat and boil for 3–4 minutes or until reduced to a syrup. Pour the syrup into a shallow tray. Place the rice paper in the syrup, then carefully lift it out, keeping the shape of the paper. Place the rice papers on a non-stick baking sheet, or a baking sheet lined with baking parchment, and sprinkle generously with candied and dried strawberries (reserving some of each for making confetti and decorating later). Bake for 3–4 hours or until crisp and rigid.

4 While the wafers are in the oven, make the compote. Put the raspberry liqueur in a heavy stainless steel saucepan with the vanilla pods, orange and lemon zests, and peppercorns. Boil until reduced to a syrup. Reduce the orange juice in a separate pan to a syrup. Mix the two syrups together in one pan and add the strawberries. Roll them in the syrup over a medium heat until they are just starting to collapse. Take the pan off the heat.

5 With a slotted spoon, transfer the strawberries and a little of their syrup to a food processor. Reserve the remaining syrup in the pan. Pulse the strawberries until crushed but not puréed, then reduce in a clean pan over a gentle heat until a compote consistency (it should just drop off a spoon when shaken). Remove the orange and lemon zests and the vanilla pods from the sticky syrup. Cut the vanilla pods into fine julienne, the same size as the zest. Put the zest and vanilla julienne on a non-stick baking sheet.

6 When the wafers are done, remove them from the oven. Put the zest and vanilla julienne in the oven and leave to dry out overnight. When the wafers are cool, slide a palette knife under the rice papers and lift them off the baking sheet.

7 To make the vanilla ice cream, heat the milk, cream and vanilla pod in a heavy saucepan over a high heat, whisking to loosen the vanilla seeds. Leave to infuse off the heat for 30 minutes. Beat the egg yolks and sugar together in a bowl, then strain into the infused mixture and mix well. Leave to cool. Discard the vanilla pod. Churn in an ice cream machine until thickened, then decant the ice cream into a clean container and place in the freezer.

8 Before serving, chill four tall sundae coupes in the freezer until ice-cold. Break the reserved dried strawberries into tiny pieces (confetti). Whip the cream to almost a stiff peak, and spoon into a piping bag fitted with a 5mm tube.

9 To finish, fill the coupes with alternate layers of sticky syrup, ice cream, whipped cream and compote. Finish with a topping of whipped cream, zest and vanilla julienne, candied strawberries, confetti and wafers. Serve immediately.

Note: I always make a larger quantity of ice cream and spiced strawberry compote than I need for this dessert, because it's always good to have a tub of home-made ice cream in the freezer, and the chilled compote is great for breakfast, either on its own or poured over plain yoghurt.

208

MUSCOVADO AND HAZELNUT TART
WITH YOGHURT SORBET

SERVES 6-8
150g dark muscovado sugar
120g plain flour, sifted
50g soft salted butter
100g whole hazelnuts, toasted
1 large egg
½ tsp baking powder
150g soured cream

YOGHURT SORBET
50g caster sugar
500ml good-quality plain yoghurt
juice of ½ lemon, strained

TO FINISH
1 tbsp dark muscovado sugar
1 tbsp whole hazelnuts, toasted

1 To make the yoghurt sorbet, add the sugar to 120ml boiling water in a small pan and bring back to the boil, stirring to dissolve the sugar. Boil for a few seconds, then remove from the heat and leave to cool.

2 When the sugar syrup is cold, mix into the yoghurt with the lemon juice. Taste and adjust with more lemon juice, if necessary. Churn in an ice cream machine for about 15 minutes or until softly set, then transfer to a container and freeze.

3 Preheat the oven to 200°C/fan 180°C/gas 6.

4 To make the tart, put the sugar, flour, butter and nuts in a food processor and blitz to a coarse breadcrumb texture. Remove half the mixture from the food processor and spread it over the bottom of a 20cm round non-stick tin that is 5cm deep (not loose-bottomed). Pat the mixture down gently with the back of a spoon as you would for a cheesecake base, without pressing too firmly.

5 Tip the other half of the mixture into a bowl. Add the egg, baking powder and soured cream, and beat to a batter. Pour this over the crumb base. Scatter over the 1 tbsp muscovado. Bake for about 25 minutes or until just firm. To check if done, push a skewer into the centre; it should come out clean.

6 Use a Microplane grater to shave the toasted hazelnuts into fine powdery shavings. Serve the tart at room temperature in wedges, with the hazelnut shavings scattered over and with a spoonful of yoghurt sorbet at the side.

210

CRANACHAN
WITH OATMEAL PRALINE

SERVES 8
3 large free-range egg yolks
25g caster sugar
35g clear honey (2½ tbsp)
5 tbsp whisky
150g crème fraîche
100g mascarpone cheese
²/₃ long gelatine leaf
2 tsp lemon juice
raspberries to serve

OATMEAL PRALINE
100g caster sugar
50g pinhead oatmeal

JELLY
250g raspberries
3 tbsp caster sugar
4 tsp lemon juice
²/₃ long gelatine leaf

1 First make the oatmeal praline. Line a baking sheet with baking parchment. Place a frying pan over a medium heat and sprinkle in the sugar. Allow the sugar to melt without stirring, then turn up the heat. As the sugar begins to caramelise, mix in the oats and stir. Carefully tip the contents onto the lined baking sheet and leave to cool completely. Once cold, break into pieces with a rolling pin, and grind in a pestle and mortar to a coarse powder. (This can be done ahead. If you don't use all the praline, it can be stored in an airtight container for future use.)

2 To make the jelly, set a medium-sized heavy pan over a gentle heat and add the raspberries, sugar, lemon juice and 6 tbsp water. Bring to the boil and simmer for 3 minutes or until the raspberries have softened. Meanwhile, soften the gelatine in a small bowl of cold water.

3 Remove the pan from the heat and rub the raspberry mixture through a fine sieve into a clean pan, to remove the seeds. You should get about 200ml of raspberry purée. Gently reheat the purée, then remove from the heat. Drain and squeeze the gelatine, add to the hot raspberry purée and stir until the gelatine has melted. Leave to set to a very soft jelly.

4 Put the egg yolks and sugar in a large heatproof bowl and whisk to combine. Mix in the honey and 3 tbsp of the whisky. Set the bowl over a pan of simmering water and beat with an electric mixer for 5–6 minutes or until the mixture starts to thicken – when you lift the beaters out of the mixture in a circular motion, you should be left with a distinct trail on the surface. (If you have a thermometer, the mix should be at 80°C.) When ready, take the bowl off the pan and allow to cool.

5 In another bowl mix the crème fraiche and mascarpone together. Soak the gelatine as before. Gently warm the remaining whisky in a small pan (don't allow it to get too hot). Lift the gelatine from the soaking water, squeeze it gently and add to the whisky. The gelatine should melt almost at once. Fold the whisky into the mascarpone

mixture, then add the cooled egg yolk mixture and the lemon juice. Carefully fold the whole lot together. Cover and keep in the fridge.

5 To serve, add a handful of raspberries to the softly set jelly. Put a couple of spoonfuls of jelly in the bottom of eight dessert glasses. Add a couple of spoonfuls of mousse on top, then sprinkle with some oatmeal praline. Add more jelly, then more mousse and another sprinkling of praline. Finish with a few raspberries.

MATT TEBBUTT

MONMOUTH PUDDING

SERVES 4

90g fresh breadcrumbs
light soft brown sugar
450ml full-fat milk
grated zest of 1 lemon
25g unsalted butter
4 tbsp caster sugar

3 large eggs, separated
100g fresh seasonal soft fruit, such
 as raspberries, strawberries, cooked
 gooseberries, blackcurrants and
 redcurrants, or your favourite
 home-made jam

1 Preheat the grill to hot.

2 Spread the breadcrumbs on a baking tray and sprinkle with a little brown sugar. Put the tray under the grill and toast the breadcrumbs for a few minutes, turning them frequently. Remove and set aside.

3 Put the milk in a medium saucepan with the lemon zest, butter and 1 tbsp of the caster sugar. Bring to a simmer. Stir in the toasted breadcrumbs. Leave to stand off the heat for 30 minutes.

4 Preheat the oven to 200°C/fan 180°C/gas 6.

5 Stir the egg yolks into the milk and breadcrumb mixture. Pour into a 900ml baking dish and scatter over the soft fruit or spread jam on top.

6 Whisk the egg whites until they form firm peaks. Fold in the remaining caster sugar, and whisk until stiff again. Spoon the meringue over the fruit to cover it completely. Bake for 10–15 minutes or until the meringue is lightly golden. Serve the pudding warm, straight from the dish.

COX'S APPLE TART

SERVES 4
250g puff pastry, thawed overnight in
   the fridge if frozen
6 Cox's apples
squeeze of lemon juice
caster sugar for sprinkling
vanilla ice cream or clotted cream
   to serve

APPLE COMPOTE
80g unsalted butter
600g Granny Smith apples, peeled
   and chopped
80g caster sugar
1 vanilla pod, split lengthways

VANILLA BUTTER
1 vanilla pod, split lengthways
100g soft unsalted butter

1 To make the apple compote, melt the butter in a stainless steel saucepan. Add the apples and sugar. Scrape the seeds from the vanilla pod into the mixture, then drop in the pod. Cook on a moderate heat for about 20 minutes to make a thick compote, stirring from time to time. If the texture is too runny, leave to cook a little longer.

2 Remove the vanilla pod, then put the apple compote into a blender and blend to a fine pulp. Rub through a fine sieve into a container and set aside.

3 Roll out the pastry on a lightly floured surface to a 50 x 14cm rectangle. Using a 12cm cutter (or by cutting around a plate), cut out four discs. Place the discs on a baking tray and let rest in the fridge for 10 minutes.

4 To make the vanilla butter, scrape the seeds from the vanilla pod and mix them with the soft butter. Set aside.

5 Preheat the oven to 220°C/fan 200°C/ gas 7.

6 Peel the Cox's apples. Slice off four even-sized apple circles, brush these with lemon juice and set aside. Core the apples, then cut them in half lengthways and slice each half thinly.

7 Remove the pastry discs from the fridge and prick them all over with a fork. Spoon some apple compote into the middle of each pastry disc, then fan the apple slices on top so they overlap tightly over the compote and pastry, starting from the middle like the spokes of a wheel. Finish by placing the reserved apple circles in the middle of each tart to cover the centre.

8 Lightly brush the apple slices with some of the vanilla butter, then sprinkle with a little caster sugar. Bake for 10 minutes, then remove and brush with more of the vanilla butter. Bake for a further 8–10 minutes or until the apples are golden. Remove from the oven and leave to rest for 10 minutes.

9 Serve the tarts with vanilla ice cream or clotted cream. (The tarts can be made and baked in advance and eaten cold, or reheated to serve hot.)

PERRY JELLY AND SUMMER FRUITS
WITH ELDERFLOWER ICE CREAM

SERVES 4

4 large gelatine leaves
500ml perry (sparkling pear cider)
75g caster sugar
125g mixed berries, such as blueberries,
  raspberries and wild strawberries

ELDERFLOWER ICE CREAM

300ml full-fat milk, preferably
  Channel Island milk
6 medium egg yolks
100g caster sugar
300ml Jersey or clotted cream, or
  a mixture of the two
200ml elderflower cordial

1 First make the ice cream. Bring the milk to the boil in a heavy saucepan, then remove from the heat. Whisk the egg yolks and sugar together in a bowl, pour in the milk and whisk well. Return to the pan and cook over a low heat for about 5 minutes, stirring constantly with a whisk. Do not boil. Remove from the heat and whisk in the cream and elderflower cordial. Leave to cool, then churn in an ice cream machine until thickened. Decant into a clean container and place in the freezer.

2 To make the perry jelly, immerse the gelatine leaves one at a time in a shallow bowl of cold water and leave for a minute or so until soft. Bring 100ml of the perry to the boil in a medium saucepan, add the sugar and stir until dissolved. Drain and squeeze the gelatine leaves, then add to the hot perry and stir until melted. Remove from the heat, add the rest of the perry and stir well. Put the pan of jelly somewhere cool, but do not let it set.

3 Divide half the berries among four individual savarin moulds or individual jelly moulds, or use one large mould. Pour in half the cooled jelly. Chill for an hour or so to set, then top up with the rest of the berries and unset jelly. (This ensures the berries stay suspended and don't float to the top.) Return to the fridge to set.

4 To serve, turn the jellies out onto individual plates and sit a ball of elderflower ice cream in the middle of each one.

RESOURCES DIRECTORY

Many of the finest foods in Britain, once only found locally, are now available nationwide, often with next day delivery. The following directory lists the producers recommended by the Great British Menu chefs.

MEAT, POULTRY AND GAME

The Aberfoyle Butcher
206a Main Street, Aberfoyle, Stirling FK8 3UQ
Tel: 01877 382473
www.aberfoylebutcher.co.uk
beef hung for the right length of time, sometimes for as long as 6 weeks. Supplier to Nick Nairn

Adsdean Farm
Funtingdon, Chichester, West Sussex PO18 9DN
Tel: 01243 575464 Fax: 01243 575586
www.adsdeanfarm.co.uk
mixed farm with pigs, cattle and 240 acres of arable crops. The bacon is home dry-cured and smoked; also cooked ham, ox tongue, salt beef, pastrami. Supplier to Stuart Gillies

Arthur Howell Butcher
53 Staithe Street, Wells-next-the-Sea, Norfolk
Tel: 01328 710228; Tel/Fax (office): 01328 711300
http://members.aol.com/angushouse100
family butchers since 1889. Bacon is smoked and gammon cooked on the premises; game from local farmers and deer from the Holkham Estate (home of the Earl of Leicester). Supplier to Galton Blackiston

Ballylagan Organic Farm
12 Ballylagan Road, Straid, Ballyclare,
Co Antrim BT39 9NF
Tel: 028 9332 2867 Fax: 028 9332 2129
www.ballylagan.com
the first farm in Co Antrim to achieve organic certification from the Soil Association in the early nineties and the first organic farm in Northern Ireland to open its own farm shop outlet. They produce and sell organic beef, lamb, pork, poultry, eggs and vegetables, as well as a variety of cheeses. Supplier to Richard Corrigan

Blackface
Weatherall Foods Limited
Crochmore House, Irongray, Dumfries DG2 9SF
Tel: 01387 730326
www.blackface.co.uk
sources quality meat direct from their own hill farms and from other carefully selected producers in south west Scotland; famous for Galloway beef and Scottish Blackface, one of Scotland's oldest breeds of sheep. Mail order lamb, mutton, haggis, Iron Age pork, grouse, partridge, Bronze turkeys and venison. Supplier to Jeremy Lee

Cornish Duck Company
Terras Farm, Grampound Road, Truro,
Cornwall TR24 4EX
Tel: 01726 882393/884086
www.cornishduck.co.uk
breeders and producers of uniquely flavoured, tender Cornish duck, reared in stress-free environment. Delivery throughout Cornwall Wednesday–Saturday. Supplier to Michael Caines

Devon Quail
Tel: 01392 202371
http://freespace.virgin.net/philip.may/index
boned and stuffed quail; oven-ready birds; fresh, smoked and pickled eggs. Weekly delivery in south and east Devon, and mail order anywhere in the UK mainland. Supplier to Michael Caines

Edwards of Conwy
18 High Street, Conwy LL32 8DE
Tel: 01492 592443 Fax: 01492 592220
www.edwardsofconwy.co.uk
award-winning butcher shop supplying a full range of meat and meat products. Welsh salt marsh lamb, lamb sausages, Welsh beef available by mail order. Supplier to Bryn Williams

Elwy Valley Welsh Lamb
Gwern Valley Farm, Henllan, Denbigh LL16 5DA
Tel: 01745 870227
www.elwyvalleylamb.co.uk
lamb from family-run hill farms in the heart of North Wales. Supplier to Richard Corrigan and Bryn Williams

L'Escargot Anglais
Credenhill Snail Farm, Credenhill,
Herefordshire HR4 7DN
Tel: 01432 760218
supplier of snails to Mark Broadbent

Farmer Sharp
Diamond Buildings, Pennington Lane
Lindal in Furness, Cumbria LA12 0LA
Tel: 01229 588299 Fax: 01229 583496
www.farmersharp.co.uk
Andrew Sharp is the public face of 27 co-operating farmers in the Lake District who produce some of the finest quality cattle and sheep the area has to offer; from these Herdwick sheep and Galloway cattle, lamb, mutton and well-hung beef is produced. Has a stall in Borough Market, London. Supplier to Mark Broadbent

Glenshane Farm
Magheramore, Dungiven, Co Londonderry BT47 4SW
Tel: 028 777 41942
info@magheramore.com
traditional mountain lamb reared in the Sterrin Hills. Supplier to Richard Corrigan

J T Beedham & Sons
556 Mansfield Road, Nottingham NG5 2FS
Tel: 0115 9605901
www.jtbeedham.co.uk
free-range meats including air-dried hams and home-cured bacon. They have won Gold awards at Newark Agricultural show, and Gold awards for their sausages. Supplier to Sat Bains

J Williams and Company
120 Vale Street, Denbigh, Clwyd LL16 3BS
Tel: 01745 812585
local beef, pork and home-made sausages, available by mail order. Supplier to Bryn Williams

Johnson & Swarbrick
Swainson House Farm, Goosnargh, Preston,
Lancashire PR3 2JU
Tel: 01772 865251 Fax: 01772 865133
www.jandsgoosnargh.co.uk
producers of free-range Goosnargh duckling, Goosnargh geese, Goosnargh corn-fed chicken, Goosnargh corn-fed turkey and game. Supplier to Mark Broadbent and Stuart Gillies

Mulholland Butchers
55 Sloan Street, Lisburn, Co Antrim BT27 5AG
Tel: 028 92664904
120 Sandy Row, Belfast BT12 5EX
Tel: 028 90327038
all meat is locally produced and much is sourced direct from farms; award-winning sausages. Supplier to Richard Corrigan

N S James
Crown Square, Raglan, Monmouthshire
Tel: 01291 690675
nsjames@ukonline.co.uk
butcher specialising in rare breed and locally sourced meats; also provide award-winning sausages and home-made faggots. Supplier to Matt Tebutt

Northfield Farm
Whissendine Lane, Cold Overton, Oakham,
Leicestershire LE15 7QF
Tel: 01664 474271 Fax: 01664 474669
www.northfieldfarm.com
multi-award-winning meat. They source and produce premium quality beef, lamb and pork. Beef is from a wide range of rare breed animals, including Dexter, and all beef is hung for 3 weeks before sale. Supplier to Sat Bains

O'Doherty's Fine Meats
Belmore Street, Enniskillen, Co Fermanagh
Tel: 028 66322152
www.blackbacon.com
small family-owned butchers offering award-winning bacon, wild venison and Aberdeen Angus beef, plus unusual meats – anything from crocodile to kangaroo. The pigs from which the bacon is produced are an old-fashioned breed, Black Saddlebacks. The pork is cured using ancient methods and natural ingredients, and is allowed to season naturally until it matures. Supplier to Richard Corrigan

Piper's Farm Butchers
27 Magadalen Road, Exeter, Devon EX2 4OA
Tel: 01392 274504
www.pipersfarm.com
multi-award-winning butcher offering full mail order service. You can order Red Ruby beef (native to Exmoor), pork, chicken, lamb, venison, geese, hams and Bronze turkeys as well as sausages, all-meat burgers made only with herbs and spices, and ready-to-go casseroles made in the farmhouse kitchens. Supplier to Michael Caines

Pugh's Piglets
Bowgreave House Farm, Bowgreave, Garstang
Preston, Lancashire PR3 1YE
Tel: 01995 601728/602571
denbyashworth@fastmail.fm
Barry and Gillian Pugh, with their son Richard and

dedicated team, personally select every pig, which ensures every order is usually from the farm to the table within 3 days. Also every product is fully traceable and guaranteed to be bred and reared within the UK. Produce suckling pig, porchetta, medallions and lamb. Supplier to Stuart Gillies

Raoul Van Den Broucke
The Wild One Ltd, 1 Alms House Road
Newlend/Coleford, Gloucestershire
Tel: 01594 835313
twolimited@waitrose.com
Raoul is an experienced forager who has foraged for some top restaurants and chefs, supplying snails, mushrooms and any kind of wild food. He offers Forager tours. Supplier to Matt Tebutt

Sheepdrove Organic Farm
Warren Farm, Lambourn, Berkshire RG17 7UU
Tel: 01488 71659 Fax: 01488 72677
www.sheepdrove.com
family-run, mixed organic farm with sheep, free-range poultry, cattle and pigs in an organic field rotation with arable crops. Online shopping plus shops in Bristol and London. Supplier to Atul Kochhar

Sillfield Farm
Endmoor, Kendal, Cumbria LA8 0HZ
Tel: 015395 67609 Fax: 015395 67483
www.sillfield.co.uk
Peter Gott keeps free-range wild boar and rare breed pigs as well as Herdwick sheep and pedigree poultry. His traditional Cumberland sausage, smoked speck and wild boar air-dried prosciutto are multi-award-winners. Supplier to Mark Broadbent

FISH

Atlantic Ocean Delights
64 Ballymean Road, Larne, Co Antrim BT40 2SG
Tel: 028 2826 0965
forage and cultivate seaweeds that are native to the Irish coast and sell 10 tons of dried seaweed and moss in Ireland every year; also send it all over the world. They even produce a smoked seaweed. Supplier to Richard Corrigan

Britannia Shellfish Ltd
The Viviers, Beesands, Kingsbridge, Devon TQ7 2EH
Tel: 01548 581186 Fax: 01548 580560
www.britanniashellfish.co.uk
fresh crab and lobster, diver-caught scallops, mussels, clams, oysters, and freshest catches of bass, mackerel, turbot, skate, lemon sole etc. Also have a fresh seafood stall at the local farmer's markets in Kingsbridge and Dartmouth. Supplier to Michael Caines

Conwy Mussel Company
The Quay, Mussel Purification Centre,
Conwy LL32 8BB
Tel: 01492 592689
www.conwymussels.co.uk
locally run business specialising in mussels in winter. During the summer the Centre is open free of charge to the public. Supplier to Bryn Williams

Dundrum Bay Oyster Fishery
24 Main Street, Dundrum, Newcastle,
Co Down BT33 0LX
Tel: 028 43751810 Fax: 028 437 51610
supplies fresh oysters, mussels, cockles and winkles by mail order throughout the UK and Ireland. Supplier to Noel McMeel and Galton Blackiston

Forman and Field
30a Marshgate Lane, London E15 2NH
Tel: 020 8221 3939 Fax: 020 8221 3940
century-old artisan business and the last salmon smokery in East London; specialises in traditional British produce from small, independent producers

Furness Fish, Poultry and Game Supplies
Moor Lane, Flookburgh, Grange-over-Sands,
Cumbria LA11 7LS
Tel: 015395 59544 Fax: 015395 59549
furnessfish@yahoo.com
producers of award-winning Morecambe Bay potted shrimps and suppliers of quality fresh seafood, smoked salmon, Lakeland game, stuffed poultry and game, three bird roasts, game pies and specialist food hampers by mail order. Have a stall at Borough Market in London. Supplier to Mark Broadbent

Iain R Spink's Original Smokies From Arbroath
Forehills Farmhouse, Carmyllie By Arbroath,
Angus DD11 2RH
www.arbroathsmokies.net
Iain Spink is a fifth generation smokie producer and uses the same methods as fishwives working in the late 1800s. His fish is sold at local farmer's markets and regional fairs. He won the highly prestigious BBC Radio 'Food Producer of the Year' Award 2006. Supplier to Nick Nairn

Loch Fyne Oysters Ltd
Clachan Farm, Cairndow, Argyll PA26 8BL
Tel: 01499 600264
www.lochfyne.com
produce oysters, mussels and a wide range of smoked fish, along with other fresh shellfish from local waters. Winner of several major awards. Supplier to Jeremy Lee

MacCallum's of Troon
71 Houldsworth Street, Glasgow G3 8ED
Tel: 0141 204 4456
John MacCallum is dedicated to providing the best quality, freshest and widest range of Scottish fish and shellfish, including lively langoustines, squat lobsters, razor fish and lobster. Supplier to Nick Nairn

Market Fisheries (Rye)
Unit 1, Simmons Quay, Rock Channel, Rye,
East Sussex TN31 7HJ
Tel: 01797 225175 Fax: 01797 222336
marketfisheries@btconnect.com
family-run business of over 30 years trading. All locally landed fresh fish; fish is also smoked on the premises. Supplier to Atul Kochhar

North Norfolk Fish Company
8 Old Stable Yard, Holt, Norfolk NR25 6BN
Tel: 01263 711913
John Griffin's fishmonger shop is in an old stable yard. He sells fresh and smoked fish and local shellfish, including oysters. The shop also has a deli section with home-made fish pies, lasagne and pâté (John's wife makes these). Mail order available. Supplier to Galton Blackiston

Penclawdd Shellfish Processing Limited
Unit 28 Crofty Industrial Estate, Gower SA4 3YA
Tel: 1792 851 678 Fax: 1792 851 657
www.penclawddshellfish.co.uk
the company was formed by a group of licensed cockle gatherers. It has a state of the art cockle cooking facility, which is capable of cooking many tons of these tasty little molluscs daily, as well as producing that peculiarly Welsh delicacy, laver bread, from locally gathered seaweed. Supplier to Matt Tebbutt

Pwllheli Seafoods Ltd
The Outer Harbour, Pwllheli LL53 5AY
Tel/Fax: 01758 614615
fish and shellfish (fresh and frozen) as well as game and poultry, terrines and pâtés, chocolates, olives, capers, oils and vinegars, smoked meats and fish. Supplier to Bryn Williams

Scot Prime Seafoods
Murray Street Fish Docks, Grimsby,
Lincolnshire DN31 3RD
Tel: 01472 357425 Fax: 01472 250356
www.scotprime.co.uk
specialist in a full range of fresh and frozen seafood, including cod, haddock, plaice, dover sole, lemon sole, turbot, skate, catfish, redfish, scallops, langoustines and prawns.

Selsey Fish & Lobster Co
Lagoon Cottage, Kingsway, Selsey, Chichester,
West Sussex PO20 0SY
Tel: 01243 607444 Fax: 01243 607333
Supplier of lobster to Stuart Gillies

Severn and Wye Eel Smokery
Chaxhill, Westbury-on-Severn,
Gloucestershire GL14 1QW
Tel: 01452 760190 Fax: 01452 760193
www.severnandwye.co.uk
situated below the salmon rivers Severn and Wye, this smoked fish business specialises in fresh and smoked wild salmon, smoked fish and smoked poultry. All are hand prepared, salted and smoked over a blend of oak chips and chipped whisky and Calvados barrels to give a unique smoked fish taste. Mail order available. Supplier to Matt Tebbutt

Shellseekers
Darren Brown
Tel: 07787 516 258
shellseekers@talk21.com
Darren is a scallop diver, and has a stall at Borough Market in London. Supplier to Mark Hix

Thornham Oysters
7 School Row, High Street, Thornham,
Norfolk PE36 6LY
Tel: 01485 512163 Fax: 01485 512027
www.thornhamoysters.co.uk
a family business supplying prime-condition fresh
oysters and Brancaster mussels to almost any
address in the UK by overnight delivery. Thornham
rock oysters are grown in the natural salt marsh
creeks that meander from the North Sea into
Thornham Harbour.

CHEESE, BUTTER AND OTHER DAIRY FOODS

Alston Dairy
Longridge, Preston, Lancashire PR3 3BN
Tel: 01772 782 621 Fax: 01772 784459
www.alstondairy.co.uk
Ann Forshaw's Alston Dairy is a long-established
dairy farm. Since the early 1980s, Ann and her family
have been producing a wide range of traditional
farmhouse yoghurts that are now selling across the
nation. She has won the Championship Yoghurt
prize at Nantwich Show for 8 consecutive years.
Supplier to Mark Broadbent

Bower Farm Dairy
Grosmont, Abergavenny, Monmouthshire NP1 8HS
Tel: 01981 240219 Fax: 01981 240219
www.bowerfarm.freeserve.co.uk
delicious Jersey cream, clotted cream and yoghurt
made entirely from milk produced by their own herd
of pedigree Jersey cows. Supplier to Matt Tebbutt

Caws Cenarth
Glyneithinog Farm, Pontseli, Boncath SA37 0LH
Tel: 01239 710432
www.cawscenarth.co.uk
small family enterprise making traditional Welsh
cheeses, including Caerffili, Perl Wen, Cenarth Brie
and Perl Las Caws Cenarth Cheese. Supplier to Bryn
Williams

Cheshire Farm Ice Cream
Tattenhall, Chester, Cheshire CH3 9NE
Tel: 01829 770446 / 01829 770995
make over 30 flavours of luxury ice cream from the
milk of their own cows, plus real fruit sorbets, with no
artificial flavours or colourings. Their Ice Cream
Parlour comprises a farm, milking parlour, ice cream
production room and tea room. Supplier to Mark
Broadbent

Country Cheeses
Market Road, Tavistock, Devon PL19 0BW
Tel: 01822 615035
www.countrycheeses.co.uk
Elise and Gary Jungheim are passionate supporters
of Devon cheeses, and their shop stocks more than
100 different varieties of British cheeses, mostly
from Cornwall, Devon and Somerset. Mail order.
Supplier to Michael Caines

Dundermotte Farmhouse Ice Cream
30 Station Road, Glarryford, Ballymena,
Co Antrim BT44 9RA
Tel: 02825 685357
small family-run business making ice cream the
traditional way, using organic milk and cream
produced onsite at Dundermotte farm. Their
speciality is Honeysuckle Ice Cream. Supplier to Noel
McMeel

Llaeth Bethesda
Sarngwm, Bethesda, Narberth,
Pembrokeshire SA67 8HG
Tel: 01437 563039
llaethbethesda@tiscali.co.uk
makes real old-fashioned farmhouse butter from its
own herd of Ayrshire cows, which won a silver award
in the True Taste Awards 2005-2006. The milk is
bottled at the farm, and the leftover cream is then
churned to make a soft creamy butter with just 1% of
sea salt added. Supplier to Bryn Williams

Llaeth y Llan Village Dairy
Tal y Bryn, Llannefydd, Denbigh LL16 5DR
Tel: 01745 540 256 Fax 01745 540 278
www.villagedairy.co.uk
suppliers of creamy dessert yoghurt, a melt in the
mouth delicacy, made from locally produced milk –
including that from Gareth and Falmai's 50 dairy
cows. You can choose from 20 different flavours.
Supplier to Bryn Williams

Neal's Yard Dairy
17 Short's Gardens, Covent Garden,
London WC2H 9UP
Tel: 020 7240 5700
www.nealsyarddairy.co.uk
pioneering company with a very wide range of British
and Irish cheeses. Supplier to Stuart Gillies

Paxton & Whitfield
6 Fosseway, Moreton in Marsh,
Gloucestershire GL56 9NQ
Tel: 01608 652090 Mail order: 0870 2642101
www.paxtonandwhitfield.co.uk
Shops in London (93 Jermyn Street, London
SW1Y 6JE, 020 7930 0259), Stratford-upon-Avon
(13 Wood Street, Stratford-upon-Avon CV37 6JF,
01789 415544), Bath (1 John Street, Bath BA1 2JL,
01225 466403) and Birmingham (The Mailbox,
27-29 Wharfside Street, Birmingham B1 1RD,
0121 632 1440)
a great source not just for artisan cheeses from the
West Country, but also the best from throughout
Britain and Europe. Supplier to Michael Caines

Woolsery Cheese
The Old Dairy, Up Sydling, Dorchester,
Dorset DT2 9PQ
Tel: 01300 341991 Fax: 01300 341991
www.woolserycheese.co.uk
all cheeses are handmade using traditional methods
and the finest fresh goat's or cow's milk, to produce
a wide range of soft to hard cheeses. Their goat's
cheese has won many awards. No artificial additives
or ingredients are used – just natural milk. Supplier
to Mark Hix

SPICES, VINEGARS AND OTHER FOODS

Blacks Delicatessen
28 The Square, Chagford, Devon
Tel: 01647 433545
www.blacks-deli.co.uk
Michael Caines' 'corner shop' on which he relies for
lots of items he may have forgotten to order. It's also
a great place to stop for everything from salads and
deli items to a cup of coffee.

Somerset Cider Vinegar Company
Westcroft Farm, Highbridge, Somerset
Postal Orders: 5 Centre Road, Edington,
nr Bridgwater TA7 9JR
www.somersetcidervinegarco.co.uk
Customers in Somerset can order from
SOMERSET FARMERS MARKET DIRECT at:
www.sfmdirect.co.uk
makes vinegar from pure Somerset cider apple juice,
fermented naturally for at least 2 years, to give it a
rich, smooth flavour. Supplier to Mark Hix

The Spice Shop
1 Blenheim Crescent, London W11 2EE
Tel: 020 7221 4448/4960
www.thespiceshop.co.uk
all herb and spice blends are freshly ground and
hand mixed, and none contains any artificial
flavours, colourings or salt. They are totally free of
wheat, starch, gluten or nuts. They contain no
animal products, so they are suitable for vegetarians.
Supplier to Stuart Gillies

FRUIT AND VEGETABLES

Andreas Georghiou & Co
35 Turnham Green Terrace, London W4 1RG
Tel: 020 8995 0140
www.andreasveg.co.uk
small independent greengrocer with an unrivalled
range of top-end, quality fruit and vegetables.
Andreas and his trusted number 2, Darren, provide a
bespoke free delivery service to domestic clients as
well as restaurants. Supplier to Mark Broadbent

Angus Soft Fruit Ltd
East Seaton, Arbroath DD11 5SD
Tel: 01241 879989 Fax: 01241 871220
raspberries and strawberries. Supplier to Nick Nairn

Blackmoor Farm Shop
Blackmoor Liss, Hampshire GU33 6BS
Tel: 01420 473782 Fax: 01420 475878
www.blackmoor.co.uk/farmshop.php
as well as the specialist fruit tree nursery, Blackmoor
Estate has been growing fruit since the 1920s and
opened its farm shop in the 1960s. The shop
specialises in fresh fruit grown in the orchards,
including pears, strawberries, plums, apricots,
quinces and many traditional apple varieties. It also
sells a wide variety of locally grown vegetables,
English wines and cider, and much more. Supplier
to Atul Kochhar

Cherry Tree Farm
Lower Road, Stone, Tenterden, Kent, TN30 7JH
Tel: 01797 270626 Fax: 01797 270050
herbs and salad leaves. Supplier to Stuart Gillies

Dorset Blueberry Company
Littlemoors Farm, Ham Lane, Hampreston,
Wimborne, Dorset BH21 7LT
Tel: 01202 891426
www.dorset-blueberry.com
the family has been growing blueberries since 1949.
They have an onsite bakery, making blueberry pies,
cookies and cakes, which are sold at farmer's
markets and local farm shops. A farm shop will be
opening Easter 2007. Juices, jams and sauces are
available by mail order. Supplier to Mark Hix

F A Secretts Ltd
Hurst Farm, Chapel Lane, Milford, Goldalming,
Surrey GU8 5HU
Tel: 01483 520529 Fax: 01483 520501
www.secretts.co.uk
third generation family business set in the heart
of the Surrey countryside selling an extensive
range of herbs, fruit, vegetables and salads.
Supplier to Mark Broadbent

Forager
www.forager.org.uk
Supplier to Stuart Gillies

Fresh Garden Produce
Broxtowe, Nottinghamshire
www.freshgardenproduce.co.uk
family-run vegetable producer that provides local
vegetable box scheme. All orders are hand picked on
the day of delivery. Supplier to Sat Bains

The Mountain Food Company
www.mountainfood.org
foraging 52 weeks a year since 1995, working
through all weather conditions – 'your hands in the
forest', tracking and picking nature's finest wild
herbs, salads and vegetables, such as wood sorrel,
pennywort, gorse flowers, hairy bittercress, cleavers
and alexanders. Free delivery on all orders and
samples sent at no charge. Supplier to Stuart Gillies

Rowswell Fruit and Vegetables
Bakers Farm, Barrington, nr Ilminster,
Somerset TA19 0JB
Tel: 01460 55504
Box Scheme: 01460 55504; 01460 52387;
01460 53835
www.rowswellsfarm.com
everything is grown and produced using a special
blend of natural fertilisers, without insecticides or
herbicides. John Rowswell grows around 50 different
types of vegetable, including nine varieties of
tomato. Buy direct or at farmer's markets in
Crewkerne and Yeovil. Supplier to Mark Hix

BREAD AND FLOUR

Ditty's Home Bakery
44 Main Street, Castledawson,
Co Londonderry BT45 8AB
Tel: 028 79 468243 Fax: 028 79 468243
www.dittysbakery.com
an award-winning family-run bakery that has
been in business for over 40 years. Supplier to
Richard Corrigan

Fisher & Donaldson
1 Ceres Rd, Cupar KT15 5JT
Tel: 01334 65255
www.fisheranddonaldson.com
fourth generation family bakery business based in
St Andrews and Cupar in the county of Fife. A broad
range of traditional Scottish, continental and
confectionery products are produced each morning
from their bakeries, including Aberdeenshire
butteries, richly fruited Selkirk bannocks, oatcakes
and highlander shortbread. Supplier to Jeremy Lee

G R Wright & Sons Ltd
Ponders End Mills, Enfield, Middlesex EN3 4TG
Tel: 020 8344 6900
Freefone orders: 0800 064 0100
www.wrightsflour.co.uk
family-run mill, the only one in London. 140 years
old this year. Flour is available by mail order. Supplier
to Stuart Gillies

Letheringsett Watermill
Riverside Road, Letheringsett, nr Holt,
Norfolk NR25 7YD
Tel: 01263 713153
www.letheringsettwatermill.co.uk
Letheringsett is now a fully functional water-
powered flour mill producing flour from Norfolk-
grown wheat. Visitors can see the mill at work and
buy bread and flour from the small shop. Producer of
spelt flour, organic stoneground flour and 100%
stoneground flour. Supplier to Galton Blackiston

CIDER, WINE AND SPIRITS

Celtic Country Wines
Windy Rise Winery, Beulah, New Castle Emlyn,
Ceredigion SA38 9QJ
Tel: 01239 85 88 88
www.celticwines.co.uk
dedicated to re-creating ancient recipes, but with
the benefit of modern wine-making knowledge and
equipment. Mail order. Supplier to Matt Tebbutt

Chilford Vineyard
Chilford Hall, Balsham Road, Linton,
Cambridge CB21 4LE
Tel: 01223 895600 Fax: 01223 895605
www.chilfordhall.co.uk/vineyard
produces a variety of dry and medium dry white
wines, rosé and sparkling rosé. Wine-tastings,
guided tours of the winery and walks in the
vineyards. Supplier to Galton Blackiston

Coddington Vineyard
Near Ledbury, Herefordshire HR8 1JJ
Tel/Fax: 01531 640668

one of the smaller commercial vineyards in the UK –
quite literally a back-garden vineyard. Recently a
small winery has been built, so owners Denis and
Ann Savage now have total control over the wines.
Four grape varieties are grown: Bacchus, Kerner,
Ortega and Pinot Gris. The wines are of a uniformly
high standard and they are very well priced (£4–6 per
bottle). Supplier to Mark Hix

Denbies Wine Estate
London Road, Dorking, Surrey RH5 6AA
Tel: 01306 876616 Fax: 01306 888930
www.denbiesvineyard.co.uk
the largest vineyard in England, representing over
10% of the plantings in the whole of the UK. All
wines are available in the shop, via mail order or
ordered from the website. Supplier to Atul Kochhar

Glengoyne Distillery
Dumgoyne, Nr Killearn, Glasgow G63 9LB
Tel: 01360 551402/01360 550254
www.glengoyne.com
unlike most other single malts, Glengoyne has been
preserving the essence of its flavour for decades by
using air-dried barley rather than barley dried using
harsh peat smoke. They have been producing single
malt scotch whisky for over 200 years. Supplier to
Nick Nairn

Minchew's Real Cyder and Perry
Rose Cottage, Aston Cross, Tewkesbury,
Gloucestershire GL20 8HX
Tel: 0797 403 4331
www.minchews.co.uk
produces the world's largest range of single variety
cyders and perries using natural methods, without
the aid of artificial additives or chemicals. All fruit is
hand-picked, hand-washed, milled in an old-
fashioned scratter and pressed on an old stone slab,
then allowed to ferment naturally in oak barrels.
Only when fermentation has naturally ceased and is
judged to be mature, is it then bottled. Supplier to
Mark Hix

Somerset Cider Brandy Company
Pass Vale Farm, Burrow Hill, Kingsbury Episcopi,
Martock, Somerset TA12 5BU
Tel: 01460 240782 Fax: 01460 249220
www.ciderbrandy.co.uk
company has been in existence for 150 years. It
grows more than 100 varieties of cider apples, and
makes cider for drinking or distilling to make
brandies. Supplier to Michael Caines and Mark Hix

Mr Whitehead's Cider Company
Hartley Park Farm, Selborne, nr Alton,
Hampshire GU34 3HS
Tel/Fax: 01420 511733
www.mr-whiteheads-cider.co.uk

Wickham Vineyard
Botley Road, Shedfield, Southampton SO32 2HL
Tel: 0132 9834042
www.wickhamvineyard.co.uk
makes a wide range of white, red and sparkling wine
using the traditional champagne method. Supplier
to Atul Kochhar

	JANUARY	FEBRUARY	MARCH	APRIL	MAY	JUNE
FRUIT & NUTS	Apples Pears Rhubarb, forced	Rhubarb, forced	Rhubarb, early	Rhubarb Strawberries	Cherries Elderflowers Raspberries Rhubarb	Cherries Elderflowers Gooseberries Redcurrants Strawberries, cultivated Tayberries
MEAT, GAME & POULTRY	Goose Hare Partridge, matured Pheasant Rabbit Venison	Goose Guinea Fowl Partridge Pheasant Rabbit	Pigeon Rabbit	Guinea fowl Lamb, Welsh Rabbit Wood pigeon	Duck Lamb, new season	Lamb, new season

VEGETABLES	Cabbage
	Carrots
	Cauliflower,
	  Cornish
	Celeriac
	Kale
	Kohlrabi
	Leeks
	Shallots
	Spinach
	Squash
	Swede
	Turnips
		Broccoli, purple
		  sprouting
		Cabbage
		Carrots
		Celeriac
		Chicory
		Leeks
		Parsnips
		Salsify
		Shallots
			Beetroot
			Broccoli, purple
			  sprouting
			Calabrese
			Carrots
			Chicory
			Garlic
			Leeks
			Mint
			Nettles
			Onions
			Parsley
			Parsnips
			Radishes
			Seakale
			Sorrel
			Spring
			  greens
				Broccoli, purple
				  sprouting
				Cabbage, spring
				Carrots
				Dandelion
				Garlic, wild
				Kale
				Leeks
				Mushrooms, wild
				  (e.g. morels)
				Potatoes (Jersey
				  Royal)
				Radishes
				Sorrel, wild
				Spinach
				Watercress
					Asparagus
					Beans, broad
					Carrots
					Cauliflower
					Mint
					Mushrooms, wild
					  (e.g. morels)
					Nettles
					Parsley
					Peas
					Potatoes, new
					Radishes
					Rocket
					Samphire
					Sorrel
					Spinach
					Watercress
						Artichokes, globe
						Asparagus
						Aubergines
						Beans, broad
						Broccoli,
						  calabrese
						Carrots
						Courgettes
						Cucumber
						Fennel, wild
						Horseradish
						Lettuce
						Peas
						Peppers
						Potatoes, new
						Radishes
						Samphire
						Watercress

CHEESE	Appleby Cheshire
	Stilton
	Wensleydale, blue
		Cheddar,
		  farmhouse
		Cheshire, blue
		Stilton
		Wensleydale, blue
			Cotherstone
			Ewe's milk
			  cheeses
			Stilton
				Ewe's milk
				  cheeses
				Goat's milk
				  cheeses, fresh
				Single Gloucester
					English soft
					  cheeses
					Ewe's milk
					  cheeses
						Cheddar,
						  farmhouse
						Ewe's milk
						  cheeses
						Goat's milk
						  cheeses, fresh

FISH & SEAFOOD	Cod John dory Lobster Oysters, native Scallops Turbot	Halibut Lemon sole, and other flat fish Mussels	Lobster Mackerel Mussels Salmon, wild Sardines Sea trout	Cockles Crab, brown Lobster Oysters, native Razor clams Salmon, wild	Crab, brown Haddock Lemon sole Prawns Sardines Sea bass Sea trout	Crab Grey mullet Hake Lobster Mackerel Salmon, wild Sardines Sea trout Whitebait

	JULY	AUGUST	SEPTEMBER	OCTOBER	NOVEMBER	DECEMBER

FRUIT & NUTS	Blackcurrants
	Blueberries
	Cherries
	Elderflowers
	Gooseberries
	Loganberries
	Raspberries
	Strawberries
		Apples
		Blackcurrants
		Blueberries, Dorset
		Cherries
		Cobnuts
		Gooseberries
		Greengages
		Loganberries
		Pears
		Plums
		  (Early Laxton,
		  Czare, and Opal)
		Sloes
		Strawberries, wild
			Apples (Worcester
			  Pearmain, James
			  Grieve)
			Blackberries
			Blackcurrants
			  and redcurrants
			Chestnuts
			Cobnuts
			Crabapples
			Damsons and
			  plums
			Elderberries
			Figs
			Greengages
			Pears
			Sloes
				Apples (especially
				  Cox's Orange
				  Pippins)
				Chestnuts
				Cobnuts
				Damsons and
				  bullaces
				Elderberries
				Figs
				Hazelnuts
				Quinces
				Rowanberries
				Walnuts
					Almonds
					Apples
					Chestnuts
					Cranberries
					Hazelnuts
					Medlars
					Pears
					Quinces
					Sloes
					Walnuts
						Almonds
						Apples
						Chestnuts
						Cranberries
						Hazelnuts
						Pears
						Pomegranates
						Quinces
						Walnuts

MEAT, GAME & POULTRY	Lamb, new season
	Venison
	Wood pigeon
		Grouse
		  (from the 12th
		  onwards)
		Hare
			Duck, wild
			Goose
			Grouse
			Lamb, autumn
			Rabbit
			Venison
			Wood pigeon
				Grouse
				Guinea fowl
				Lamb
				Partridge
				Pheasant
					Goose
					Grouse
					Mallard
					Partridge, grey
					Pheasant
						Duck, wild
						Goose
						Pheasant
						Turkey

VEGETABLES	Artichokes,
	  globe
	Aubergines
	Beans, broad,
	  French and
	  runner
	Cauliflower
	Cucumber
	Fennel
	Garlic
	Lettuce
	Peas
	Radishes
	Sage
	Samphire
	Shallots
	Sweetcorn
	Tomatoes
	Watercress
		Aubergines
		Basil
		Beans, French
		  and runner
		Beetroot
		Courgettes
		Cucumber
		Fennel
		Leeks
		Lettuce
		Mushrooms, wild
		  (e.g Scottish
		  girolles/
		  chanterelles)
		Peas
		Peppers
		Potatoes
		  (Pink Fir Apple
		  and Ratte)
		Samphire
		Squash
		Sweetcorn
		Tomatoes
			Beetroot
			Cauliflower
			Chard
			Cucumber
			Kale
			Mushrooms, wild
			  (e.g. ceps)
			Onion
			Pumpkin
			Salad leaves
			Spinach
			Sweetcorn
			Tomatoes
				Beetroot
				Broccoli
				Cabbage, red
				  and Savoy
				Cardoons
				Chicory
				Courgettes
				Jerusalem
				  artichokes
				Kale
				Marrows
				Mushrooms, wild
				  (e.g. ceps and
				  girolles/
				  chanterelles)
				Parsnips
				Pumpkins
				Salsify
				Squashes, winter
				Tomatoes
				Watercress
					Beetroot
					Brussels sprouts
					Cabbage
					Cauliflower
					Celery
					Jerusalem
					  artichokes
					Leeks
					Mushrooms, wild
					Parsnips
					Potatoes
					Pumpkins
					Swede
					Turnips
						Beetroot
						Brussels sprouts
						Cabbage, red
						Celeriac
						Garlic
						Jerusalem
						  artichokes
						Kale, curly
						Leeks
						Parsnips
						Pumpkins
						Spinach
						Swede
						Turnips

CHEESE	Goat's milk
	  cheeses
		Cheddar,
		  farmhouse
		Goat's milk
		  cheeses
			Cheshire,
			  farmhouse
			Double
			  Gloucester
					Ribblesdale	Stilton
						Wensleydale,
						  blue

FISH & SEAFOOD	Clams Crab Lobster Pike Pilchards Prawns Squid, Scottish Trout	Crayfish Dover sole Haddock Herring John dory Mullet, red Pilchards Salmon, wild Trout	Clams Dover sole Eel Mussels Oysters, native Pilchards Plaice Prawns Sea bass Trout, brown	Cod Crab, brown Dover sole Eels Mussels Oysters, native Squid Turbot	Halibut Herring Lobster Mackerel Sea bream	Carp Mussels Oysters Sea bass Skate Turbot

Sat Bains is Chef/Proprietor of Restaurant Sat Bains with Rooms.
Trentside, Lenton Lane, Nottingham, Nottinghamshire NG7 2SA
(0115 9866 566; www.restaurantsatbains.com)

Galton Blackiston is Chef Patron at Morston Hall Hotel and Restaurant.
Morston, Holt, Norfolk NR25 7AA
(01263 741041; www.galtonblackiston.com, www.morstonhall.com)

Mark Broadbent is Executive Chef at Bluebird.
Gastrodrome, 350 Kings Road, London SW3 5UU
(020 7599 1156; www.conran-restaurants.co.uk)

Michael Caines is Executive Chef at Gidleigh Park and Director
of Food & Beverage, ABode Hotels.
Gidleigh Park, Chagford, Devon TQ13 8HH
(01647 432367; www.gidleigh.com)
Michael Caines at ABode Exeter, Cathedral Yard, Exeter, Devon EX1 1HD
(01392 223638; www.michaelcaines.com/exeter)
Michael Caines at ABode Glasgow, 129 Bath Street, Glasgow G2 2SZ
(0141 572 6011; www.michaelcaines.com/glasgow)
Michael Caines at ABode Canterbury, High Street, Canterbury CT1 2RX
(01227 826684; www.michaelcaines/canterbury.com)
Manchester opening September 2007; Chester opening early 2009
(www.michaelcaines.com)
All ABode properties sit side-by-side with the Michael Caines
concepts and house a selection from: Michael Caines Fine Dining, MC
Champagne Bar, MC Cafe Bar, MC Vibe Bar, MC Boutique, MC Tavern

Richard Corrigan is the Chef/Owner of Lindsay House and Bentley's.
Lindsay House, 21 Romilly Street, London W1D 5AF
(020 7439 0450; www.lindsayhouse.co.uk)
Bentley's Oyster Bar and Grill, 11-15 Swallow Street, London W1B 4DE
(020 7734 4756; www.bentleysoysterbarandgrill.co.uk)

Stuart Gillies is Executive Chef at Boxwood Café.
The Berkeley, Wilton Place, Knightsbridge, London SW1X 7RL
(020 7235 1010; www.gordonramsay.com/boxwoodcafe)

Mark Hix is Chef-Director of Caprice Holdings Limited and oversees
all the restaurants and events in the Caprice Group.
Bam-Bou, 1 Percy Street, Fitzrovia, London W1T 1DB
(020 7323 9130; www.caprice-holdings.co.uk)
Daphne's, 112 Draycott Avenue, South Kensington, London SW3 3AE
(020 7589 4257; www.daphnes-restaurant.co.uk)
J Sheekey, 28-32 St. Martin's Court, London WC2N 4AL
(020 7240 2565; www.j-sheekey.co.uk)

Le Caprice, Arlington House, Arlington Street, London SW1A 1RJ
(020 7629 2239; www.le-caprice.co.uk)
Rivington Grill, 28-30 Rivington Street, London EC2A 3DZ
(020 7729 7053; www.rivingtongrill.co.uk)
Scott's, 20 Mount Street, London W1K 2HE
(020 7495 7309; www.scotts-restaurant.com)
The Ivy, 1-5 West Street, London WC2H 9NQ
(020 7836 4751; www.the-ivy.co.uk)
Urban Caprice, 63-65 Goldney Road, London W9 2AR
(020 7286 1700; www.urbancaprice.co.uk)

Atul Kochhar is Chef-Owner of Benares.
12a Berkeley Square, London, W1
(020 7629 8886; www.benaresrestaurant.com)

Jeremy Lee is Head Chef at Blueprint Café.
28 Shad Thames, London SE1 2YD
(020 7378 7031; www.conran-restaurants.co.uk/restaurants/
blueprint_cafe/home)

Noel McMeel is Executive Head Chef at Castle Leslie and runs
the Castle Leslie Cookery School.
Castle Leslie, Glaslough, County Monaghan, Ireland
(+353 (0) 47 88100; www.castleleslie.com)

Nick Nairn runs his own cookery school.
Nick Nairn Cook School
Port of Menteith, Stirling FK8 3JZ
(01877 389900; www.nicknairncookschool.com, www.nairnsanywhere.
com, www.nicknairn.tv)

Matt Tebbutt is owner and Head Chef at The Foxhunter.
Nantyderry, Abergavenny, Monmouthshire NP7 9DN
(01873 881101; www.thefoxhunter.com)

Marcus Wareing is Head Chef at The Savoy Grill and at Pétrus.
The Savoy Grill, The Strand, London WC2R 0EU
(020 7592 1600, Banquette 020 7420 2392; www.marcuswareing.com)
Pétrus, The Berkeley Hotel, Wilton Place, Knightsbridge, London SW1X
7RL (020 7235 1200; www.marcuswareing.com)

Bryn Williams is Head Chef at Odettes.
130 Regents Park Road, Primrose Hill, London NW1 8XL
(020 7586 8569; www.odettesprimrosehill.com)

INDEX

pancakes, boxty 91–2
pannacotta, almond 177–8
pâté, hot spider crab 113
pears: almond pannacotta 177–8
  poached pear in mulled red wine 195
peas: ham, egg and 37
  mousse of Norfolk-grown peas 35
  pea and leek tarts 47–8
  roast scallops with English peas 98–100
perry jelly and summer fruits 214
pie, rabbit and crayfish stargazy 164–5
pigeon: pigeon with Ayrshire bacon 168–9
  salad of slow-roasted wood pigeon 50–51
  warm seared pigeon 58–9
polenta crumble, rhubarb and ginger 190
pork: belly pork, langoustines and lardo 40–41
  crackled pork with beetroot 154–5
  crubeens and beetroot 56–7
  pan-roasted scallops with crisp smoked belly pork 108–10
  a plate of Scottish pork 156–7
  pork cutlets with celeriac and apple mash 146
  pot roast pork belly cooked in cider 148–9
  roast rack of pork with crackling 152–4
  roasted loin of suckling pig 142–3
  slowly braised belly and roasted loin chop of pork 150–51
  smoked eel and crisp pork belly 36–7
potatoes: boxty pancakes 91–2
  colcannon soup 59
  crab cakes and mayonnaise 28–9
  cullen skink 62
  fillet of beef with traditional champ 121–3
  lobster mash 76–7
  olive oil mash 152–4
  potato drop scones 34–5

salad of potatoes, Arbroath smokies and Ayrshire bacon 92
soused mackerel with potato salad 93
potted salt beef 54
prunes, iced whisky creams with 196

quail, galantine of 43–5

rabbit: rabbit and crayfish stargazy pie 164–5
  saddle of rabbit in Savoy cabbage 166–7
raspberries: almond and raspberry tart 199
  cranachan with oatmeal praline 210–11
  English trifle 173–5
  raspberry shortcake 184
  raspberry sponge with goat's milk ice cream 202–3
  raspberry trifle 194–5
ravioli, crab 106–8
rhubarb: rhubarb and ginger polenta crumble 190
  trio of rhubarb 187–8

salads: asparagus and wild herb 38
  crab and wild cress 111
  crisp-fried South Coast squid 26
  duck livers, hearts, snails and bacon 46
  glazed asparagus and herb 47–8
  potatoes, Arbroath smokies and Ayrshire bacon 92
  slow-roasted wood pigeon 50–51
  soused mackerel with potato salad 93
  warm salad of hot-smoked sea trout, asparagus and cucumber 68
  warm salad of lobster 24
salmon: pan-fried wild salmon with Conwy mussels 86
  whole poached wild salmon and duck egg dressing 74–5
salmon trout, cured slices of 32

salt beef, potted 54
scallops: pan-roasted scallops with crisp smoked belly pork 108–10
  roast scallops with English peas 98–100
  scallops, lobster and spider crab 102
  seared scallops with grape and mint dressing 30–31
sea bass, mousse and fillet of 70–71
sea trout: cured slices of salmon trout (sea trout) 32
  lightly cured sea trout 25
  sewin and soused vegetables 80
  warm salad of hot-smoked sea trout, asparagus and cucumber 68
seasonal food 218–20
sewin and soused vegetables 80
shellfish, a broth of Scottish 97–8
shortcake, raspberry 184
skate wing with nut brown butter 81
smoked eel and crisp pork belly 36–7
smoked eel mousse 91–2
smoked haddock: cullen skink 62
  see also Arbroath smokies
snails: poached fillet of Welsh Black beef 124
  salad of duck livers, hearts, snails and bacon 46
sole: lemon sole and oysters 72–4
soufflé, strawberry 186
soups: cawl cennin with Caerphilly cheese 63
  colcannon soup 59
  cullen skink 62
  mussel bree 60
  Uncle Arwyn's beetroot soup 64
squid: salad of crisp-fried South Coast squid 26
stargazy pie, rabbit and crayfish 164–5
strawberries: strawberry knickerbocker glory 206–7
  strawberry soufflé 186

tarts: almond and raspberry 199
  caramelised red onion 58–9
  Cox's apple 212
  crab and tea-smoked mackerel 22–3
  Cromer crab 112
  muscovado and hazelnut 208
  pea and leek 47–8
tea cream, Earl Grey 204–6
Tebbutt, Matt 13, 36, 63, 80, 111, 124, 127, 190, 211, 222
terrine of ham hock 51–3
toffee apple sundaes 200
tomato and fennel essence with oysters, Dublin Bay prawns and crab 101
tongue: rack of lamb, sautéed tongue and sweetbreads 127
trifles: Dorset blueberry trifle 182–3
  English trifle 173–5
  raspberry trifle 194–5
turbot: fillet of turbot in red wine 78–80
  poached turbot and cockles 84–5

Uncle Arwyn's beetroot soup 64

vanilla and gingerbread cheesecakes 176–7
vegetables: langoustines with summer vegetable stew 103–5
  piccalilli 51–3
  see also asparagus, potatoes etc
venison: carpaccio of cured venison 42

Wareing, Marcus 14, 22–3, 32, 78–80, 88–9, 150–51, 160–62, 177–8, 204–5, 222
watercress: crab and wild cress salad 111
whisky creams, iced 196
Williams, Bryn 12, 24, 64, 86, 106–8, 116–17, 139, 186, 198, 222

ACKNOWLEDGMENTS

Dorling Kindersley would like to thank the following:

Alex, Emma, Helen, Jim, Katrin and Saskia at Smith & Gilmour; Nicola Moody, Raewyn Dickson, Ross Blair, Christopher Monk, Sam Knowles, Vanessa Land and Karen Taylor at Optomen Television; Roz Denny and Val Barrett for recipe testing; Bex Ferguson and Clemmie Jacques for assisting with the recipe testing; Country Cheeses and Sue Proudfoot (Whalesborough Farm), Kathy Hayward and Ken Hayward at Thornham Oysters, Roger Olver and Tanya Dalton at Cornish Duck Company, and Jackie Thompson and Paul Booker at Letheringsett Watermill for help with location photography; and Hilary Bird for the index